THE

ENGLISH IN WESTERN INDIA.

THE

ENGLISH IN WESTERN INDIA;

BEING THE

EARLY HISTORY

OF THE

FACTORY AT SURAT, OF BOMBAY,

AND THE SUBORDINATE FACTORIES ON THE WESTERN COAST.

BY

PHILIP ANDERSON, A.M.

GYAN

Published by

GYAN

Gyan Publishing House
5, Ansari Road
Daryaganj, New Delhi-110002
Phone: 011-47034999, 9811692060
E-mail: books@gyanbooks.com

Distribution Network
gyanbooks.com
India, USA, Canada, UK, Australia, France

ISBN: 978-81-212-7117-2 (PB)
First Published, 1854

2nd Impression 2024

Printed at: Gyan Press, Delhi.

THE ENGLISH IN WESTERN INDIA
Author: PHILIP ANDERSON

THE
ENGLISH IN WESTERN INDIA.

PRINTED AT THE

" BOMBAY GAZETTE" PRESS.

THE

ENGLISH IN WESTERN INDIA;

BEING THE

EARLY HISTORY

OF THE

FACTORY AT SURAT, OF BOMBAY, AND THE SUBORDINATE FACTORIES ON THE WESTERN COAST.

FROM THE EARLIEST PERIOD UNTIL THE COMMENCEMENT OF THE EIGHTEENTH CENTURY.

Drawn from Authentic Works and Original Documents.

BY

PHILIP ANDERSON, A.M.,

ONE OF THE HONORABLE COMPANY'S CHAPLAINS IN THE DIOCESE OF BOMBAY, AND A VICE-PRESIDENT OF THE BOMBAY BRANCH OF THE ROYAL ASIATIC SOCIETY.

BOMBAY:

SMITH, TAYLOR AND Co.

LONDON: SMITH, ELDER AND Co., 65, CORNHILL.

1854.

PREFACE.

The following pages will not, it is hoped, be thought uncalled for, as they fill an hiatus in Indian History. They contain facts which have been hitherto buried in old Manuscripts or in such printed works as are not accessible to many persons. It has been thought that when such are given for the first time to the world, they should be clothed, as far as possible, in simple and unadorned language. They may thus form a groundwork for those whose object is philosophical inquiry, and to trace the progress of Anglo-Indian civilization.

The various authorities have been carefully examined, accurately quoted, and a diligent attempt has been made to estimate their true value. First in importance are the Records of Government, permission to consult which was conceded with liberality, and accepted with gratitude. Next in importance comes Bruce's Work, which is simply an analysis of those Records. The third place must be assigned to writers who have consulted those Records, and made use of them to a limited extent;—such are Orme, Macpherson, Milburn, Grant Duff, and Kaye. In the fourth class are personal narratives; such as those of Herbert, Roe, Fryer, Terry, Ovington, and Alexander Hamilton. These have different degrees of anthenticity, which we must determine in various ways. There is no reason to question the truth of their accounts, when they declare that they were eye-witnesses of the facts which they record. But when their information was gained at second hand, we know that they were liable to be imposed upon. Hamilton especially had a particular bias, and was a prejudiced, although probably an honest man. The books of least importance in the compilation of this little work have been standard histories; for they are not drawn from original sources, and sometimes their facts are squeezed into a shape which best suits their writer's purpose, or is most ornamental to his pages.

In searching original Manuscripts, the object has not been to note down facts, which have already appeared in the pages of authentic writers. That would have consumed much time, with no other result than the correction of a few and unimportant mistakes. The aim has simply been to supplement histories, and to record circumstances which had been concealed from observation through the neglect of inquirers, a low estimate of their value, or timidity in exposing nude and ugly truths.

Bacon has broadly stated it as his opinion, that " a mixture of a lie doth ever add pleasure" ; and that although truth may be as much valued as a pearl, which shews best by day, it will never rise to the price of a diamond, which shews best in varied lights. This hint appears to have been taken by some modern historians, who have converted history into romance, and set off facts with ornaments of imagination. Perhaps, however, some sober-minded readers will be satisfied with knowing, that as the writer of the following Chapters cannot offer the attractions of such authors, so neither has he been led away by their peculiar temptations. He has not endeavoured to walk on the stilts of fancy ; but has been satisfied with the secure footing of plain dealing and truth.

One circumstance to which his attention has been obligingly drawn may be here noticed.—The troops which Sir Andrew Shipman brought with him from England (see page 52 &c) formed the Honorable Company's First European Regiment, and are at this day represented by the gallant Fusiliers. It appears that two Regiments had been raised in England. One was sent to Tangier, and when that place was abandoned, having returned to England, obtained infamous notoriety as " Kirke's Lambs." This body of men is now represented by the Second or Queen's Regiment. The other Regiment, which was raised in 1638, afterwards comprised the European officers and soldiers who are mentioned in this work. When Bombay was transferred to the Company, only ninety-three soldiers were living of the five hundred which had left England ; but few as they were, these must be regarded as the Corps which has since gained so many laurels in various parts of India.

CONTENTS.

CHAPTER I.

1612—1616.

CHAPTER II.

1616—1630.

CHAPTER III.

1630—1662.

CHAPTER IV.

1662—1685.

CHAPTER V.

SAME PERIOD.

CHAPTER VI.

SAME PERIOD.

CHAPTER VII.

1685—1697.

CHAPTER VIII.

SAME PERIOD.

CHAPTER IX.

1698—1701.

PAGE

CHAPTER X.

SAME PERIOD.

CHAPTER XI.

1703—1708.

THE

ENGLISH IN WESTERN INDIA.

CHAPTER I.

1612—1616.

CONTENTS:—Object of the Writer—Progress of the British Power in India; its incongruous character; its moral force—Early European travellers: Sir John Mandeville, Friar Odoricus, The Portuguese, Cæsar Frederick—Early English Travellers: Thomas Stephens; his valuable letters; Leedes, Fitch, Newberry, a painter and others—English Prisoners at Goa; their harsh treatment—Mildenhall arrives by the overland route; his crimes and death—Captain Hawkins and his wife—William Finch—Sir Henry Middleton—Best—Defeat of the Portuguese—Receipt of a firmán—First establishment of English reputation—English Factors: Starkey, Canning, Aldworth, and Withington; their adventures—Downton—Second defeat of the Portuguese—Sir Robert Shirley and Sir Thomas Powell; their misfortunes—Edwards' mission to the Great Mogul; his presents—Sir Thomas Roe; arrives at Surat; reception at Burhámpúr and Ajmír; his presents; revelries; jealousy of the Factors—Roe's subsequent history—Treaty with the Zamorin—Factory established at Cálicot—Sea fight: Portuguese gallantry—Sketch of the Portuguese—Establishment of a Dutch Factory; their economy; Van den Broeck—English Shipping.

THE history of the English in Western India may be divided into Five Periods. The first period commences with the establishment of a Factory at Surat; the second with the formation of a settlement at Bombay; the third with the supremacy which the Government of Bombay was authorized by the Honorable Company to assume over its other factories and settlements in India; the fourth with the annexation of territory in the neighbourhood of Bombay, Gujarát, and other places; the fifth, with the loss of that supremacy which Bombay for long enjoyed, and its subjection to the Governor-General of India. The following History is designed to embrace the three first of these periods.

The narrative of an Empire's rise and progress usually tells how the brook became a river, and the river became a sea. But the history of British India is peculiar and incongruous. It began without a strip of territory. A warehouse was expanded into a province; a province into an

Empire. I propose to collect some tales of the Warehouse, and to record the early history of the Province; but I do not aspire to relate the annals of an Empire.

My aim, moreover, is to furnish a few sketches of men and manners without devoting an exclusive attention to the great and illustrious. In most historical pictures, kings, statesmen, and warriors stand conspicuous, whilst the multitude are grouped together, and their separate features are scarcely perceptible. But in modern ages a spirit of research has led students to inquire into the habits and characters of the many, and their minute discoveries have supplied defects in History, throwing, as they do, light not only upon heroes, but on Man.

The following work is not indeed antiquarian, but yet its design is to exhume from the graves in which they have been buried, the motives and acts of individuals. As students of antiquity, by finding a bone here, a piece of tesselated pavement there, in another place some pottery or rust-eaten weapons, have caught glimpses of the Roman's domestic life and social condition; so now it is hoped, that by collecting heterogeneous facts from new and old books, and from mouldy records, we shall be able to form a museum, in which will be exhibited the social and moral condition not only of the architects by whom the foundations were laid, and the building superintended; but also of those who were work-people in the construction of our Anglo-Indian Empire. And when expatiating "free o'er all this scene of man," it will be an object to shew, that although "a mighty maze," it is "not without a plan."

In writing the word "Empire" we are reminded how ill it assorts itself with the facts which are here to be recorded. The word conveys ideas of grandeur, wealth, and power; whereas this and the two following Chapters are annals of mediocrity and weakness, sometimes of drivelling baseness. The instruments, which Providence employed to create a British power in India, were often of the basest metal. But such answer the same purposes as the finest in the hands of Infinite Wisdom. And though we may feel disappointed, we ought not to be surprised, when we see little to admire in the pioneers of our Eastern empire, and find that some were amongst the meanest of mankind.

Yet, bad as were such agents, it will, I think, appear in this work that British power has been established by the moral force of British character. A writer of Anglo-Indian History must indeed soil his paper with narratives, from which virtue and honesty turn with disgust. But here is a distinction. Truth and sincerity have been, in the main, characteristics of the British, and the opposite vices exceptions. With the Oriental races amongst whom they have been located, fraud, chicanery and intrigue have been the usual engines of State policy; truth and sincerity have been rare as flowers in a sandy soil. When British merchants or statesmen have formed compacts, given pledges, or made promises, they have usually —though not in all instances—observed their compacts, redeemed their pledges, and fulfilled their promises, and the natives have generally acknowledged this: so that, although their confidence has been sometimes misplaced, and has received a few severe shocks, they have continued to rely upon the good faith of Englishmen. On the other hand, they have rarely placed dependence on one another, and although some have been distinguished for their virtues in private life, their rule has ever been, to regard each other with suspicion and mistrust.

But let us see the steps which led to the first establishment of the English in India. So early as the commencement of the fourteenth century, certain Europeans, who have left accounts of their travels, visited the Western Coast, and mentioned places well known at the present day —such as Cámbái, Bassein, Choul, and Thána. In the marvellous history composed A. D. 1325 by Sir John Mandeville of St Albans, there is a vague description of these parts; but the credulous knight does not state whether he had himself visited them. There is also a curious and fragmentary narrative published about 1330 in Latin, which sets forth that it was taken by William de Solanga from the lips of Odoricus, an Italian friar of the order of Minorites or *fratres minores*, a branch of the Franciscans. From Ormus, Odoricus passed in twenty-eight days to Thána, where four of his Christian brethren suffered martyrdom. He specifically calls the ship in which he sailed a 'jaház,' the generic name by which vessels of all kinds are known in India, and he was surprised, as many other Europeans have been, to see that such were made of bámbús without any appearance of being fastened by iron bolts.* He also notices with quaint brevity the flying foxes, and bandicote rats, which were so large that cats could not kill them, the tulasi tree standing before the houses of idolaters, and their superhumane practice of feeding ants and pismires.

Soon after the Portuguese had discovered the passage by the Cape of Good Hope, they formed settlements at Diu, Damán, Goa, Cálicot, Cochin, and other places on the Western coast. The deeds of high daring which they wrought, and the wealth which their deeply laden carracks bore to Europe, spread their reputation far and wide, and inspired the English in particular with a desire to share the risks and profits of Eastern adventure.

In 1563 Master Cæsar Frederick, a Venetian merchant, travelled by way of the Persian Gulf to these parts. He describes Cámbái, where the marine supremacy of the Portuguese was acknowledged, and Ahmedábád, both of which places were remarkable for their extensive trade. When journeying in a palanquin from Ankola to Goa, he was assailed by robbers, stripped naked, and would have been plundered of all that he possessed, if he had not, before starting, taken the precaution to conceal his valuables in a bámbú.

Thomas Stephens is the first Englishman of whom we are sure that he visited the Western shores of India. When there, he was only known as a Jesuit, but he had been originally educated at New College, Oxford. On the fourth of April 1579 he sailed from Lisbon, and the following October reached Goa, where he lived many years. A letter

* "In hâc terrâ homines utuntur navigio, quod vocatur Jase, sutum sparto. Ego autem ascendi in unum illorum, in quo nullum ferrum potui reperire, et in viginta octo diebus perveni ad civitatem Thana, in quâ pro fide Christi quatuor de fratribus nostris martyrizati sunt." Hakluyt's Voyages, Vol. II. The same is noticed in "the Voiage and Travail of Sir John Mandevil, Kt."

which he wrote to his father, a London merchant, soon after his arrival, is printed in Hakluyt's collection of Voyages. It not only contains a particular and interesting description of his perilous navigation round the Cape, but many sage remarks are made in quite a mercantile spirit on the state of Portuguese trade, of which he evidently desires that his countrymen should obtain a share. The reader is surprised to find a Roman ecclesiastic entering with such eagerness and penetration into commercial affairs. Probably Stephens' advices were the strongest inducements which London merchants had been offered to embark in Indian speculations, and certainly they began from this period to fit out expeditions for the East. Pyrard de Laval, who was a prisoner at Goa in 1608, states that Stephens was then Rector of a College on Salsette, by which he probably means the province of that name in the Goanese territory. The English Jesuit was a kind-hearted man, and true friend in need to several of his countrymen, who within the space of a few years found their way to India. * The advance guard to an army of English adventurers now made their appearance.

In 1583 Leedes, Ralph Fitch, John Newberry and some others, entered India by the route which Cæsar Frederick had followed. A suspicion that they were engaged in trade was sufficient to alarm the jealous Portuguese, and no sooner did they reach Goa, than they were thrown into prison. They tell us that first of all they were "examined whether they were good Christians or no," and, as they never hesitated to tell a lie, their Christianity was approved. In fact, they passed themselves off as "real Catholics," although strongly suspected of English heresy. One of their party had some skill in painting, and as his art was in great request at Goa for the decoration of its magnificent churches, he was induced to regain his liberty by becoming a Jesuit, and naturalized inhabitant of the place. Indulgence was also shewn to the rest through the good offices of Thomas Stephens, and after enjoying partial freedom they at last contrived to effect their escape, leaving the painter behind them. When too late he repented of having changed his religion, and although he had no intention of leaving Goa, persuasion was in vain used to retain him in a cloister. He opened a shop, carried on a lucrative business, and married the daughter of an Indo-Portuguese. As for Fitch he returned to England after a lengthened peregrination, and Leedes entered the service of the Great Mogul. †

Pyrard de Laval, who, combining business with pleasure, left St. Maloes on the 18th May 1601, and stayed many years at Goa, met there with Spaniards, Venetians and other Italians, Germans, Flemings, Armenians, a few English, and only three Frenchmen. ‡ The English were chiefly prisoners, who had been surprized at the bar of the Surat river by a cowardly stratagem of the Portuguese. Probably they had belonged to the expedition of Captain Hawkins, whose long-boat with twenty-seven

* Histoire generale des voyages ; par C. A. Walckenaer. Hakluyt's Voyages.

† Hakluyt's Voyages. Oriental Commerce : By William Milburn, Esq. Vol I.

‡ Voyage de François Pyrard de Laval. Seconde partie, Chap II. Historical Fragments of the Mogul Empire. By Robert Orme, Esq.

men and some valuable goods was seized. Laval merely states that they had been employed in traffic, and a gentleman who had come with them had gone on to the Great Mogul's Court, where he had been well received. Whilst their ships were at anchor, seventeen persons had left them in two boats laden with merchandize, which they intended to exchange for Indigo. Their movements, however, had been watched from some Portuguese coasting vessels, the commander of which bore down upon them, cut off their retreat, and carried them all to Goa. Confinement and neglect soon brought on disease, and in a short time there were but six or seven survivors.

Six months before he left Goa, Pyrard met another English prisoner, who seemed a person of some distinction, and had been surprized in the same way as the others, when he was taking soundings. He accused the Portuguese of savage ferocity, declaring that they had slaughtered his cousin in cold blood, and placed his head upon a pike as a trophy. His own life had been in great danger, for his captors, knowing that he had been surveying the coast, regarded him with peculiar suspicion. After a long imprisonment he was suffered to depart.

Four months after this gentleman had been seized, the unlucky ship to which he belonged was wrecked on the coast. The crew, twenty-four in number, having contrived to reach the shore near Surat with their money and other property, were well treated by the native authorities. They then divided themselves into two parties ; the more adventurous spirits making an attempt to return home by way of Tartary, the others remaining at Surat. The former were enabled by passports, which they procured at the Mogul's court, to pass through his dominions, but were not permitted to enter the country of the Tartars, and after a fruitless journey they returned to Surat. All the survivors repaired to Goa, and sailed from thence to England. * Every Englishman on whom the Portuguese could lay their hands was treated by them as a prisoner, and when Laval was about to leave India, several Englishmen were actually brought on board in irons. † Yet even when in this sad plight they appeared to him a proud set, who took every opportunity of shewing their contempt for Frenchmen. ‡

Such was Portuguese hospitality ! Shipwrecked mariners, instead of receiving from them generous fare and clothing, or at least protection and sympathy, were condemned to eat the bread and water of affliction in a dungeon, and if they survived such treatment, were sent to their own country with ignominy. Exclusiveness and illiberality are the sure forerunners of degeneracy, and the English are avenged. Being now the dominant party, they can return good for evil by blessing the descendants of these persecutors with religious toleration and political freedom.

Mildenhall, a London merchant, was sent out from that capital by a commercial association in 1599 ; but, as he travelled overland and was frequently delayed, he did not reach Agra until 1603 ! His object was to obtain from the Emperor a firmán, authorizing the English to trade

* Pyrard de Laval. Troisième partie, Chap. xx.
† Ib. Chap xxi.
‡ Ib. Seconde partie, Chap. vi.

in his dominions. After waiting three years, and defeating the machinations of Jesuits and two Italian merchants, he was satisfied with his success, and returned to England. We hear of him as being again at Agra in 1614, but have no very clear account of his history. It is said that he went in 1610 to Persia, where he was joined in a commission with two young men, whom he poisoned, and having possessed himself of their property repaired to Agra. Religion of course sat loosely on such a character, and as soon as he found it convenient to be a Roman Catholic, he threw off his Protestant faith. It was not long before he was himself poisoned, and dying left his money to a Frenchman, whose daughter he had intended to marry. *

Two years after Mildenhall had left Agra to give an account of himself in England, Captain Hawkins of the ship 'Hector' came to Surat. He tells us that he was kindly received by the natives "after their barbarous manner;" but was much harassed by the Portuguese, who, however, permitted him to land his iron and lead with some treasure. As soon as possible he started with a letter from King James to the Great Mogul for Agra, where he arrived at the end of May 1609, after being in continual fear that he would be assassinated by his attendants at the instigation of the Portuguese. His reception at Court was flattering, and he was assured that he should have permission to establish a Factory at Surat. The Great Mogul wishing to engage his services and keep him in the country, offered him a pension and a wife. Hawkins was not averse to either. Although he called himself an English ambassador, he did not scruple to accept a salary, which, however, was very irregularly paid; and as the imperial harem contained a large assortment of ladies varying in race, colour, and religion, he was provided with a bride to his taste who was both a Christian and a maiden. He seems to have really loved his wife, and to have resolved not to forsake her. Still he did not forget the interests of his English employers. He repeatedly demanded the privileges which they required, was frequently promised them, and as frequently disappointed. At last, baffled by the intrigues of the Portuguese, and disgusted with the wavering counsels of the Emperor, he gave up his efforts in despair, and requested his dismissal. The Indian potentate did not condescend to give any answer to King James's letter, and Hawkins, after a protracted contest with his wife's brothers, who wished to prevent her from leaving the country, contrived to take her on board an English ship at Cámbái, from whence he sailed with her on the 26th of January 1612 to Europe. †

William Finch and three or four English servants had been left by Hawkins at Surat when he went up the country, that they might dispose of such goods as he had landed. Whilst they were there the ship 'Ascension' was wrecked at Gandaví, and happily they were enabled to succour the crew, seventy-five of whom escaped from the wreck, and, not being suffered to enter Surat, were maintained for some time by Finch at a neighbouring village. They were afterwards dispersed over the country. Some were probably the persons whom Laval met at

* Historical Fragments of the Mogul Empire. By Robert Orme, Esq.

† History of the European Commerce with India. By David Macpherson. Orme's Fragments.

Goa. Finch was summoned in January 1610 by Hawkins to Agra, and travelled by way of the Panjáb and Persia to England. *

Expeditions from England to the Western coast of India became now more frequent. The object of all was purely commercial, but it was an ominous fact that Englishmen only obtained respect and influence amongst the natives by means of hard fighting. Their laurels were first gathered at Swally near Surat. The managers of a Factory which had a few years previously been established at Bantam in Java, had recommended that a trade should be opened at Surat and Cámbái for the sake of supplying them with cloths and calicoes. Sir Henry Middleton endeavoured to comply with their suggestion in January 1612; but his efforts were frustrated, partly through his own unfair dealing and insolent treatment of native chiefs, partly by Portuguese intrigue. More successful, however, was one of those daring spirits, which have never been wanting to the British in their hour of need. Captain Best was determined to open a passage to Surat with his two ships, the 'Dragon' and 'Hosiander.' He reached the coast on the 28th October 1612. Two Portuguese armaments successively threw themselves in his way at the river's mouth; but after severe struggles the skill and courage of himself and men prevailed against both. The great Mogul then sent down to him a firmán authorizing an English Minister to reside at Court, and opening to English subjects the trade of Surat. This imperial ordinance was forwarded to Best as an ordinary letter, but he had by this time become aware of his own power, and of the impression which a little display makes upon native minds. He therefore wisely insisted that the usual ceremonies should be observed, and the firmán was formally presented to him by the Governor of Surat, who came in state to Swally for the purpose. Best then sailed away, first leaving at Surat ten persons to dispose of the goods which he had brought, and with a stock of four thousand pounds to purchase the manufactures of India. That was the first rising of the British star, and the Portuguese paled before it. In vain did they afterwards endeavour to undermine by intrigue the influence which was built upon conduct and bravery. Englishmen had left an impression which was never to be effaced. †

The principal Factors left in 1613 by Best at Surat, were Andrew Starkey, Canning, Aldworth, Withington, and Kerridge. Starkey had orders to proceed overland to England with intelligence that a Factory had been established, but, as is asserted, he was poisoned on the journey by two friars. Canning, being sent with a king's letter to Agra, was attacked on the road by robbers, who wounded him and another Englishman, and killed one of his escort. He carried with him a present for the great Mogul, but it was of so little value that it was received with contempt, and the disappointed monarch asked if *that* was sent by the king of England. He was in constant dread of being poisoned, and

* Orme's Fragments.

† Annals of the Honorable East India Company. By John Bruce, Esq. Vol. I. Orme's Fragments. Description of Hindostan. By Walter Hamilton. Appendix to a Treatise on the wealth, power, and resources of the British Empire. By P. Colquhoun, LL.D.

as he died on the 29th of May, the Portuguese Jesuits, whom the Factors believed capable of committing any crime, were suspected of having caused his death.

Aldworth and Withington travelled in November from Surat to inspect Baroch, Jambúsír, Baroda, and Ahmedábád, with a view to ascertain the state of their markets. At Baroch and Ahmedábád they hired houses on the Company's account, and left brokers to transact their business. Aldworth was for some time the principal merchant at Surat, and died in 1615 at Ahmedábád.

At this place Withington heard a report that three English vessels were lying in the Indus, and immediately started on a most perilous journey overland to assist them with his counsel. He had better have remained where he was. He never reached the Indus, but being plundered by the predatory tribes of all that he possessed, and reduced to sustain life by begging alms, was compelled to retrace his steps. After an absence of a hundred and eleven days, during which he had suffered intense misery, he thought himself lucky in April 1615 to set his foot again in Ahmedábád. Soon afterwards he was sent for to Agra, that he might secure the effects of Mildenhall, who had lately deceased.*

This season Captain Nicholas Downton sustained the reputation of which Captain Best had laid the foundation. He was the chief commander, or, as such officers were then styled, "the General" of four English ships. At Surat he found three English Factors, Aldworth, Biddulph, and Richard Steele, the last of whom had lately come from Aleppo. His first step was, to demand redress for extortion in the customs; his second was to require, like a true Englishman, that a market for beef should be established at Swally. The first application was met by evasion; the second by a declaration that beef could not be had, as the banyás, by whom the preservation of animal life was regarded in the light of a religious duty, had paid a large sum to prevent bullocks from being slaughtered.

The Emperor and petty princes of the Deccan were united in an attempt to drive the Portuguese out of India, and no sooner had Downton arrived, than the Governor of Surat invited his co-operation. But as Portugal and her possessions were then subject to the Spanish crown, and there was peace between Spain and England, the English Captain declined this invitation, which so annoyed the Governor, that he in turn refused him all assistance, and on a frivolous pretext threw the English Factors into prison. Downton's forbearance was but ill-requited by the Portuguese; for they falsely represented to the Governor that he had consented to join them in an attack upon Surat. Their own acts, however, soon refuted this calumny. With six galleons of from four to eight hundred tons burden, three other vessels of considerable size, and sixty smaller ones, mounting in all a hundred and thirty-four pieces of ordnance, the viceroy of Goa attacked the four English ships, which could only mount eighty guns of inferior calibre. To the astonishment of the natives, the assailants were defeated as signally as in the previous year, so that their glory and renown were for ever transferred to their conquerors. Downton was

* Orme's Fragments.

no longer treated with roughness and insolence, but before leaving Surat received from the pliant Governor and principal men of the place, distinguished marks of courtesy and respect. He died at Bantam on the sixth of the following August, "lamented, admired, and unequalled."*

The report which had induced Withington to attempt his hazardous journey, was an exaggeration; but one English ship had actually arrived at the Indus. On board were Sir Robert Shirley, who was returning from England whither he had been sent as the king of Persia's Ambassador, and Sir Thomas Powell, who had been sent to that monarch on an embassy by King James. Debarred by the Portuguese from passing the Straits of Ormus into the Persian Gulf, the two ambassadors and their wives attempted to land in Balúchisthán, where they narrowly escaped being murdered. At last they disembarked at Diul on the Indus, and there again were ill-treated and detained by the Governor, whom the Portuguese had either bribed or intimidated. Sir Thomas Powell and one of his followers died; but Sir Robert Shirley persisted in setting off for Persia. No sooner, however, had he put off from the shore, and was afloat on the river Indus, than an armed force brought him back. A fray ensued, in which his companion, Mr. Ward, fired his pistol in the face of a trooper, and was instantly shot dead by another trooper. At this juncture Sir Thomas Powell's widow was confined, and died with her infant, as did also Michael, the brother of Sir Thomas. Shirley at length escaped from the hands of his barbarous tormentors, and reached Agra, where he was courteously received by Jehángír, who sent him forward on his journey with rich presents, equipages, provisions, and an escort.†

By this time a regular Factory had been established at Surat. It was usually styled 'the English House,' and was presided over by Kerridge. A Factor named Edwards had also been left at Ahmedábád. It was arranged between these two that Edwards should proceed on a mission to the Mogul Court. He was provided with a letter from King James; and Kerridge having an eye to business made him take with him an investment of cloths, looking-glasses, and sword-blades. Half Ambassador and half hawker, he thus went to Agra, where he was presented to the Emperor by Asof Khán, the Prime Minister and favourite Sultána's brother. By a judicious distribution of presents he obtained all that he asked. To the Emperor himself he delivered portraits of King James and the Royal family. But his most acceptable offering was a large mastiff, of which Kerridge wrote as follows:—

"Mr. Edwardes presented the Kinge a mastife, and speakinge of the dogs courage, the Kinge cawsed a yonge leoparde to be brought to make tryall, which the dogge soe pinchtt, thatt fewer howres after the leoparde dyed. Synce, the Kinge of Persia, with a presentt, sent heather haulfe a dozen dogges—the Kinge cawsed boares to be brought to fight with them, puttinge two or three dogges to a boare, yet none of them seased; and rememberinge his owne dogge, sentt for him, who presently fastened on

* Orme's Fragments. Macpherson's History. Colquhoun's Treatise.
† Orme's Fragments.

the boare, so disgraced the Persian doggs, wherewith the Kinge was exceedingly pleased. Two or three mastiffes, a couple of Irish greyhowndes, and a couple of well-taught water spanyells, wold give him greate contente."

No needy client ever studied a patrician's whims and caprices more attentively than did the English Factors study the Great Moguls. In 1612 they had specially recommended that toys and bull dogs should be sent for presents to him and his courtiers ; and now Edwards desired that landscapes, such pictures as represented the manners and customs of England, portraits of the nobility, and some fine beaver hats, should be forwarded.*

Although Hawkins, Canning, Kerridge, and Edwards had assumed the imposing title of Ambassador, yet they were merely humble agents of the Company. It was now resolved to try what effect the dignity of a Royal Embassy would have. Sir Thomas Roe was chosen to make the experiment, and there could scarcely have been a better selection. The object of his Embassy was twofold—to arrange the terms of a treaty, and to recover large sums of money due to the Company from persons about the Court. He brought with him the draft of a treaty comprising nineteen articles, the first seventeen of which related to the protection and encouragement of trade, the last two to an alliance offensive and defensive between the Emperor and the English people.

Having left England on the sixth of March he arrived at Surat on the twenty-fourth of September 1615, and was received in an open tent by the chief Officers of the city with distinguished honour. On this, as well as all other occasions—whether he was admitted to interviews with great Chiefs, the Prince Royal, or the Emperor himself—he refused to compromise the dignity of England by making those slavish prostrations which Indian despots expected from the representatives of foreign powers.

From Surat Sir Thomas marched to Burhámpúr, where he was most courteously and honourably received by Parvíz, one of the Emperor's younger sons. The Prince's Court had no pretensions to splendour, but parade was by no means neglected. A hundred native gentlemen on horse back formed a lane in the outer court of the palace, through which the Ambassador was conducted. Parvíz himself sat under a canopy in the inner Court, and his nobles were ranged on either side of him, according to their rank. An interpreter standing upon the steps of the throne was the medium of communication. Many of the usual ceremonies were dispensed with, that the Prince might pay Sir Thomas the compliment of receiving him according to the customs of England.

The Emperor was residing at Ajmír. The day before the Ambassador arrived there he was met by Edwards and Coryat. He found the Court in the midst of joyous festivities, and was well pleased with his reception ; but complained that the meanness of the presents which he took with him, proved a serious drawback. In spite of the care with which their Factors had drawn their attention to the subject, the Company did not understand how to gratify the taste of an Oriental potentate. The presents

* Bruce's Annals, 1614-15.

were ill selected, unworthy of the monarch by whom Sir Thomas was accredited, and, as he well knew, were spoken of with contempt by the Emperor. An English carriage was accepted graciously, but was not sufficiently gaudy to please a native of India. As before, so now, some noble mastiffs had an irresistible charm for the Imperial sportsman, who was however much disappointed when he found there was no "great English horse," for which he would have given a lakh of rupees. And then his inquisitive Majesty began to fumble in the Ambassador's chests, until by ill-luck he drew out a picture. The subject was 'Venus leading a Satyr by the nose.' "What is the meaning of this?" asked Jehángír. The Ambassador really did not know. His Chaplain was then asked for an explanation; but he also pleaded ignorance. So the Emperor pertinently demanded why they brought to him things which they did not understand. His suspicions soon suggested to him an interpretation. He decided that it was an allegory and caricature of himself and people. The Satyr was black; so he must represent the Natives of India. Venus leading him by the nose symbolized the great influence which women were supposed to exercise over men in Hindústán. His Majesty was in high dudgeon for some time after the discovery of this ingenious solution. It was natural that it should occur to the husband of the beautiful and all powerful Núr Jehán, better known to the readers of English poetry by the name of Nourmahal, "his harem's light."

Sir Thomas Roe's liberality was soon exhausted in attempting to cram the maw of an Indian Monarch and his greedy courtiers. On new year's day he had so little left that he could only offer the Emperor "a couple of fine knives, and six glasses," to Asof Khán "a pair of gloves, and a curious nightcap," the former of which was returned as "of no use in India." The neglect with which he was occasionally treated, was attributed by him to these evidences of poverty; yet on the whole he was honoured with marked distinction.

In his case there were few of those barriers which are now raised between Europeans and Natives. He did not indeed, when invited to great men's houses, partake with them of the same dishes; but sat with his Chaplain at a separate table; except in one memorable instance, when Asof Khán listened to his remonstrances, and shared a meal with him. But this restriction upon social intercourse at formal banquets was amply compensated by the admission which he freely gained to drinking bouts. Like the *symposia* and *commissationes* of the Greeks and Romans, these were separate entertainments, conducted with the utmost freedom and joviality. For although Jehángír and his courtiers were strict observers of the Kurán by day, at night they felt absolved from all attention to its abstemious principles. The Ambassador's wine of Alicant was in great request, and accepted without scruple; but "the Lord of the world" called also for a more potent draught. The liquor of which he drank deep was so strong that the mere fumes made the Ambassador sneeze. Then his Imperial Majesty passed through the stages of intoxication, known as "laughing" and "crying drunk." Now in the warmth of his heart he vowed that he would recognize no distinctions between Christians, Moors, and Jews, for that all should share his favour equally; now "sighs stole out, and tears began to flow." The Ambassador having thus discovered his taste, took the hint as usual, and in writing to the Directors of the East India Company offered them his advice thus :—" There is nothing more welcome here, nor did I ever see men so fond of drink, as the King and Prince are of red wine, whereof the Governor of Surat sent up some bottles ; and the King has ever since solicited for more. I think four or five casks of that wine will be more welcome than the richest jewel in Cheapside."*

Although Sir Thomas was mortified by many refusals and evasions, yet he obtained more success at last than he could have anticipated. He so completely brought Asof Khán over to his interests, that even a stout opposition of the heir to the throne was overcome The separate articles of his treaty were indeed rejected ; " yet by piecemeals," he wrote, " I have got as much as I desired at once. I have recovered all bribes, extortions, and debts made and contracted before my time till this day, or at least an honorable composition." He gained also permission to establish a Factory at Baroch, which, although its fortunes varied, was so flourishing in 1683, that an investment of fifty-five thousand pieces of cloth was sent from it in that single year to England.

Sir Thomas was much vexed and retarded in his operations by difficulties which the Factors of Surat threw in his way, probably at the suggestion of their English masters. The East India Company have always been jealous of such servants of the Crown as have been mixed up with their affairs, and the Ambassador was convinced that they were so in his case. He writes:—

" Your Factors sent me four or five clauses of your commission that concerned Persia, a fort, a plantation in Bengala, all which they knew were not of use ; with no other proposition or resolution they will acquaint me. They cannot abide I should understand or direct them. If they resolve of anything in their opinion for your profit, I will effect the court part ; but you will find in my letters and journay how they use me, which doubtless at first was sowed by some jealousy of yours, which will cost you dearly,"

It is creditable to the good sense of both parties that they understood each other at last, and when Sir Thomas left the country the Factors parted with him on good terms.

On the whole, the result of the Embassy must be pronounced a triumph of diplomacy. Its display was indeed insignificant as compared with the

* That Roe's narrative is not a libel against Jehángír is evident from that Monarch's own confessions. He acknowledges in his autobiography that when on a hunting expedition he had for the first time drank a cup of wine, at the recommendation of the Commandant of Artillery, who assured him he would be much refreshed by it, he found it so delicious, that he afterwards repeated the draught. Increasing his potations gradually, he at last drank wine in large quantities, and it had no effect upon him. Then he craved a stronger liquor. " Constantly, for nine years, he drank of double distilled spirits, fourteen cups in the day, and six cups at night, which, he says, were altogether equal to six Hindostan seers, or English quarts." The result was the same as in Falstaff, who had but " one half pennyworth of bread to an intolerable deal of sack." Jehángír suffered loss of appetite, and contracted such a nervous affection, that he was obliged to have the cup lifted to his mouth.—*Gladwin's History of Jehanguire.*

splendour of the Court to which it was dispatched, and at one time it was on this account threatened with failure. Yet such as it was, it proved in the end so expensive, that—as the thrifty King threw the burden upon the Company—their finances were drained alarmingly. Happily, Sir Thomas Roe was gifted with judgment and tact, and he had the good fortune to visit a communicative and sociable, if not a liberal and enlightened Emperor. So that, although eighty years or more afterwards the character of the British nation was lowered by an Embassy entrusted to the vacillating and misguided Sir William Norris, it was at this time exalted. The condescension, affability, even friendliness, with which Sir Thomas was received by the occupant of the peacock throne, caused the English to shine in Native eyes with lustre reflected from Imperial glory.*

So highly were the Company pleased with Sir Thomas Roe's conduct, that when he returned to England they paid him the compliment of offering him an honorary seat in their Court of Committees, and more substantially rewarded him with a pension of two hundred pounds per annum. † He afterwards obtained a seat in Parliament, where he supported the Company's interests. ‡ So late as 1643 his name appears in English history. He was then sent as Ambassador Extraordinary by Charles the First to the Emperor and Princes of Germany; and was the subject of unjust accusations, which were secretly submitted by the French Ambassador to the English Parliament. §

In March 1616 Keeling, "the General" of the four ships with which Sir Thomas Roe arrived at Surat, made a strenuous effort to establish a Factory at Cranganor. The Zamorin, as the ruler of the country was styled, having heard the fame of Downton's exploits, sent his Minister to meet Keeling at Cálicot, and invited him to a conference. The English Captain took the precaution to secure a hostage for his safe return, and then went to the neighbourhood of Cranganor, which the Zamorin was besieging. He was received with great politeness, and soon concluded a treaty, which commenced with the heathen ruler's words, thus :—"As I have been ever an enemy to the Portuguese, so do I purpose to continue for ever." He then promises to give the Fort of Cranganor— when captured—the islands, and nine miles of coast to the English; also with their aid to take Cochin, and then transfer it to them with all its territory; finally he stipulates to exempt them from all payment of duties and customs. It is scarcely necessary to say that these terms were too favourable for the English to be observed. However, Keeling left at Cranganor three Factors and a lad, as also a gunner who entered the Zamorin's service. It was not long before the Factors found themselves the victims of gross extortion, instead of being encouraged. They seized the first opportunity of escaping with their goods to Cálicot, where they remained in spite of the many difficulties

* Journal and Letters of Sir Thomas Roe in Churchill's Collection of Voyages. The History of Hindóstan; translated from the Persian. By Alexander Dow, Vol. iii. Chap. iii The View of Hindostan. By Thomas Pennant, vol. i.

† Macpherson's History.

‡ Robert Grant's "Sketch of the History of the East India Company," Chap. 1.

§ Clarendon's History of the Rebellion, Book vi.

with which they had to contend. Thus the English Factory of Călicot had its origin.* The place, we may be sure, was celebrated for the produce of its looms from the fact of its name having been given to our ordinary cotton fabrics.

As these pages contain much that is discreditable to the Portuguese it is a pleasure now to chronicle an action which redounds to their honour. Four English ships, in one of which was Terry, afterwards Sir Thomas Roe's Chaplain, were bringing to India merchandize, and the presents which the Embassy was to take charge of for the Emperor. All were under the command of General Joseph. At the head of the channel between Madagascar and the African coast, they descried a Portuguese carrack of enormous size, which proved to be commanded by Don Manuel de Menezes. Although England and Portugal were at peace, yet in the Indian Seas there was a smouldering enmity between the seamen of the two nations, which was always ready to burst into a flame. The *Globe*, a small but fast sailing vessel of Joseph's squadron, gave chase to the carrack, and on coming up was saluted with opprobrious language, and an order to fall to leeward. As obedience was not promptly paid, the Portuguese fired five large shot at her. By this time Joseph himself had come up in his large ship, the *Charles*, and called out that the Commander of the carrack must come on board. As the excuse was made that they had no boat, Joseph sent his own, which brought three officers with a message, "that Don Menezes had promised his master, the King of Spain, not to quit his ship, out of which he might be forced, but never commanded." Joseph replied, "that he would sink by his side, or compel him." After these words of defiance had been exchanged, the fight began. Joseph was killed in a few minutes, and his command assumed by Captain Pepwell. Night came on; but the chivalrous Menezes scorned to skulk away in the darkness, and hung out a light to guide his enemies. The following day and night passed without any continuance of the struggle, but it was renewed at sunrise on the second morning. Pepwell was wounded in the jaw and leg, and his eye was struck out. The carrack's main and mizen masts were brought down, and her fore top shot away. Seeing their foe in this plight the English sent a boat to him, with Mr. Cormack, the principal merchant, bearing a flag of truce, and Menezes received him courteously, but declared his resolution to renew the contest on the morrow. Unhappily for the gallant Don, his ship struck on the rocks during the night. The crew set her on fire, and made their escape with treasure to a large amount, but being overpowered and plundered by the natives were reduced to great distress. Menezes at last contrived to reach Goa, where he was received with great respect on account of his valour and misfortunes. He was also much honoured on his return to his country, and, as his force had been far inferior to that of his enemies, his defeat was considered equivalent to a victory.†

One of the most peculiar features in this early part of English history is the evidence of a jealousy and hatred with which all who were in the

* Orme's Fragments.
† Orme's Fragments. Terry's Voyage.

Company's employ, and their rivals in trade, mutually regarded each other. The French had not yet appeared in India, if we except the three whom Laval met at Goa, and a few whom Bernier found employed by the Emperor as cannoniers. But the Portuguese had been there so long that they had passed their zenith, and were in the descendant. They had formed settlements at Cálicot, Mangalor, Goa, Bombay, Salsette, Bassein and Damán. As they always seemed ignorant how to use victory with moderation, their haughtiness and insolence had prepared the natives to look with favour upon any rival, who should contest with them the privileges of trade and command of the sea. In 1508 they had taken and plundered Dábhol, and in 1510 under Albuquerque surprised and conquered Goa. As early as 1512 they pillaged Surat, and nearly destroyed it.* The inhabitants then spoke of them as "the vile miscreants," and when a Turkish Admiral arrived welcomed him as a deliverer from their odious tyranny. The Admiral himself,—who has left us an account of his voyage,—always uses the word 'miscreant' as a synonyme for 'Portuguese.'† Bombay was occupied by them in 1532. The same year they burned the whole of the towns on the coast between Chicklí Tárapúr and Bassein, and in 1548 all between the neighbourhood of Goa and Bánkot. Although their chief possessions were at a distance from Surat, yet we have seen them using all their power to prevent the English from entering its port. However, the power of these dreaded plunderers was shown by a succession of naval defeats to have been over estimated. "On my word they are weak in India," wrote Sir Thomas Roe, "and able to do your fleet no harm, but by supplies from Lisbon.‡ At last in 1630 they procured a reinforcement from Europe, and with nine ships endeavoured to destroy a fleet of five English ships as it approached Swally. Their efforts were baffled, and then the superiority of British seamen was for ever established.§

Lest it should be suspected that our opinion of the Portuguese is dictated by national prejudices, the testimony of their own countrymen and intelligent Frenchmen is appealed to. Much of the above account is taken from their historian De Faria. The biographer of Francis Xavier dwells upon their moral degradation, and declares that they "lived more like idolaters than Christians." He adds that they had imitated the depraved habits of the heathen, that wedded chastity was little esteemed amongst them, that they were even proud of the number of their concubines, and nothing could be more corrupt than their whole lives. ‖ Father leGobien traces the aversion with which they were regarded by the natives to the violence which they had employed, and Father de Fontenay makes special mention of their dissolute behaviour.¶

* Conquêts des Portugais par Lafitou. Maffeei Historiarum Indicarum, Lib x. This Jesuit gives detailed accounts of their plundering expeditions, without expressing any disapprobation.

† Vogages de Sidi Aly par M. Moris. Grant Duff's History of the Mahrattas, Vol. I. Chap. 2.

‡ Sir Thomas Roe's Letters to the Company.

§ Mill's History of India, Book I Chap. 2.

‖ S. Xaverii Vita, auctore Tursellino. Lib ii. cap. i.

¶ Choix des lettres edifiantes, tom. iv.

The Abbè Raynal enters into the subject, and his testimony is very decided. He regarded the Portuguese as a decaying race. The religious zeal which once inspired them with energy and generous courage was afterwards manifested only in ferocity, and served to stifle all scruples about pillaging, cheating, and enslaving idolators. As they pretended to have been endowed with authority over the kingdoms of Asia by a decree of the Pope, they chose to suppose that a power to seize the property of individuals was also conferred upon them. Demanding tribute from the ships of every country, ravaging the coasts, and insulting native chiefs, they became the scourge and terror of all the nations bordering upon the ocean. Nor was their treatment of one another better than of foreigners. They were divided into factions, and amongst all, avarice, debauchery and cruelty prevailed. Many of them had seven or eight concubines, whom they employed as menial servants. Effeminacy pervaded their armies, and they lost the courage for which they had long been celebrated. "No Portuguese pursued any other object than the advancement of his own interest; there was no zeal, no union for the common good. Their possessions in India were divided into three governments, which gave no assistance to each other, and even clashed in their projects and interests. Neither discipline, subordination, nor the love of glory, animated either the soldiers or the officers. Men of war no longer ventured out of the ports; or whenever they appeared, were badly equipped. Manners became more and more depraved. Not one of their commanders had power enough to restrain the torrent of vice; and the majority of these commanders were themselves corrupted. The Portuguese at length lost all their former greatness, when a free and enlightened nation, actuated with a proper spirit of toleration, appeared in India, and contended with them for the empire of that country."*

The first Dutchman who attempted to open a trade at Surat was Van den Broeck. He was favourably received on the second of August 1616 by the Governor, and permitted to dispose of his goods; but when he craved permission to establish a Factory, as well as the English, he was told that a reference must be made to the Great Mogul. His failure at that time is attributed by him in great measure to the success of English intrigue. However, when he went away he promised that he would return, and left behind him three Factors with a Chief. Accordingly he did return in 1620, and declared himself Director of the Dutch trade in all those parts of the East. From that year he kept a diary, which has been published. Della Valle describes him as "a gentleman of good breeding and very courteous."†

Before Van den Broeck's return to Surat, an accident, turned to account with remarkable adroitness by the Dutch, had gained them a secure footing. One of their ships having been wrecked in July 1617 on the neighbouring coast, the merchants were allowed to dispose of its cargo in the city, and as they quickly discovered how valuable traffic there would prove, they left behind them ten

* A Philosophical and Political History of the Settlement and Trade of Europeans in the East and West Indies. By the Abbè Raynal.

† Voyage de Pierre Van den Broeck. Recueil des Voyages, Tome vii.

persons with instructions to make arrangements for the establishment of a Factory.* As they were more powerful, and soon proved themselves more skilful in trade than the Portuguese, the English did not fight them, but endeavoured to supplant them by base and underhand means. Sir Thomas Roe used every art to prejudice the Mogul government against them, his object being, as he said, "to disgrace them," and "turn them out," if he could do so without risk.† Referring to the arrival of a Dutch ship at Surat he writes thus: "This I improved to fill their heads with jealousies of the designs of the Dutch, and the dangers that might ensue from them, which was well taken; and being demanded, I gave my advice to prevent coming to a rupture with them, and yet exclude them the trade of India."‡ When the crafty ambassador said that he *improved* a fact, he simply meant, that he perverted the truth. However, his illiberality was neither more nor less than was shewn at that time by the representatives of other European nations in India.

The Dutch appear to have had the advantage of the English in the superior management of their Factories, and sagacity in all commercial transactions. The large capital which their Company possessed, and their economy in disposing of it, enabled them to compete successfully at Surat, so that the English Factors were reduced to utter puerile complaints, that their rivals bought Indian goods at a higher rate, and sold European goods at a lower rate than themselves.§ But after some years this opposition ceased, and the two nations joined their arms against the Portuguese.‖

At this period the Dutch were distinguished chiefly for their enterprizing spirit, and republican simplicity of manners. This simplicity was probably accompanied by rudeness, and some years later fell under the lash of Dryden's satire.¶ Their Governor General's salary was at the rate of £91. 13s. 4d. *per annum*, with the liberty of private trade, which, however, was afterwards withheld from all their Company's servants. Even at Batavia, their chief settlement, the members of Government dressed, we are assured, like common sailors, and before the year 1650 not one remarkable fortune had been made. But this state of affairs did not continue very long. At Surat they soon affected some style, and finally luxury and magnificence were introduced.**

As the reader will probably be glad to gain some idea of the English shipping which visited the coast of India, I conclude this chapter with an extract from a curious pamphlet entitled "Trades Increase" published at that time. "You have built," writes the author, apostrophizing the Company, "more ships in your time, than any other merchants' ships, besides

* Bruce's Annals, 1617-18.
† Letter to the East India Company.
‡ Sir Thomas Roe's Journal.
§ Mill's History.
‖ Van den Broeck.

¶ "With an ill grace the Dutch their mischiefs do:
They 've both ill nature, and ill manners too.
Well may they boast themselves an ancient nation,
For they were bred ere manners were in fashion.
And their new Commonwealth has set them free,
Only from honour and civility."

Satire on the Dutch.

** Raynal's History.

what you have bought out of other trades, and all those wholly belonging to you. There hath been entertained by you since you first adventured, one and twenty ships, besides the now intended voyage of one new ship of seven hundred tons, and happily some two more of increase. The least of all your shipping is of fourscore ton; all the rest are goodly ships of such burthen as never were formerly used in merchandize; the least and meanest of these last is of some hundred and twenty ton, and so upward even to eleven hundred ton. You have set forth some thirteen voyages; in which time you have built of these, eight new ships, and almost as good as built the most of the residue, as the Dragon, the Hector, &c." Respecting a ship called like the pamphlet, "The Trades Increase," the writer adds: — "It was a ship of eleven hundred ton, for beauty, burthen, strength, and sufficiency surpassing all merchants' ships whatsoever. But alas! she was but shown; out of a cruel destiny, she was overtaken with an untimely death in her youth and strength."*

* This pamphlet was published in 1615. Robert Grant's "Sketch of the History of the East India Company."

CHAPTER II.

1616—1630.

Contents:—Arrangements of the Factory.—President Kerridge; his character.—Joseph Salbank; his complaint.—Presidents Rastell and Wyld.—Business of the Factors; their private trade and inadequate salaries; their social position; aims solely mercantile.—Domestic Economy of the Factory.—Dress of the period adopted in India.—Society; a wedding banquet; no English Ladies; history of a Portuguese damsel; intemperance.—Legal powers to restrain offenders; escape of a Dutch murderer.—Religion; the Clergy; the Rev. Henry Lord; his oriental researches; Lescke and John Hall: Terry; his history; his sermon before the Company; Copeland; Dr. John Wood's good opinion of the Company.—Conversion of the natives; Salbank's pious letter.—Native opinions of English Christianity; the Knight of the Golden Rapier's opinion; account of this personage—Three portraits; Tom Coryat; his travels and eccentricities; death and burial; the reckless son of an English Baron; a rollicking cook—Della Valle's visit to Surat; his romantic history—Sir Thomas Herbert's visit; his history—Two speculators; scheme for navigating the Indus—Piracies by the Company's Captains—Reflections on English character.

It has been shewn in the preceding pages that an English Factory had been established at Surat under encouraging auspices. Through the efforts of Best, Downton, and Roe, the Factors had attained by proxy to a high degree of reputation. English courage and naval skill were feared; and even the inferior pretensions of the Embassy to magnificence, patronized as it had been by the great Mogul, were respected. Let us now enter the Factory's gates, and endeavour to ascertain its internal economy, with the qualities, characters, and employments of its occupants.

The persons who superintended the Company's affairs were, according to the humour of the times, variously styled Presidents, Agents, or Chiefs. In 1616 the title of President was given to Thomas Kerridge, the first Superintendent, by his own subordinates, and many of his successors are so addressed in the Company's records. The little we know of this Kerridge is much to his credit. He came to India in Best's ship, the *Hosiander*, September 1612. For some time his residence was at Agra, and then he managed a Factory at Ahmedábád, where he suffered much from the oppression of Mogul Officers. His integrity and ability were unquestionable, and—which was scarcely to be expected under the circumstances—he had an inquiring and literary turn of mind. As Europeans, before his time, had been sorely perplexed by the various castes into which the natives are divided, and had in vain attempted to thread the mazes of their idolatory, he urged Henry Lord, "Preacher to the Honorable Company of Merchants," to explore the whole of Hindú and Pársí mythology, and himself supplied the student with all the information which his position enabled him to obtain.*

Joseph Salbank, a man of observation, though somewhat illiterate, whose testimony we shall have occasion to cite hereafter, was in 1617 a Factor at Surat. He wrote to England a grievous complaint of the way in which he had been treated by "proud Captain Keeling," who as General of the Fleet appears to have had a controlling power over the Company's servants on shore. Poor Joseph maintained that he had carried himself "very genteelly" towards Keeling, and indeed had shown an excess of humility, but yet suffered the indignity of being placed under "punies and younglings," for whose grandfather he might have passed, so much was he their senior.†

Thomas Rastell seems to have succeeded Kerridge in the Presidency, in 1623, and he was succeeded by Wyld. The narratives of two visitors will presently introduce us to the acquaintance of these individuals.

To house for exportation the calicoes and produce of the country was the business in which the community engaged on their principal's account. These goods were paid for in money, or else by the exchange of spices and the manufactures of England and China.‡ With this business of the Company, the Factors combined a profitable trade on their own account, and, as might be expected, considered their own interests, without paying too exclusive an attention to those of their employers. Indeed, unless they had had this recourse, they could scarcely have hoped to obtain a bare subsistence,—so beggarly were the salaries which they received,—much less could they have amassed fortunes. By the bad policy of the East India Company their servants were thus driven to consult more for themselves than the public good. That judicious observer, and their true friend, Sir Thomas Roe, foresaw this consequence. He therefore strongly urged the Directors to increase their Factors' salaries, and then to prohibt them, under severe penalties, from engaging in private trade. He also justly remarked, that if they complied with his recommendation, they must select persons of respectability for their service, such as would only be induced by the offer of liberal payment to come to India; but when once there would regard high wages as a compensation for the loss of other profits, and would honestly devote their time and ingenuity to fulfil their employers' intentions. §

This advice was not followed, and after a very few years the servants of the Company were obscure individuals, whose characters were either unknown, or only known to their disadvantage. Gentlemen they did not pretend to be; for even their masters did not aspire to such a title. It was an age when the occupation of a merchant was still looked upon as

* A discovery of two forreigne sects in the East Indies, by Henry Lord Churchill's Voyages. Bruce's Annals.

† Letter from Joseph Salbank to the Company, quoted in Kaye's "Administration of the East India Company."

‡ Mokreb Khán complained to Sir Thomas Roe that the English brought "too much cloth and bad swords." He recommended that they should import rarities from Japan or China, and from England the richest silks and cloth of gold.—*Sir Thomas Roe's Journal.*

§ Letter to the East India Company.

decidedly vulgar.* The persons who formed the Company were known by the name of "adventurers," and so far from seeking for men of rank, they regarded gentle blood and noble race as disqualifications for their service. When the crown proposed that they should employ Sir Edward Michelbourne, they looked upon the prefix to his name with suspicion and low-minded jealousy. It was their resolution, they declared, "not to employ any gentleman in any place of charge," and they requested that they might "be allowed to sort theire business with men of their own qualitye, lest the suspicion of the employment of gentlemen being taken hold upon by the generalitie, do dryve a great number of the adventurers to withdraw their contributions."† So that the first English Factors were above, or, perhaps we should say below, all suspicion of being gentlemen.

But what the Directors most dreaded was, that their servants might be animated with a martial spirit. They repeatedly warned them against any appeal to arms, even for their own defence. They declared that war and traffic were incompatible, and in this instance at least attended to Sir Thomas Roe's counsel, who, when recommending the Company to confine their attention to trade, had referred to the examples of the Portuguese and Dutch. "The Portugueses," he wrote, "notwithstanding their many rich residences, are beggared by keeping of soldiers ; and yet their garrisons are but mean. They never made advantage of the Indies, since they defended them. Observe this well. It has also been the error of the Dutch, who seek plantations here by the sword. They turn a wonderful stock ; they prole in all places ; they possess some of the best ; yet their dead pays consume all the gain." With even more prudence, the ambassador points out the uselessness of expensive Embassies. He himself had obtained solid advantages for the Factory ; but he thought that in future they should be content with employing a native agent at Court on a low salary.‡ The wisdom of this opinion was subsequently proved, when Norris frittered away large sums of money, and only brought contempt upon himself and his countrymen.

Books and records enable us to catch but few glimpses of English manners at this early period. We may represent the Factory as a mercantile house of agency, in which the President or Chief was head partner. He and his junior partners, who were called Factors, lived under the same roof, each having his own private apartments ; but all assembling for meals at a public table, maintained by the Company. They were also expected to meet at a certain hour every day for prayers. Such carriages and cattle as they possessed, were part of the common stock. Horses were expensive luxuries, used only by the Chief and some of his friends. Bullock Carts were in ordinary use. For space and furniture the English and Dutch houses excelled all others in the city. The President affected some style. When he went into the streets, he was followed by a long

* The word "merchant" is frequently used in Shakespeare as a term of contempt. Thus in the first part of King Henry the Sixth, Act II. Sc. 3, the Countess of Auvergne when perplexed by Talbot calls him "a riddling merchant ;" and in Romeo and Juliet, Act II. Sc. 4, the nurse calls Mercutio "a saucy merchant."

† Mill's History, Book I. Chapter 2.

‡ Roe's Journal and Letters.

train of persons, including some natives, armed with bows, arrows, swords, and shields. A banner or streamer was borne, and a saddle-horse led before him. His retainers were numerous; and as each only received three rupees *per mensem* for wages, the whole cost but little. There were also many slaves, whose clothing was white calico, and food rice with a little fish.*

The English had not yet properly adapted their mode of dress to the climate. The costume of the seventeenth century must have been found peculiarly cumbersome and oppressive in a tropical climate. Old prints represent Europeans in India with large hose, long waisted, "peasecod-bellied" doublets, and short cloaks or mantles with standing collars. Then there were ruffs, which Stubbs says were "of twelve, yea sixteen lengths a piece, set three or four times double"; and he adds that the ladies had a "liquid matter, which they call starch, wherein the devil hath learned them to wash and dive their ruffs, which being dry will then stand stiff and inflexible about their necks." Breeches, too, were worn by gentlemen preposterously large, and their conical-crowned hats were of velvet, taffata, or sarcenet, ornamented with great bunches of feathers. † Probably, however, this dress approved itself to Native taste better than ours. At least Fryer, when at Junar, flattered himself that Nizam Beg, the Governor of the Fort, admired both *the splendour* and novelty of his costume. ‡ Sir Thomas Roe and his suite, as we are informed, were all clothed in English dresses, only made as light and cool as possible. His attendants wore liveries of "red taffata cloaks, guarded with green taffata," and the Chaplain always appeared in a long black cassock. §

Society was of the free and jovial kind. There were no English ladies, and if the Factors wished to enjoy the conversation of the gentler sex, they must resort to the Dutch Factory. We have an account of a wedding party there. The bride was an Armenian; the bridegroom a Dutchman. All the Europeans of the place were invited, and every lady came; so there were present one Portuguese and one Dutch matron, a young Maronite girl, and a native woman who was engaged to marry a Dutchman.

The circumstances under which the Portuguese lady was brought there are so characteristic of the times, that they should be narrated. The King of Portugal was in the habit of giving a dowry every year to a few poor but well-born orphan girls, whom he sent to assist in colonizing the settlements of India. A ship which was conveying three of these maidens had been intercepted and seized by the Dutch, who immediately carried their prizes to Surat. A supply of ladies was naturally received with avidity in that time of dearth, and the most eminent of the merchants became candidates for their hands. Two were taken, we know not where; but Donna Lucia, the third, married a rich Dutchman, and was a guest at the wedding banquet. She seems to have been contented with her lot. The affection of her Protestant husband led him to tolerate her religion in

* The Travels of Signor Pietro della Valle, Letter I. Sir Thomas Herbert's Travels, page 43.

† See the History of British Costume in the Library of Entertaining Knowledge.

‡ Fryer, Letter iii. Chap. 5.

§ Roe's Journal.

private, although she was compelled to observe in public the forms of the Dutch Reformed Church.

The reason why there were ladies in the Dutch, and not in the English Factory, was, that the Government of Holland encouraged the matrimonial desires of their Company's servants. At Java such as had wives and families could claim peculiar privileges ; *and on that account* many came to Surat, merely that they might marry native women and take them to Batavia.*

Sir Thomas Roe remarked with disgust the prevalence of intemperance amongst Europeans at Surat, and wondered that it was tolerated by the native Government. Drunkenness, he writes, and " other exorbitances proceeding from it were so great in that place, that it was rather wonderful they were suffered to live." The manners of the young men in the Factory were extremely dissolute, and on that account they were continually involved in quarrels with the natives. Even the President, after passing the night on board the ship which brought Della Valle, no sooner rose in the morning than he began drinking " burnt wine." This was a hot mixture flavoured with cinnamon, cloves, and other spices, and, we are told, was " drank frequently in the morning to comfort the stomack, sipping it by little and little for fear of scalding."†

Where intemperance prevailed to such an extent, there must also have been a considerable amount of crime ; but it is difficult to determine what were the legal powers with which the Company were invested for the punishment of criminals. In 1616 a formal trial was held, and sentence of death passed against one Gregory Lellington, who was charged with murdering Henry Barton in Surat. The Court assembled on board the ship *Charles* at Swally. The prisoner having confessed his guilt, was sentenced to be taken ashore the next day, and there shot to death by the musketeers of the guard.‡ This appears to have been a Court Martial ; but in 1622 James the First authorized the Company to chastise and correct all English persons residing in India, who should commit misdemeanours. Yet the Company could not have considered that they had authority to visit with severe punishment any who were convicted of grave offences, as in 1624 they petitioned for the establishment of martial and municipal laws, which at a still later period were sanctioned by Parliament.§ It is probable that in some instances the Factors adopted summary measures, without troubling themselves about the slow processes of law. When one of Van den Broeck's seamen had killed an English gunner, the enraged countrymen of the latter insisted upon having the Dutchman executed at once. In vain did Broeck beg that the forms of justice might be employed. Nothing would do but immediate execution, until the crafty Dutchman devised a plan which shewed that he relied upon English generosity. He declared that the sailor had been condemned to be drowned. No sooner had the Factors heard this, than their

* Della Valle, Letter I.

† Roe's Journal. Terry's Voyage. Della Valle, Letter I.

‡ Consultation held on board the ship *Charles*. Extracted by Mr. Kaye from the Records of Government.

§ Morley's Digest of Indian Cases, Vol. i. Mill's History, Book I. Chap. 2.

thirst for blood was allayed. Believing that there was really an intention of putting the man to death, they relented, interceded for his life, and he was pardoned. *

Where the execution of human laws was so vague and uncertain, the milder influences of Religion were the more required. And indeed the inmates of the Factory regularly engaged in devotional services, and forms at least were scrupulously observed. In the first Charters no ecclesiastical establishments were provided ; but, when possible, the good offices of a clergyman were always obtained. Every Portuguese, Dutch or English vessel of large size had its minister on board. The French only, Laval remarked, were without the fear of God, and never cared to have divine service performed in their ships. On b ard an East Indiaman, belonging to the English Company, a clergyman was usually to be met with, and if, when such an one arrived at Surat, there happened to be a vacancy in the Factory, he was easily induced to become a resident pastor. This was the case in 1616 with Henry Lord, who tells us that he had left one of the English ships for a charge of souls upon shore. He was both a studious and practical man, and his researches have been the means of preserving his name for posterity. Kerridge urged him to redeem the omissions of his predecessors, and make himself thoroughly acquainted with the religions of the Banyás and Pársís. Lord's curiosity had been excited so soon as he set his foot upon Indian soil ; he therefore readily undertook the task. The commencement of his work gives us some idea of the impression made upon an Englishman at his first arrival.

" According to the busie observance of travailers, inquiring what noveltie the place might produce, a people presented themselves to mine eyes, cloathed in linnen garments, somewhat low descending, of a gesture and garbe, as I may say, maydenly and well nigh effeminate ; of a countenance shy and somewhat estranged, yet smiling out a glosed and bashful familiarity, whose use in the companies affaires occasioned their presence there. Truth to say, mine eyes unacquainted with such objects, took up their wonder and gazed, and this admiration, the badge of a fresh travailer, bred in mee the importunity of a questioner. I asked what manner of people those were, so strangely notable, and notably strange? Reply was made, They were Banians."

After the worthy preacher had stared sufficiently at these effeminate and smirking dealers in cloth, he set to work with his book ; and as he remained in the Factory several years, during which he diligently inquired into native customs, the book proved to be very valuable. As was to be expected, he could not clearly distinguish the difference between the numerous sects of Hinduism, but his knowledge of their literature, mythology, and cosmogony was extensive. To him Sir Thomas Herbert was indebted for the information which his work contains regarding the Pársís ; and half a century later, Bernier acknowledged with gratitude his obligations to " Monsieur Henri Lor."†

In the same year there was also a Chaplain named Lescke at Surat. The Ambassador, too, brought with him the Reverend John Hall,

* Voyage de Van den Broeck.

† Lord's Discovery of two forreigne Sects. Bernier's letter to M. Chapelain.

Fellow of Corpus Christi College, Oxford, who soon fell a victim to the climate. His place was immediately supplied from an English ship then at Swally, and Terry was installed into the Chaplaincy of the Embassy. He also recorded what he saw, and has left us a work which proves the soundness of his principles, and accuracy of his judgment. He was afterwards Rector of Great Greenford in England, and in 1649 preached at the Church of St. Andrew Undershaft before the East India Company after the safe return of seven ships. His discourse, whch is still to be met with in print, was earnest and impressive. After exhorting his hearers to shew their gratitude for the Divine mercies which had been vouchsafed to them, the preacher impresses upon the Company that it is their duty to employ only such Presidents, Ministers of the Word, Factors, and other servants as may "take special care to keep God in their families," and not "play the heathens," when professing themselves Christians.*

When Lord and Terry must have both been in the country, a clergyman named Copeland came to Surat in the *Royal James* East Indiaman. It was the custom before the Company's ships left England for some minister of the Church to preach a farewell Sermon on board. When Copeland was leaving in 1618, Dr. John Wood intended to have discharged this office, as he "had divers times before," but being prevented on this occasion, he published his sermon in the form of a pamphlet, entitled "The true honour of navigation and navigators; or holy meditations for seamen." In this he declares that he has been an eye-witness of the care which the Company had taken to provide all things necessary for the bodies and souls of those who sailed in their fleets. In 1622 we find Copeland preaching at Bow Church, before the Virginia Council, and we are told that he was constituted Member of the Council of State in Virginia, and Rector of a College established for the conversion of American Indians.†

In these early days, much more than at a later date, the conversion of the natives was regarded by some pious Christians with interest and hopefulness. Amongst the Company's records for the year 1617 is a curious letter recounting the conversion of "a Mogul atheist." On this subject, too, Joseph Salbank wrote to the Directors with an earnestness and urgency which we are surprised to find in a commercial adventurer. He implored them to send "preachers and ministers," who might "break unto the Factors the blessed manna of the Heavenly Gospel." In the first place, he said, let us have "sufficient and solid divines, that may be able to encounter with the arch-enemies of our religion, if occasion should so require, those main supporters of the hierarchy of the Church of Rome; I mean the Jesuits, or rather (as I may truly term them) Jebusites, whereof some are mingled here in several places in the King's dominions amongst us." In the next place he asked for "godly, zealous, and devout persons, such as may, by their piety and purity of life, give good example to those with whom they live, whereby they will no less instruct and feed their little flock committed unto them, no less by the sincerity of the doctrine they teach them."‡

* A history of the Church of England in the Colonies and foreign dependencies of the British Empire. By the Rev. James S. M. Anderson, Vol. ii. Chap. xv.

† Anderson's Colonial Church, Vol. i. Chap. x., and Vol. ii. Chap. xv.

‡ Joseph Salbank to the Company. Extracted by Kaye.

But according to Terry, the natives had formed a mean estimate of Christianity. It was not uncommon to hear them at Surat giving utterance to such remarks as :—" Christian religion, devil religion ; Christian much drunk ; Christian much do wrong, much beat, much abuse others." Terry admitted that the natives themselves were " very square, and exact to make good all their engagements ;" but if a dealer was offered much less for his articles than the price which he had named, he would be apt to say :—" What! Do'st thou think me a Christian, that I would go about to deceive thee ?"

There was at least one European also who had no higher opinion than natives of Englishmen's religion, as will appear from the following anecdote. When Terry was in Surat a certain Spaniard presented himself at the Factory, and asked for employment. He gave out that he was by birth an Hidalgo, which, as our author explains, " signifies in Spanish the son of somebody." He had all that national fondness for exaggeration, and recklessness of assertion, which so fatally imposed upon the English at the commencement of the last Peninsula war, but in his case were inoffensively ridiculous. He tried to pass himself off as a hero and the flower of chivalry. Butler has given us his portrait, as if it were taken from the life :

" A wight he was, whose very sight wou'd
Entitle him mirrour of knighthood ;
That never bent his stubborn knee
To anything but chivalry ;
Nor put up blow, but that which laid
Right worshipful on shoulder blade—
But here our author's make a doubt,
Whether he were more wise or stout ;
Some hold the one, and some the other,
But howse'er they make a pother,
The difference was so small, his brain
Outweigh'd his rage but half a grain ;
Which made some take him for a tool,
That knaves do work with, call'd a Fool ;
And offer'd to lay wages, that
As Montaigue, playing with his cat,
Complains she thought him but an ass,
Much more she would Sir Hudibras."

This strange character gave his name as " the Knight of the Golden Rapier," and declared that having come with the Spanish Viceroy to Goa, he had, in defence of his spotless honour, fought so many duels there, that he had been placed in confinement, and required by the priests to atone with penances for the indulgence of his sanguinary propensities. No sooner was he set at liberty, than his honour was again injured, and having slain his adversary, he was compelled to fly the country. Such was the story of this mock hero, who added that he was now resolved " not to live any longer amongst the Christians, but that he desired to live amongst the English." " But the English are Christians," some one replied. " Jesu Maria !" exclaimed the amazed Spaniard ; he had never before heard that such was the case. Eventually he was received into the Factory, where he remained for some time. When about to leave, he assigned a reason for his departure, which gives us a peep into the Factors' mode of living. His pride was hurt, because at meals he was not permitted to occupy a place of honour ; but he, an Hidalgo of Spain, was required to sit with menials at the lower end of the table.*

Writers of the period have painted three portraits of the English in India, which shall be presented to the reader, although it must be admitted, that they would add but little ornament to a gallery of national characters.

Tom Coryat, " our English Fakier," as Fryer styled him, was the most conspicuous. A short sketch of his life was made by Terry, his companion and fellow traveller ; it well deserves a page in the history of his times. This eccentric man was born in 1577 at Odcomb in Somersetshire, and having early in life set his heart upon visiting foreign countries, he began with Europe. On his return he published a laughable account of his travels styled " Coryate's Crudities." Prefixed to the book were about forty copies of verses written in various languages, by the most witty persons of the day. Amongst other strange matters the author declares, that he had walked nineteen hundred and seventy-five miles in one pair of shoes, which he had occasion to mend but once. He is also said to have hung these shoes up in the church of his native village, as a donarium in token of gratitude for his safe return, a fact recorded by his biographer with sufficient gravity to shew, that he had an admiration both for old shoes and pedantry.

Tom desired to know and to be known, so as to obtain contemporary and posthumous fame. Unrestrained by poverty, he again started with a determination of traversing Asia, limiting his expenses to two pence a day, which he expected to procure by begging. His designs were vaster than his actual labours ; for he planned not only a journey through Tartary and China, but also a visit to "the Court of Prester John, in Ethiopia."

It is not our business to trace minutely his wandering steps ; but we will follow him hastily to the scene of our narrative. In 1612 he sailed from London to Constantinople ; thence to Alexandria. After seeing enough of Cairo and the Pyramids, he explored all the venerated places of the Holy Land, and then passed with a caravan from Aleppo to the sites of ancient Nineveh and Babylon. Persia, Candahar, Lahore, and Agra—where he found an English factory—were all traversed by him. Mixing with the natives of the countries through which he passed, he acquired with facility a knowledge of many foreign languages. Some acquaintance he had with Turkish and Arabic ; but in Persian and Hindústání his proficiency was considerable. At Agra he appeared before the Great Mogul, and pronounced an oration in florid Persian. The Mohammedan potentate was pleased to hear himself compared by Coryat to Solomon, and to be told that as the Queen of Sheba had heard of the Jewish monarch's fame, so the Englishman had heard of the Emperor's, and like her acknowledged, that what he saw far surpassed all that had been reported. The flatterer was rewarded with a hundred rupees, and thus enabled to prosecute his travels.

Less remunerative, but more amusing and creditable to him as a

* Terry's Voyage.

linguist, was his next feat. Having joined Sir Thomas Roe's suite, he found amongst them a washerwoman, whose native language was Hindústání, and who was celebrated for being a fluent and pertinacious scold. One day, writes his companion, Tom "undertook her in her own language, and by eight of the clock in the morning so silenced her, that she had not one word more to speak."

On another occasion he heard a Múlá uttering from the summit of a mosque his usual call to devotion. Suddenly all Coryat's religious fervour was awakened, and standing on an eminence opposite the Mussulman devotee, he cried out at the top of his voice, "Lá aláh, alá, aláh, Hazrat Isá Banaláh!"—there is no God, but God, and Christ the Son of God; adding moreover, that Mohammed was an impostor. With another Múlá he entered into argument, and after both the disputants had become very hot and very angry, Tom closed the controversy by asserting, that he himself was the orthodox Mussulman, or true, true believer, and the Múlá was the pseudo-Mussulman, or false true believer. Happily for himself he was considered a lunatic, and, as before the introduction of European reforms, such persons belonged in all Mussulman countries to a privileged class, and were allowed to do almost as they pleased, so Tom's insults were left unrevenged, and he could indulge his freaks without paying the penalty of a broken head.

Inordinate vanity seems to have been the motive cause of all his eccentric acts. Great men must feel an interest in him, and the world must regard him as a distinguished traveller—this was his aim. What then was his delight to be told by Richard Steele, the merchant, that King James had inquired about him. The eager fop immediately wished to know all his Majesty's words, but alas, after hearing that Tom was well, all that the monarch said was, "Is that fool yet living?" Equally mortified was he to discover, that in a letter which Sir Thomas Roe had written on his account to the Consul at Aleppo, he was styled "an honest poor wretch."

Tom's vagaries were brought to an abrupt termination at Surat in December 1617. His health had for some time been failing when he arrived, and his death was hastened by an act of imprudence. Although ordinarily a temperate man, he could not resist the seductions of a little sack which he heard was to be had in the Factory. Forswearing for the time all "thin potations," he began to soliloquize upon good liquor. "Sack, sack," exclaimed the thirsty wanderer, "is there any such thing as sack? I pray you give me some sack." The unusual draught was too much for his weak stomach. He was taken ill and died, as Fryer says, "killed with kindness by the English merchants, who laid his rambling brains at rest." He was buried on the shore near Swally, where there is a small hill at the left side of the road leading to Baroch. As no one was to be found who could and would engrave an epitaph, his name was unrecorded. Sir Thomas Herbert writes of him as one with whose reputation he supposes his readers to be acquainted, and adds that his grave was known "but by two poor stones that speak his name there, resting till the resurrection." A Persian in the Ambassador's suite, who had accompanied Herbert from England, and whose conduct having been such that he dreaded to meet his royal master, destroyed himself at Swally by eating opium, and was buried about a stone's cast from Coryat's remains.*

Coryat's follies were harmless; not so those of another man who visited Surat about this time. He was an English Baron's son who had fallen at home into such reckless habits, that his angry father sent him to find either reformation or a grave in India, as that country was considered by many, we are told, an excellent field for sowing wild oats. During his passage out he had at first been appointed to wait upon the Commander of the vessel, but as the young aristocrat was soon found unworthy even of such menial employment, he was afterwards sent to work as a common seaman before the mast. At last Sir Thomas Roe chanced to meet him in Surat, and having been acquainted in England with his family took him under his protection. But the scapegrace was continually embroiling himself with those around him. When travelling in the Ambassador's train, he one day flew into a terrible rage, because the servant of a native prince refused to hold his horse after he had dismounted. Not only did he ply his horsewhip over the servant's shoulders, but fired a pistol at him as he was running away in terror. Happily the ball only grazed the man's knuckles, and broke his bow. "Young bedlam's" companions instantly disarmed him, and did their utmost to hush the matter up; but it gave rise to a serious disturbance. This wild youth was fortunate in living long enough to be sent home by the Ambassador. †

We have thus seen a specimen of the English middle class, and one of their aristocracy in India. The third and last of those, whose pranks have appeared in print, was an English cook. He had been brought out by Sir Thomas Roe, and was at least as anxious to provide good liquor for himself as savoury viands for his master. Surat must have offered few attractions to such a thirsty soul, for when Fryer visited it some years later, he saw an Armenian flogged through the city, simply because detected in the act of selling liquor. But Akbar, the late Emperor, had published a decree permitting intoxicating spirits to be sold to Europeans, because, he said, "they are born in the element of wine, as fish are produced in that of water," "and to prohibt them the use of it is to deprive them of life." In consequence of Akbar's consideration for a national failing, the cook was so lucky as to light upon a shop where they sold what was called Armenian wine. ‡ "But," remarks Terry, "I do believe there was scarce another in that populous city of that trade; the greater shame for those, whosoever they be, that suffer so many unnecessary tippling-houses (in the places where they have power to restrain them), which are the Devil's nursery, the very tents wherein Satan dwells, where Almighty God receives abundance of dishonour; drunkenness being a sin which hath hands and fingers to draw all other sins unto it; for a drunkard can do any thing or be any thing but good." After making these moral reflec-

* Terry's Voyage. A new account of East India and Persia; By John Fryer. Some years' travels into divers parts of Africa and Asia the Great, by Sir Thomas Herbert. The View of Hindoostan, by Thomas Pennant, Vol. i. I have tried to reconcile Fryer's and Herbert's accounts of Coryat's burial place.

† Terry's Voyage.

‡ That is, wine made by Armenians at Shiraz; according to Hamilton's "New Account of the East Indies," Chapter ix.

tions by the way, Terry records that the English cook got very drunk, and sallied out into the streets. As he staggered along he met the Mogul Governor's brother with his attendants. Balancing himself upon his sheathed sword the drunkard cried out: "Now, thou heathen dog!" The Native gentleman did not understand him, and civilly inquired what he wanted. The cook's reply was, a stroke with his sword and scabbard, upon which the bystanders interfered, seized and carried him to prison. When the account of this awkward occurrence was brought to the Ambassador, he begged the Governor's brother to deal as he pleased with his insolent retainer. However, the fellow met with more consideration than he deserved, being set at liberty without suffering any punishment. *

But passing from buffoons and debauchees we next meet with two visitors at Surat who made some figure in their day, and whose slight sketches of English society deserve on that account the more attention. Pietro della Valle, surnamed Il Pellegrino, was here about the year 1623. This remarkable person was born at Rome of a patrician family in 1586, and had been distinguished early in life for his literary attainments. In 1614 he set out on his travels, and hearing whilst on his route to Bagdad that there was at that place a young Maronite lady of extraordinary beauty, named Maani, he soon found her out, and offered her his hand, which was accepted. She accompanied him on his journey, and was cherished by him with the greatest affection.

Della Valle tells us that when he arrived at Swally the ship was immediately visited by the English President "with one of their Ministers—so they call those who exercise the office of Priests—and two other merchants." Rastell, the President, spoke Italian with fluency, and was very polite, "shewing himself in all things a person sufficiently accomplished and of generous deportment, according as his gentile and graceful aspect bespoke him." The English and Dutch Presidents contended for the honour of shewing hospitality to the noble stranger. Rastell first invited him to the English Factory, but Della Valle objected to take his young and timid bride where there were only men. Anxious, however, not to give offence, he begged a friend to engage a private house for him. His friend acting in concert with the Dutch President, contrived to bring him near the rival Factory, when the President hurried out in his shirt sleeves, and clutching the bridle of Della Valle's horse, urged the reluctant stranger to go and live with him. Further resistance was useless. Della Valle yielded; but next day went to make his peace with the English President. Rastell was in such high dudgeon that he refused to see him, and was with difficulty induced to read a letter of apology. At last, on the Dutch President's mediation, Rastell relented, and not only forgave the deserter, but also invited him and his friends to supper. He treated them "very splendidly, and every thing ended in jollity and friendship, as at first."

It was not long before poor Della Valle lost his young Maani. She died near the Persian Gulf. Her husband had her remains embalmed, and carried them about with him until he returned to Rome. He then had them interred with great pomp in the Church of Ara Cœli, and pronounced over them a funeral oration, which was printed. He afterwards married a

* Terry's Voyage.

Georgian who had been a friend of his first wife, and who also travelled with him. He wrote an account of his travels, which was published at Rome in 1650, and which shews considerable knowledge and love of natural history. Pope Urban the Eighth made him gentleman of the bed-chamber, but having in a fit of anger killed a coachman, whilst the Pope was blessing the people in the Place of St. Peter, he was banished. He soon returned, and died in 1652 at Rome.*

Mr. Herbert, afterwards Sir Thomas, a cadet of the house of Pembroke, was at Surat about this time. He was born in 1606, and educated at Jesus and Trinity Colleges, Cambridge. In 1626 he left England with Sir Dodmore Cotton, Ambassador from Charles the First to the king of Persia, and travelled for four years in Asia and Africa. On the 17th of November he touched at Goa, which, and not Baroch, he supposed to be the Barigaza of antiquity. On the 29th he went to Swally, where he found six English and seven Dutch ships, most of which were of a thousand tons burden. He travelled, as he says, to Surat in "a chariot drawn by two Buffollos," and attended by "some pe-unes, or olive coloured Indian foot-boys, who can very prettily prattle English." He was hospitably received at the Factory by the President, whom the young aristocrat describes with transparent condescension as "one master Wyld, an ingenious and civil merchant, to whose kind respect I owe acknowledgment." Herbert published in 1634 a book of Travels, which was translated into French. In the civil war he took the Parliamentary side, and was appointed one of the Commissioners with the army of Sir Thomas Fairfax. Being afterwards placed in attendance on the imprisoned Charles, the fallen monarch's misfortunes so enlisted his sympathies, that he treated him with the greatest respect, and afterwards published his Threnodia Carolina, being an account of the two last years of Charles the First. In acknowledgment of these services, Charles the Second made him a Baronet. He was held in much repute by the literary men of his time, and assisted in the composition of many learned works.†

Even at this time a few persons disregarded the Company's monopoly, and endeavoured to push their fortunes by carrying on a private trade. Richard Steele seems to have deserted the Factory, and with a person named Jackman to have traded in pearls. The two also projected extensive water works with a view of increasing the demand for lead. It is a curious fact also, that some adventurers submitted to Sir Thomas Roe a project for opening a trade on the Indus. They recommended that the merchants of Persia and Candahar should be induced to ship their goods on the Indus, instead of bringing them by Lahore and Agra to the towns of lower India. English vessels would then be lying at the mouth of the Indus, and transport the merchandize to the Persian Gulf. The one serious obstacle to this plan was, the difficulty of returning against the stream, and it has been reserved for our days and the force of steam to shew that this is not insuperable.‡

* The Travels of Sig. Pietro della Valle. Biographical Dictionary, by the Rev. Hugh James Rose.

† Herbert's Travels. Rose's Biographical Dictionary.

‡ Sir Thomas Roe's Journal.

As the number of adventurers increased, the reputation of the English was not improved. Too many committed deeds of violence and dishonesty. We can shew that even the commanders of vessels belonging to the Company did not hesitate to perpetrate robberies on the high seas or on shore when they stood in no fear of retaliation. During a visit which some English ships paid to Dábhol the officers suddenly started up from a conference with the native chiefs, and attacked the town, having first secured some large guns in such a manner that they could not be turned against them. Their attempt failed, but after retreating to their ships they succeeded in making prizes of two native boats. Della Valle declares that it was customary for the English to commit such outrages.*

And although this last account may be suspected as dictated by the prejudices of an Italian, we can see no reason to question Sir Thomas Herbert's veracity. Sailing along the coast with several vessels under the command of an English Admiral, he descried, when off Mangalore, a heavily laden craft after which a Malabar pirate was skulking. The native merchant in his fright sought refuge with the Admiral, but, writes our author with confessed grief, his condition was little better than it would have been, if he had fallen into the pirate's hands. After a short consultation, his ship was adjudged a prize by the English officers. "For my part," proceeds Herbert, "I could not reach the offence : but this I could, that she had a cargo of cotton, opium, onyons, and probably somewhat under the cotton of most value, which was her crime it seems. But how the prize was distributed concerns not me to inquire ; I was a passenger, but no merchant, nor informer." The whole account would be incredible if not given on such good authority ; but as it is, we must regard it as a blot upon the English character, and some justification of the Mogul officers when they afterwards brought charges of piracy against the Company's servants. Sixty of the native seamen, concluding from the churlish conduct of the English that mischief was intended, and that they would be sold as slaves to the people of Java, trusted rather to the mercy of the waves than of such Englishmen, and threw themselves into the sea, "which seemed sport to some there," writes Herbert, "but not so to me, who had compassion !" Some were picked up by canoes from the shore, and some by English boats ; but the latter were so enraged with the treatment which they had received, that they again endeavoured to drown themselves. A terrible storm which followed was regarded by the narrator as a token of God's severe displeasure.†

Such were the English at their first appearance on the Western coast of India. It must be confessed that the natives had before them a strange variety of models from which to form in their minds the character of an Englishman. Roe and Herbert, the acute diplomatist and the polished gentleman ; Best, Downton and other valiant mariners ; the inquiring and literary Kerridge ; hard headed, ungrammatical and religious Joseph Salbank ; wine-bibbing Rastell ; Mildenhall cheat and assassin ; preachers or gospellers half Anglican and half Zuinglian ; orthodox chaplains ; a few scampish reckless travellers ; and piratical, merciless captains—such a

* Della Valle's Travels.

† Sir Thomas Herbert's Travels.

medley could scarcely leave any well-defined impressions upon the native mind. Probably opinions were decided by circumstances. The jovial Jehángír found that an Englishman was a well-trained courtier and good boon-companion ; the banyás of Surat found that he was a clever tradesman, and a hard driver of a bargain. But doubtless at first the popular feeling was one of fear, afterwards of contempt. Hindús and Mussulmans considered the English a set of cow-eaters and fire drinkers, vile brutes, fiercer than the mastiffs which they brought with them,* who would fight like Eblis, cheat their own fathers, and exchange with the same readiness a broadside of shot and thrusts of boarding-pikes, or a bale of goods and a bag of rupees.

As time wore on, the estimation in which the English had been held, declined. After a few years there were but certain illiberal merchants, struggling that they might keep the market of Surat to themselves, and exclude by fair means or foul the Portuguese and Dutch. The celebrity which their naval skill and courage had gained for them soon passed away ; the glory reflected on them from a royal embassy was soon forgotten. They were only known as shrewd and vulgar adventurers who had opened warehouses in India. Their existence was scarcely heeded by the Mogul despot, whose imperial sway was one of the most extended, and his throne one of the most splendid on the face of the earth. Yet that sway was destined to fall into their grasp ; that throne to depend upon the forbearance and magnanimity of the successors of those peddling traders. These English were indeed regarded as men of an insignificant country, dissolute morals, and degraded religion ; yet they were the pioneers of a Company which now possesses territory more than four times the size of France, and seven times that of Great Britain and Ireland.

Let the British Empire in the East, then, be compared to Gothic architecture, which began with its wooden buildings, thatched roofs, and rush strewn floors, but was gradually refined into the groined roofs, elaborate mouldings, stately pillars, and delicate tracery of our magnificent cathedrals. Joseph Salbank and his contemporaries were of the ruder, not to say of the baser sort ; but now the Empire is a noble structure, the style and order of which remain to be further developed by ingenuity and labour ; nor have they, we thank God, yet reached a period of debasement and decline.

* "Tetræ belluæ, ac molossis suis ferociores." So says Salmasius of the Regicides ; quoted by Carlyle in his "Oliver Cromwell's letters and speeches."

CHAPTER III.

1630—1662.

CONTENTS.—A dark age—Oldest despatch extant in India—Surat becomes the Company's chief place of trade—Description of Surat; its population and trade—The use and exportation of tea; orders from England for tea—Swally; description of the port and roads—English accounts of the state of the country; the Emperor's wealth; inventory of his jewels; various opinions; oppression; unsettled state of the provinces; dangers of travelling; thuggism; highway robbers: a bloody nách; the markets: awkward position of foreigners—Presidents Methwold, Fremlen, Breton, Blackman, Revington, Wyche, and Andrews—Speculation in a Diamond—Weddel and Mountney, agents of a new Company—Pusillanimity of the President and Factors—Expedients of the new Company; piracy—Sufferings of the Factors—Union of the two Companies—Interlopers—Question of monopoly stated and considered—Failure and triumph of monopoly—First collision with Sivají—Factories at Rájapúr, Carwar, Cochin, and Ponáni—Improvement in the social position of the Factors; their mal-practices—Private trade—Surgeon Boughton's adventures—Davidge's mission—Internal economy of the Factory; regularity of prayers; religious tone; Sunday sports; refreshments—Dutch hostility.

WHEN writing the two last chapters I was the more anxious to give the reader all the information I could glean respecting the habits, occupations, and characters of Englishmen in India, as I knew that we were approaching a period of which it would be difficult to gain any historical details. The first half century of Anglo-Indian history may remind us of the Hindús, who profess to trace with great exactness events, which they throw back into remote antiquity; but are utterly unable to distinguish facts in the foreground of comparatively modern ages. The days of Best, Downton, and Sir Thomas Roe, are the "twilight of gods." They are followed by the darkness of Erebus. The affairs of the East India Company were so unskilfully managed, their reverses so severe and frequent, that at this period they were hidden under a cloud, and the world saw little of them. Such records as are preserved at the East India House are meagre, and wide gaps in them remain unfilled; until at last for several years after 1642 no account even of the annual equipments is to be discovered.*

The oldest despatch, of which a copy is extant in the books of the Surat Factory, was forwarded to London by Thomas Rastell, and was dated the twenty-sixth of July 1630, on board the Ship *James* in St. Augustine's Bay, Madagascar.† It throws no light upon the history of the time; but we learn from other documents that the Company's agents were then

* Mill's History, Book i. Chapter 3.

† Outward Letter Book of the Surat Factory.

engaged in negotiating with the officers of the Great Mogul and the King of Golconda an extension of their trade in Hindústán.* Surat was gradually acquiring importance in the Company's estimation; thither their largest fleets were despatched, and they now styled the principal person in the Factory "Chief for the Honorable Company of English Merchants trading to the East."† As Bombay was held by another European nation, the Directors could find no place so well suited for the attainment of their objects as Surat; and intimately connected as it became from this time with the English nation, it claims from us a particular description.

Surat had been from remote antiquity celebrated not only for the number of its inhabitants, and the beauty of its gardens rich with an alluvial soil; but also for its commercial wealth, and the concourse of foreigners who thronged its streets. Situated on the left Bank of the Táptí, its walls extended six miles in a semicircle, of which that river was the chord. As the city was about fourteen miles from the sea, it offered a secure haven, and the navigation of its waters was sufficiently easy for such barks as were anciently employed in the Indian ocean. Seaward it drew riches from those ancient ports of Sinde, Gujarát, and the coast of Málabár, which were known even to the classical writers of Greece and Rome. Its inhabitants had also opened communications with the coasts of Africa, Arabia, and the Persian Gulf. From the land side the produce of the interior was carried down the valley of the Táptí, or in a journey of a few miles was transported from the still more famous valley of the Narmadá.

At the period now under consideration the streets—as is usual in Oriental countries—were narrow. The houses, writes Herbert, were "indifferent beautiful;" and, if we may form an opinion from the statement of an Italian who visited the place forty years later, they were mere cottages, with the exception of a few, belonging to European and Mussulman Merchants, which were lofty and spacious.‡ Mosques were numerous, but displayed little of that elegance and airy stateliness for which such buildings are often distinguished, and still less worthy of admiration were the temples of Hindus. The principal objects of attraction were the Mussulmans' houses, gardens, and artificial lakes in and about the suburbs.

Perhaps no city in the world contained a more varied and mixed assemblage of people. In the thoroughfares were to be seen not only natives of the Gujaráthí and Maráthí provinces; but also Sindians, Persians, Arabs, Armenians, Pársís and Jews, together with English, Dutch, and Portuguese. Here were Christians, who acknowledged the authority of the Pope, the Patriarchs of Constantinople and Antioch, and the Catholicus of Armenia; Christians also who disowned them all, agreeing only with the thirty-nine articles of the Anglican Church, the confession of Westminster Divines, or the Synod of Dort. Mussulmans also there were of both Súní and Shía sects, and a large number of industrious, intelligent Boharás. The bazaars teemed with riches, and no better market could be found

* Mill's History.

† Inscriptions in the English cemetery at Surat.

‡ A Voyage round the World, by Dr. John Francis Gemelli Careri, Part iii. Herbert's Travels, page 43.

in India for the sale or purchase of indigo, spices, pepper, lead, quicksilver, tin, copper, porcelain, Cashmere shawls, silks, Chinese satins, Oriental jewels, mother of pearl cabinets, ivory, ebony and sandalwood manufactures. *

One article of commerce, which was imported to Surat from China at the commencement of this period, although not exported to England for many years after, deserves more lengthened notice. The herb, which we now call tea, derives its name from a word ordinarily used at the present time in India, through a variety of formations all found in the works of old authors. According to the dates at which they wrote they styled it chah, cha, chia, thea, thè, thee, tey, or tea. So early as 850 A. D. two Arabian travellers described it under the name of *chah.* In 1633 Olearius, a German, having been in Persia, wrote that "they drink a kind of black water, prepared from a decoction of a certain shrub, called *cha* or *chia*, which the Usbeck Tartars import from China." The introduction of it into Europe was much opposed by medical practitioners. In 1635, Simon Pauli published a treatise to shew that its effects were injurious,† and it became ridiculed in Holland under the name of *hay water*. But in 1641 Tulpius, a celebrated physician of Amsterdam, came forward to maintain the virtues of *Thee*. At last we find it in 1664 exported from Surat to England ; but how great a rarity it was considered will be shewn by the following extracts from the records at the East India House :—

"1664 July 1.—Ordered, that the master attendant do go on board the ships now arrived, and enquire what rarities of birds, beasts, or other curiosities there are on board, fit to present to his Majesty, and to desire that they may not be disposed of till the Company are supplied with such as they may wish, on paying for the same."

"22nd August. The Governor acquainting the Court that the Factors have in every instance failed the Company of such things as they writ for, to have presented his Majesty with, and that his Majesty may not find himself wholly neglected by the Company, he was of opinion, if the Court think fit, that a silver case of oil of cinnamon, which is to be had of Mr. Thomas Winter for £75, and some good *thea*, be provided for that end, which he hopes may be acceptable. The Court approved very well thereof."

Accordingly, in the Secretary's accounts for the 30th September 1664, there is entered a charge of four pounds five shillings "for 2lbs 2oz of *thea* for his Majesty ;" and on the 30th June 1666, "for 22¼lbs of *thea*, at 50

* When the first ships arrived in India from Europe, the Merchants inquired chiefly for *anile* or indigo, which had been since the earliest periods exported from Cámbát. The names *nil*, *anile* and *indigo* all denote its origin. Rhases, who lived at the end of the tenth century, calls it "nil, alias Indicum" Salmasius suggests that the names *nil* and *nir* arose from the Latin word *niger* ; but if he had known Sanskrit he would not have thought of such a forced etymology (Sanskrit, níl). In 1631 large cargoes of indigo were imported to Holland from Gujarát, and other countries in the East Indies

Tin was at first brought by Europeans to Surat ; but it was soon found that there were mines in countries near India.

Tavernier mentions sal ammoniac as amongst exports from Ahmedábád ; but although it was known in India, it does not seem to have been exported to England. Beckmann's History of Inventions.

† The treatise was styled "Comment. de Abusa Tabacca et *Theæ*."

shillings per lb, £56 17s. 6d." and "for the two chief persons that attended his Majesty, *thea* £6 15s."

The first order received from the Company was in 1667, when the Factors were desired "to send home by these ships 100lbs weight of the best *tey* that they could get." In 1680 a hundred and forty-three pounds were imported from Surat. In 1686 the Court sent an order to Surat, from which we conclude that this herb had hitherto been considered an article of private trade; for they desire that in future it should form part of the Company's imports. In 1687 they write an order "that very good *tea* might be put up in tutinague potts, and well and closely packed in chests or boxes, as it will always turn to accompt here, now it is made the Company's commodity; whereas before there were so many sellers of that commodity, that it would hardly yield half its cost; and some trash *thea* from Bantam was forct to be thrown away, or sold for 4d. or 6d. per lb." From this time until the Company opened their trade with China, the exportation of tea from Surat to England gradually increased, and in 1690 upwards of forty-one thousand pounds were forwarded.* But a desire of giving a connected account of this interesting trade has led us much beyond the period with which we are concerned in this chapter.

Swally was the seaport of Surat, and was a village situated about twelve miles west of the city. The only anchorage for vessels was in a road, seven miles in length and a mile and a half in breadth, between the shore and a sand bank which was dry at low water. About midway up this channel was a cove called Swally Hole, where a fleet could lie in tolerable security. At one time all large vessels which brought cargoes for the market at Surat were permitted to remain there; but as the situation offered the commanders convenient opportunities of defrauding the revenue, this permission was restricted after the year 1660 to such as were in the service of the English and Dutch Companies who had built warehouses there and laid out pleasant gardens. Fryer tells us, that the whole place was infested by "two sorts of vermin, fleas and banyans." When any ships arrived from Europe, which ordinarily they did between the months of September and March, banyás crowded to Swally, and there pitched tents and booths or built huts, so that it resembled a country fair in England. Boys also, called "pe-unes," were in waiting and ready for four pice a day to act as interpreters or run errands for strangers.†

Leaving the spots at which the English were located, and following travellers to the interior, we regard their evidence as particularly valuable, to shew the actual condition of the country under Native rule. On two points all were agreed,—the enormous wealth of the great Mogul, and the lawless unsettled state of his provinces. Hawkins was astonished beyond measure at his riches, of which he seems to have obtained a pretty exact account from documents preserved at Court. According to him the Emperor's inventory was as follows:—

"Of jewels composed solely of diamonds, one batman and an half—a

* Oriental Commerce. By William Milburn, Esq. vol ii Macpherson's History.

† This account of Surat and Swally is taken from a Description of the coasts of Malabar and Coromandel, by Philip Baldaus, Thevenot Liv i. ch. 16, &c. Voyage de Gautier Schouten aux Indes Orientales, Tome i. Sir Thomas Herbert's Travels, and Orme's Fragments.

batman is five and fifty pounds weight English—these are rough, and of all sorts and sizes, but none of less than two carats and an half. Of balass rubies, two thousand. Of pearls, twelve batmans. Of rubies of all sorts, two batmans. Of emeralds of all sorts, five batmans. Of eshime, which stone comes from Cataga, one batman. Of stones of Emen, a kind of red stone, five thousand. Of all other sorts, as coral, topazes, &c. the amount is innumerable.

" Of jewels wrought in gold—two thousand and two hundred swords, the hilts and scabbards set with rich stones : two thousand poinards in like manner ornamented. Of saddle drums of gold, used in hawking, set with stones, five hundred. Of rich broaches for the head, in which their feathers are set, two thousand. Of saddles of gold and silver set with stones, one thousand. Of tuikes, five and twenty. This is a great lance covered with gold, the fluke set with precious stones; they are carried before him when the king goeth to the wars. Of gold parasols of state, richly set with diamonds, one hundred. Of gold chairs of state, one hundred and five. Of large agate chrystal vases for wine, adorned with gold and jewels, one hundred ; of drinking cups of gold five hundred, of which are fifty exceedingly rich, all of one stone, as beryl, sapphire &c. Of gold chairs strung with pearls, and rings set with jewels, the number is infinite. Of gold plate of all kinds exquisitely wrought, as dishes, goblets, basons, three thousand batmans." This account, we are told, relates only to the palace at Agra ; but the great Mogul had also palaces at Delhi, Cabul, and Lahore, where also vast treasures were accumulated. *

Although Joseph Salbank did not enter so far into particulars as Hawkins, yet his sentiments on this subject seem to have been formed as deliberately, and expressed as judiciously. He admits that exaggerated accounts of the great Mogul's wealth had been sent to England ; but yet he was sure that it was vast. He also explains the two methods by which it had been raised. The first was the rent of land ; the second, the appropriation of deceased persons' estates, which in most cases reverted to the sovereign. The autocrat's wealth consisted of ready money, with which his coffers were filled, and which was continually being imported into the country, but never was exported ; and also of precious stones, pearls, and jewels, which he possessed in greater abundance than any other prince.†

To these testimonies we may add that of Gemelli Careri, who, half a century later, derived his information from abundant sources, examined the matter closely, and after discussing the question fully, summed up in these words :—" I am of opinion, that next to the Emperor of China, no monarch in the world is equal to the Great Mogul in strength and riches."‡

With regard to the condition of the country, although there may be some minor differences of opinion, yet the facts and arguments of European writers all shew that the people suffered from tyranny and bad Government. Lodovico Barthema, otherwise called Lewes Vertomannus, one of the first Europeans that visited Gujarát, thought well of the people, and was sure that they would be saved by their good works, if they were only

* Purchas his Pilgrims Vol. i.

† Letters from Joseph Salbank to the Company ; extracted by Kaye.

‡ Voyage round the World, Book ii. Chap. vi.

baptized. But their very virtues aud mild dispositions made them the unresisting victims of a cruel monarch, named Machamuth,—as he styles Mahmúd Begarra,—whose ferocity was incredible. His appearance was sufficient to justify a spectator's worst apprehensions. A long beard fell down to his waist, and his moustachios were of such prodigious length that he fastened them over his head like a lady's hair. Deadly poisons were his ordinary food. He was continually masticating betel, and when sitting in judgment condemned criminals to death by the simple process of squirting the juice at them—a sentence which was executed within the half hour. The grave author further tells us, that this Bluebeard maintained between three and four thousand women in his seraglio, and the one upon whom he bestowed his favours, was certain to be found dead in the morning.* If the reader wishes to know how the lady's death was caused, I must refer him to the lines in Hudibras, beginning,

> "The prince of Cambay's daily food
> Is asp, and basilisk, and toad."

This story may be taken for what it is worth. It will probably be received as evidence to shew that, when Europeans first became acquainted with the country, they found oppression rampant. The same is true of the middle of the seventeenth century. The Mogul empire was mighty and extensive ; but it could only be held together by an able and powerful ruler. The native chiefs of distant provinces were always ready to seize opportunities of disowning allegiance. As there was no fixed law of succession, wars were continually breaking out amongst the members of the reigning family, and the prince who had the most talent for military tactics or intrigue grasped the reins of Government. In the meanwhile, and until some successful usurper overcame the other contending parties, the provinces were involved in the worst disorders. Travelling in the interior was most dangerous, and Thuggism, which has made the robbers of India infamous above those of all other countries, was very frequent.† Salbank described the roads as swarming with robbers, who would at any time cut a man's throat for "the third part of a penny sterling." One Englishman had been robbed on the road between Surat and Agra, and when charitable persons offered him money, he refused to take it, knowing that it would only be stolen, and his life endangered by it. "Howbeit," adds this pious writer, "I for my part passed through all those hellish weapons that these cannibal villains used to kill men withal securely enough, through the tender mercies of my gracious God." There can be little doubt that this description was accurate, and it must not be forgotten, that when written the Mogul Empire was not in its lowest condition, but the power of

* Nauigation and Vyages of Lewes Vertomannus, Gentilman of the citie of Rome ; Hakluyt's Voyages. It must be admitted that some of these Roman Catholics were peculiarly addicted to the marvellous. When Terry was endeavouring with laudable curiosity to acquaint himself with the country, Francisco Corsi, a Jesuit missionary at Agra, supplied him with marvels to his heart's content. Amongst other stories the Jesuit told him, that on the Western coast of India there was a race of men descended from persons who had stamped St. Thomas to death. The right legs of all were deformed ; but the left were like other men's. Terry's Voyage, Section xxx.

† Les Voyages de M. de Thevenot aux Indes Orientales. There is a curious account of the Sirens whom the Thugs employed to entrap their victims.

Jehángír was considerable, although not properly consolidated or vigorously employed.*

The testimony of other English Factors corresponds with Salbank's. Canning, when on his journey to Agra, was assaulted and wounded by robbers. Starkey was poisoned. The caravan which Withington accompanied was attacked in the night at the third halting place, and the next day they met a Mogul officer returning with the heads of two hundred and fifty coolies who had been plunderers. In Rájpútána the caravan was attacked twice in one day. Between that and Tatta the son of a Rájpút Chief professed to escort them with fifty troopers, but designedly led them out of their way into a thick wood. He there seized all the men, camels, and goods, and strangled the two Hindú merchants, to whom the caravan belonged, with their five servants. Withington and his servants having been kept for twenty days in close confinement, were dismissed, to find their way home as they best could. After this, when Edwards was travelling to Agra, the escort which he took from Baroch was found to be in league with fifty mounted freebooters, who hovered about them at night, and were only deterred from attacking them by seeing their bold attitude. When Aldworth and his party were returning from Ahmedábád, their escort was increased by the orders of Government, because robberies and murders had been committed two nights before close to the city. Between Baroda and Baroch they were attacked in a narrow lane, thick set on either side with hedges, by three hundred Rájpúts, who with their lances and arrows wounded many of them, and succeeded in rifling two of their heavily laden carts.† Gautier Schouten, a servant of the Dutch Company, who was at Surat in 1660, confirms all these accounts, and declares that when the English and Dutch went to Agra they always joined themselves to native caravans. Even then they had frequently to defend themselves against Rájpúts, who descended from their mountains to plunder travellers.

One anecdote affords us some idea of the local Government at Ahmedábád. When Mandelslo was there, he was invited, together with the English and Dutch Factors, by the Governor to a native entertainment. As is usual on such occasions dancing girls exhibited their performances. One troop having become fatigued, another was sent for. The latter however having been ill requited on a former occasion refused to attend. What measure then did the Governor adopt? A very summary one indeed. He had them dragged into his presence, and then after taunting them for their scruples ordered them to be beheaded. These reluctant ministers of a despot's pleasure pleaded for mercy with heartrending cries and shrieks. Their appeal was vain, and eight wretched women were actually executed before the company. The English Factors were horror struck; but the Governor merely laughed, and asked why they were troubled. This account, given by an eye witness whose veracity has been ordinarily admitted, is in itself a commentary upon the records of Native rule.‡

* Salbank's Letters. Kaye. † Orme's Fragments.

‡ Les Voyages Du Sieur Albert de Mandelslo.

Bernier, a Frenchman, arrived at Surat in 1655. He was an observant man, who made notes of all that he saw, and took an especial interest in the bazaars. He leads us to conclude that Europeans had not as yet been able to provide themselves with edibles suited to their tastes and habits. The grandees of the country lived in luxury; but others could scarcely provide themselves with the necessaries of life. "At Delhi there is no mean," he wrote, "there you must either be a great lord or live miserably; for I have experienced it myself, in a manner dying of hunger this good while, though I have had considerable pay, and was resolved to spare nothing that way, because commonly there is found nothing in the markets but the refuse of the grandees."*

Europeans suffered almost as much as Natives from the misrule of the age, and that not only when they left home, but at times also when they remained in their Factories. Of this we shall see abundant proofs as we proceed. The distant dependencies of the empire were left to the caprices of their Governors just so long as they could bribe the Court to overlook their delinquencies. Foreigners at Surat, therefore, had a difficult and delicate part to play. As they had no power to awe the Governor, they could only retain his favour by considering his interests, for which they often resorted to artifice and corruption.

We have no complete list of the officers who superintended the Company's affairs at this period. We find that in 1636 Methwold was president, and that having repaired to Goa he there arranged a convention with the Viceroy on the basis of a treaty which had been concluded between England and Spain.†

On leaving for Europe in 1638, he was succeeded by William Fremlen, who, together with his council, urged the Directors to establish a central management of their affairs at Surat. After him comes Francis Breton, whose unostentatious monument may still be seen in the cemetery at Surat.‡ The inscription states, that after he had "for five years discharged his duties with the greatest diligence and strictest integrity, he went unmarried to the celestial nuptials on the 21st of July in the year of Christ 1649." Captain Jeremy Blackman was appointed President in 1651. Restrictions were then for the first time placed upon private trade, and his salary was fixed at £500, to be considered due from the date of his leaving England, and to be continued until his return. This was thought a handsome allowance and fair compensation for the loss of private business. Blackman was ordered to make a survey of all the dependencies of Surat.§ Revington and Nathanael Wyche also presided over the Factory during the time of Cromwell's Protectorate. The latter was succeeded by Andrews. It has been stated that Revington was the last who was styled "Agent" and Wyche was the first "President," but this is not correct. The Principals of the Factory received from the commencement the titles of President, Chief or Agent, according as their friends or the Directors were pleased to honour them.||

* Bernier's Letter to M. de la Mothe le Vayer.
† Bruce's Annals 1635-36.
‡ Bruce's Annals 1637-38.
§ Bruce's Annals 1650-51.
|| Epitaphs at Surat. Tavernier's Voyages, Chapter ii. Kaye's History.

Tavernier—who was in India at various intervals between the years 1642 and 1666,—gives a curious account of a speculation into which Fremlen and Breton entered, and which ended in a mortifying failure. In conjunction with a Jew trader named Edward Ferdinand, they had purchased a stone, supposed to be a diamond of the purest water, of good shape, and forty-two carats in weight. This was entrusted to Ferdinand, as he was going to Europe, in order that he might dispose of it to the best advantage. On arriving at Leghorn he exhibited it to some of his Israelitish friends, who offered him for it nearly twenty-five thousand piastres ; but as he was unwilling to take less than thirty thousand, he carried it with him to Venice. There it was placed on the wheel previous to being set. Alas for his fond hopes ! The supposed diamond was broken into nine pieces.

During this period a new association, at the head of which was Sir William Courten, had obtained from Charles the First a licence to engage in the Indian trade. In 1636 Captain Weddel and Mr. Mountney being sent out, declared that they were under the protection of the English Crown. Weddel addressed a letter to the President and Council at Surat, and at the same time forwarded the copy of a letter from King Charles. His Majesty avowed that he had a particular interest in the new Company, and requested that if they were in any distress, the President would afford them assistance. At the same time Weddel took the opportunity to express his desire of living on good terms with the old Company.

The President, having received no information from his superiors in England, either could not or would not believe that a new Company had been formed. He told Weddel as much, adding that two Companies could not carry on trade in the East Indies, and desiring to know what privileges had been granted to the new Company. The following year a letter from the Secretary of State shewed that there could be no doubt of the innovation. The Factors were then thrown into a state of despondency and wrote thus : —" Wee could wish that wee could vindicate the reputacon of our nation in these partes, and do ourselves right, for the loss and damage our estate, in those partes, have susteyned ; but of all these we must beare the burthen, and with patience sitt still, until wee may find these frowning tymes more auspicious to us, and to our affayres." Their hands were tied, or they would have attempted to ruin the new Company. They then fell into despair, and proposed to give up the trade ; but the Court urged them to continue, and even allowed them to grant bills on England for any money which Weddel might lodge in their hands, and to purchase from him goods at reasonable rates. They could, however, scarcely restrain their indignation when they heard that the innovators were trading at Rájapúr, which they regarded as their domain, and that they had established Factories at Batticolo and Carwar. The new association was afterwards styled " The Assada Merchants," and in 1645 formed the plan of a colony at St. Augustine's Bay, Madagascar, which was soon reduced to great distress. Their agent then offered to sell the Factory at Carwar to the President of Surat; but his offer was declined. To relieve their embarrassments the colonists tried the desperate expedient of coining native money, but they only brought themselves into disgrace with the people of India, and indeed left a stain on the English character.

It was charged against some of the servants of this new Company, that, by committing acts of piracy, they caused those misfortunes which at this time fell upon the Factory of Surat ; but the case against them has not been properly established. It was said that one of their commanders, instead of waiting for the fair profits of commercial enterprize, had plundered two native vessels belonging to Surat and Diu, and even tortured their crews. Probably this was partly, if not wholly, untrue ; but the native Governor of Surat chose to believe it, and pretended to be, or really was, so incensed, that he ordered the Chief of the Factory and his Council to be thrown into prison, where he detained them two months, decreed the confiscation of all the old Company's property, and only suffered it to be redeemed by a payment of seventy thousand rupees.*

It may be imagined that this misfortune raised the old Company's spirit of hatred and opposition against Sir William Courten and his associates to the highest pitch. Trading operations were completely suspended in the Factory, and it was feared that they would never be renewed. Happily, harmony was in some measure restored when in 1650 terms of agreement were settled by the two Companies. Still some adventurers, who had belonged to Courten's association, continued to prowl about the Indian seas.†

But if the Factors had not suffered at all, or had not pretended to trace their sufferings to the acts of the new comers, they would have regarded them with the same jealousy. Competition was always dreaded by those who traded with the Company's licence ; and from this time, Englishmen who ventured to approach the shores of India were stigmatized as "Interlopers"—a name, which they who are acquainted with the history of England, remember was invented there by the monopolists of that age. All such intruders were persecuted with virulent hostility, and under the Charter of Charles the Second could be seized and sent in custody to England.

And, as in the course of our inquiries we shall meet with repeated instances of determined resistance to all free trade, and indeed of a jealousy on that point which in these days must astonish us by its sensitiveness, we may inquire, once for all, how far such narrow policy could under the circumstances be justified. The arguments by which the original establishment and protection of a monopoly were defended, may now be easily refuted. It was asserted that it was necessary in order that the Company might be enabled to support the expenses of a Factory. But the reply is, that in most places Factories were not required, and were mere loads upon trade ; where they were required, their charges might have been defrayed just as well by the contributions of several mercantile houses, as by an exclusive Company. An equally satisfactory reply may be made to the argument, that the concentric powers of a Company were necessary to protect its commerce from the rivalries and assaults of European ene-

* Bruce's Annals 1636-1650. Pietro della Valle (Letter viii) says that in 1624 the Mogul caused all the English at his Court to be put to death, and the Factors at Surat to be imprisoned, because they had made reprisals on native vessels for alleged injuries. However, we have no account of this in Bruce's authentic Annals or other works.

† The union was not completed until 1657. The old Company could not have been possessed of much property, for their forts, privileges, and immunities in Persia and India were valued at only twenty thousand pounds.

mies, as well as from piratical surprises. There is no doubt that such protection could have been more efficiently rendered by a small naval force, which, for a consideration, the British Government would have gladly placed at their merchants' disposal. These arguments, then, which were urged in favour of an exclusive trade, may be pronounced weak and untenable.

Yet it must be admitted, that when once a monopoly was legally established, an invasion of its privileges became an insult upon the majesty of law. The agents of the Company in India, therefore, were fully justified in resenting the intrusions of "interlopers." Their masters had entrusted to them the defence of a monopoly, which, however objectionable to those who had no share in its advantages, was a species of property which had been obtained with all the forms of law and justice. Moreover, their establishment was maintained at a great expense, and they often disbursed large sums of money to procure and retain the favour of a corrupt Court in England, and a still corrupter Court in India. The Factors were, as it were, keepers of a Manor, for which the tenants, their masters, paid a high rent, and which they farmed at a heavy cost. Interlopers, then, were to them as poachers, who must be warned off, and if they persisted in their depredations, strenuously attacked with fire and sword, or prosecuted in Courts of law as enemies not only of the East India Company, but also of the British nation.

For a considerable part of the time embraced in this Chapter, all exclusive privileges met with such rude treatment in England, that the Factors must have been disheartened in their attempts to support them, and private adventure was proportionately encouraged. There was no strong Government to enforce restrictions upon trade. Politicians dared to argue upon liberal principles, and to maintain that the Company's Charter was an encroachment upon public liberty. Speculators took advantage of these political innovations, and, without asking leave of the Company, sent their ships with rich cargoes to India. So well did their enterprizes succeed, that the imports from the Eastern seas were doubled, and the English contrived to sell Oriental goods so cheaply, that the Dutch were supplanted in all European markets. At length Cromwell was induced to sanction the East India Company, and finally, after the Restoration, an exclusive Charter given by authority of the King and Parliament, was feebly opposed by the defenders of popular rights, and the Court of Common Pleas arrived at the strange decision, that the Prince had authority to prevent his subjects from holding commerce with infidels, lest the purity of their faith should be contaminated.*

A few years after the Factors had emerged from the troubles in which they maintained that the interlopers had plunged them, and when their exclusive privileges of trade had been again recognized, they were threatened with new perils by the aggressions of the celebrated Maráthá usurper, Sivají. The English came for the first time in contact with him in 1661. Having assassinated the King of Bijapúr's general, defeated his army, and escaped from a second and more considerable force which that monarch had sent against him, this chief of plunderers appeared be-

* Raynal, Book iii.

fore the town of Rájapúr, where the English had established a small Factory. Suspecting—and with some reason—that the Factors had assisted his enemies with mortars and shells in laying siege to Panála, from which he had just escaped, he was resolved to have his revenge. After taking, therefore, and plundering the town of Rájapúr, he plundered also the English Factory, seized the Factors, and confined them for two years in a hill fort. They were not released until a ransom had been paid for them, and the losses sustained by the English were estimated at ten thousand pagodas. Their Factory of Rájapúr was in consequence closed.*

Of subordinate Factories Carwar was the most important. It was pleasantly situated on an arm of the river in the midst of a piece of ground which had been originally granted by the King of Bijápúr to a Cornish gentleman, named Cutteen. By its means the Company carried on an extensive trade in cloth, for the manufacture of which they employed about fifty thousand people of the country, and no place in India was more celebrated for fine muslins. But about the year 1660 the whole territory was overrun by Aurangzíb's army, whose rude soldiers pillaged the houses of the industrious inhabitants, and scared the weavers from their looms. Their subtle general expressed a desire to arrange with the Factors terms on which their commerce should for the future be conducted, and, as if with that view, invited them to an entertainment in his tent. Secretly, however, he sent a party of troops, who plundered and burnt the Factory. The English afterwards mounted some small cannon on two bastions, but these fortifications were of little use, as they were built a league from the sea, the communications with which could easily be intercepted by an enemy.

A Factory which had been established by the English at Cochin was closed about the year 1660, when that town was taken from the Portuguese by the Dutch, who immediately ordered the Factors to remove with their effects. They accordingly retired to a small Factory at Ponáni.†

Although the Company had not been for many years so successful as at the commencement of its operations, and its affairs were sadly depressed, yet the members were becoming men of mark and consideration in society. They no longer shrank with plebeian modesty from the name of *gentlemen.* In 1637 the adventurers included both noblemen and gentlemen, and in 1647 it was thought good policy to enrol as many members of parliament as possible amongst the subscribers to the stock.‡ The Company's servants in India also, in spite of their misfortunes, were gradually rising to a higher position. By the Charter of 1661 they were authorized to make peace and war with any prince or people not being Christians, and to administer justice for themselves and their dependants.§ These privileges transformed a body of warehousemen into a political corporation, which might almost be called a Government.

However, the Factors were by no means so exalted as to be above betraying the confidence reposed in them by their English masters. For

* Grant Duff, Chapters v. and viii.

† Hamilton's "New Account of the East Indies," Chapters xxii and xxvi. Fryer, Letter iv. Chap. i.

‡ Mill's History, Book i. Chap. 3.

§ Ib. Chap. 4.

long they had concealed their mal-practices by mutual agreement, and this did very well whilst they were united in friendship ; but as soon as a misunderstanding arose, they became the accusers of one another, and shewed that they had grossly neglected the Company's affairs to care exclusively for their own. Gibson, who had been sent from Surat as Agent to Persia, was found after his death to have defrauded the Company by employing twelve thousand pounds of their money in the Dutch trade. The Persian Government professed to be so offended at his dishonesty, that the President and Council of Surat became alarmed, and declared that the trade would be ruined, unless a person of good character was appointed to the agency. These scandalous proceedings of their servants led the Court to require from them all an oath that they would not engage in private trade, and this, in spite of their Anabaptist members, who pressed hard for the substitution of a mere declaration.*

Still the practice was only checked for a time, and not suppressed. Honour was at such a low ebb, and profits were so large, that oaths were ineffectual. When we consider that both the Company and their servants frequently traded on borrowed capital, for which they paid a very high rate of interest, we conclude that their business must have been stopped unless their gains had been immense. Eight or nine per cent were paid even for loans taken up on account of the Company, and so unsettled was the state of the country that many capitalists preferred burying their money to advancing it on the best investments. In spite of this, the Factors contrived to raise capital, and to trade with it on their own account, for we find in 1659 an order again issued on the subject, and these sorts of engagements strictly prohibited.†

In the midst of storms which threatend to tear up the Company's trade root and branch, the seed of their sovereignty was silently sown. From a small source in Surat sprang that Anglo–Indian power which rapidly became a torrent, and bore away all that checked its progress. To Gabriel Boughton, Surgeon of the Company's ship *Hopewell*, more than to any other individual, must the British admit that the origin of their valuable privileges, and consequently of their territorial possessions, is to be traced. On the application of a nobleman at the Court of the Emperor Sháh Jehán, the Chief and Factors of Surat gladly seized the opportunity of sending Boughton to Delhi in 1636, that he might confirm the reputation which medical practitioners from England had already gained. He had the good fortune to attend the Emperor's daughter, and so much were his skill and attention appreciated, that Imperial favours were liberally bestowed upon him, and in particular he obtained a patent permitting him to trade, without paying any duties, throughout the Mogul's dominions. The benefit of this would probably have been doubtful, if his good fortune had not

* Bruce's Annals, 1637-38. Anderson's Colonial Church, Vol. ii. Chap. xv. The following is a curious extract from Evelyn's Diary—" 1657. Nov. 26. I went to London to a court of ye East India Company on its new union, in Merchant-taylors' Hall, where was much disorder by reason of the Anabaptists, who would have the adventurers oblig'd onely by an engagement, without swearing, that they might still pursue their private trade ; but it was carried against them."

† Letter of Nathanael Wyche to the Company ; dated 14th February 1658-59. Mill's History, Book i. Chapters 3 and 4.

followed him to Bengal, where he cured a favorite mistress of the Nawáb, who in gratitude confirmed all his privileges. The generous surgeon did not in prosperity forget his former employers, but advanced the Company's interests by contriving that his privileges should be extended to them. Having done so, he wrote an account of his success to the Factory of Surat, and the next year a profitable trade was opened in the rich province of Bengal.*

The mission of Mr. Davidge, who went from Surat to the Court of Delhi, was also eminently successful, and did much towards repairing the Company's shattered condition. He obtained the protection of Sultán Dárá, the Emperor's eldest son, and after a prolonged negotiation, received five separate firmáns granting the Company licence to trade, exemption from duties, protection for their servants, and safe conduct for their merchandize.†

Let us now again take a walk into the Factory, and observe its internal economy. A learned traveller who visited it at this time was highly pleased with the good order which prevailed. He was also struck with the deference shewn to the Chief and Chaplain.‡ He admired the regularity of attendance at prayers, which were offered twice every day—at six in the morning, and eight in the evening. On Sundays divine service was celebrated three times, and once a Sermon was preached.

And, indeed, few as are the records still extant of this period, all who read them at the present time must be struck by their religious tone. They prove that it was an age of religious profession, if not of moral practice. Puritanism was dominant, or at least had not given way to that open profligacy, that ridicule of sacred things, and contempt of religion, which disgraced the reign of Charles the Second. In India religious men did not blush to own their fear of God, and it suited the purposes of irreligious men to imitate them. Official correspondence even was devout. Thus when Rastell had arrived in St. Augustine's Bay on his passage to Surat, he commenced his homeward despatch with these words :—" It hath pleased Almighty God in his great goodness to protect us hither in safety, and in blessed union and concord together, the 14th day of this present month ; our people generally then in reasonable good plight, and without the loss of any more than five men in our whole fleet, for the which His mercies may His Blessed Name be magnified for ever." And he concludes by declaring, that he humbly commends his masters in his prayers, entreating God to bless them, and direct their counsels and affairs. When announcing the

* Orme's History of Indostan, vol. ii. sect. i. Bruce's Annals, 1644-45.

† Bruce's Annals, 1650-51.

‡ The reader will pardon my digression if I remind him that this and the three following chapters include the period to which Macaulay refers, when he describes with such exaggerations the degradation of the Clergy. He writes :—" The Clergy were regarded as, on the whole, a plebeian class. And indeed, for one who made the figure of a gentleman, ten were mere menial servants." And again ;—" A young Levite might be had for his board, a small garret, and ten pounds a year," for which he was expected to live as a servant. These statements are taken from a satire of Oldham's and given as grave history. Yet at the same time a German traveller noticed the great respect shewn at Surat to the Clergy, and it is a fact, that when Oxenden, Aungier, Streynsham Master—all men of good families—were there, the Chaplain received higher pay than all the senior Factors, and took precedence after the Members of Council. Is there any reason to suppose that the East India Company delighted more than others to honour the Clergy ?

death of a subordinate in 1630 the Chief of the Factory writes thus :—"The death of Mr. Duke was very unwelcome unto us, as being sensible of the want you will find by the missing of so able an assistant in that place where he hath been long acquainted. God of His mercy so direct our hearts, who must follow him, that we may be always ready for the like sudden summons." The same style is observable in all official letters, and the usual formula with which they conclude is, "Commending you to the Almighty's protection," or "Commending you to God's merciful guidance."*

Yet these pious adventurers had notions of their own about the observance of the Lord's Day. Although they were scrupulous in attending Divine Service, in the disposal of the rest of their time they preferred "The Book of Sports" to the "Lesser Catechism." After Sermon on Sundays they used to repair to the suburbs, where they amused themselves in a garden by shooting at the butt. And—which was still less to be defended—they indulged to some extent in gambling. Their visitor, who has told us these little facts, was so skilful in shooting that he contrived to win a hundred mamoudis or five pistoles almost every week. †

Each inmate of the Factory had his allotted hours for work and recreation. On Fridays, after prayers, the President and a few friends met for the purpose of drinking to the health of their wives, whom they had left in England.

The liquor in which they ordinarily indulged was arak, of which Bernier said that it was "a drink very hot and penetrant, like the brandy made of corn in Poland. It so falls upon the nerves, that it often causeth shaking hands in those that drink a little too much of it, and casts them into incurable maladies." "The soul of a feast, which is good wine," was to be found no where but in the English and Dutch Factories. At Ahmedábád and Golconda they had wine of fair quality, which had been made in the country, but it was usually imported from Shiraz or the Canaries at so great expense, that six or seven crowns were charged for a bottle. What they called "pale punch"—a compound of brandy, rose water, lime-juice and sugar—was also in great favour. So early as 1638, when tea was unknown in England, it was much drunk in the Factory at Surat. "It acts as a drug," writes the traveller, who highly approved of the decoction, "for it cleanses the stomach, and dissipates the superfluous humours by a temperate heat peculiar to it."‡

The Dutch were still successful rivals of the English, and the Portuguese were endeavouring to regain their lost ascendancy. The chief reason why the English Company had directed their main efforts to Surat was, that they could find no more suitable place, after they had repeatedly failed in

* Outward Letter Books of the Surat Factory for the years 1630-1673.

† Mamoudis were only current in Surat and the neighbourhood ; each was worth rather less than an English shilling ; but their value varied. In 1663 two hundred and twenty mamoudis were exchanged for a hundred rupees. See Fryer's account of coins, weights, &c., in India.

‡ Les Voyages du Sieur Albert de Mandelslo, Liv i. Bernier's Letter to M. le Vayer. The common belief has been that tea was first introduced into England from Holland by the Lords Arlington and Ossory in 1666. What is stated above in the account of the tea trade will be found correct.

attempts to divide with the Dutch the profits of their trade in the Spice Islands. For the same reason they concluded a treaty in 1634 with the Portuguese, who then opened to them ports, where their enterprizes could not be foiled by the greedy and active republicans. During the war with Holland, which in Europe terminated so gloriously for the British Navy, the English Factories suffered considerable injury. In 1653 the Factors of Surat were thrown into the utmost consternation by the appearance of a Dutch fleet; they found it impossible to carry on the coasting trade except at a risk, which they were unwilling to run, and all their commerce was suspended. In 1656 they were equally alarmed by hearing that the Dutch meditated an attack upon the island of Diu, which, if successful, would have enabled them to demand the payment of such heavy duties from all ships entering the river of Surat, that the English trade must inevitably have been ruined.

The Dutch Company was at this time very powerful, and their Factors ventured to dictate terms of peace and war even to the Great Mogul. In consequence of some injuries inflicted upon them by the Governor of Surat, they equipped four ships in 1649 to make reprisals, until the Governor or Sháh Jehán should give them satisfaction. Two native vessels, the *Ganjwar* and *Sáhibí*, were seized by them, and all the ready money found on board was held in pledge. The result was a firmán from the Emperor, conceding a portion of the Hollanders' demands.*

* Baldæus.

CHAPTER IV.

1662—1685.

CONTENTS.—*Bombay*; origin of the name. Its importance; at first little appreciated. Description. The Company desire to obtain it; their plans and proposal. Ceded to England. Arrival of an English fleet. The Portuguese refuse to evacuate. English fleet sails with the troops to Swally; thence to Anjídeva—Bombay resigned to the English under Cook; his absurd treaty. Appearance of the new possession. Sir Gervase Lucas succeeds Cook as Governor; his history and death. Captain Gary; his character; his claim to the Governorship disputed. Bombay transferred to the Company. Commission sent from Surat. Bombay governed by Commissioners. Deputy Governors Gray, Gyfford and Henry Oxenden. Court resolves to improve Bombay. Military arrangements; the Militia; the regular Troops; first European Regiment. Fortifications, and other Defences. Threatened attack from a Dutch fleet. Development of the Resources of Bombay Natives invited to settle. Trade encouraged. A Mint. Courts of Judicature. The first Judge. Unhealthiness of the climate; Cholera; its cure; causes of unhealthiness: intemperance of sick Soldiers; an Hospital built. A Church proposed; the rise of Christianity; a Bishop at Kalyán; Martyrs at Thána; description of Christian worship; the Portuguese; English place of worship; general anxiety to build a Church. Improved condition of the Island: the Revenues; Increase of trade. New View of Bombay and its neighbourhood. Expenses of the Works on the Island. Measures to increase the Revenue.

AMONGST the foreign dependencies of the British Crown none are of greater and more increasing importance than Bombay. The growth of the Australian Colonies has been indeed far more rapid, and their sudden acquisition of wealth more astonishing, than any progress which has been made in India. But the possession of Australia and other colonies is not essential to the maintenance of England's power and glory; if their independence were to be at once proclaimed, no serious consequences need be apprehended on her account. It is, however, essential to her prosperity that she should preserve her Indian Empire, and every year strengthens the conviction of thinking men, that whether that Empire be regarded from a political or commercial point of view, its most important possession is the island of Bombay.

Bombay—or Bombaim, as it is called by old writers—has been naturally supposed by Europeans to derive its name from the Portuguese, and to have denoted an advantage of its geographical position. But Briggs declares—without, however, giving his authority—that in ancient days part of the island was called Mahim, and part "Mumbaye" from an idol.* And, certainly, an old temple, dedicated to Múmbá Deví, or the goddess Múmbá, formerly stood on the plot now called the Esplanade. About a century ago it was taken down and rebuilt at some distance from its former site. The place where it now stands is well known.†

For many years the English had been anxious to lay their hands upon this treasure; yet strange to say, when they had obtained it, its value remained for a while hidden from the penetration of their statesmen, the practised eyes of their naval and military commanders, and the keen avidity of their enterprizing merchants. Its retention was considered scarcely worth a struggle, and the question whether it should be resigned was actually debated. Even the Dutch historian of the age, a shrewd and accurate man, considered that this possession was worthless.‡

Yet where is there a site more calculated not only to strike the eye of a casual observer, but to grow in the estimation of a well-informed and scientific resident, than Bombay? Two centuries ago its distinguishing features must have been the same as they are at present; for they could only be altered by the disturbances and revolutions of a geological era. The deep capacious harbour, with its channel so narrow, but safe for careful and well-trained pilots; the false harbour of Back Bay, offering to inexperienced mariners or threatening invaders a tempting and dangerous lure; the Eastern hills which rise in rugged and fantastical shapes one behind another, until at noonday they are lost in misty heat; their feet fringed with palm trees, their summits crowned with primeval forests, or here and there with the ruins of ancient fortresses—all form a scene which promises strength and security to the inhabitants; and if it had but the exquisite associations of classic antiquity, or the decorations of Italian taste, might be thought by a lover of the picturesque to rival even the place where Virgil sleeps and the Siren sang—beautiful Parthenope.

But although the outlines of the distant scenery are bold, the appearance of the island when approached from the sea is somewhat insignificant. Flat plains, in some places below the level of high-water mark, are slightly relieved by low ridges of trappean rock, the highest point of which is called Malabar Hill, and that does not exceed a hundred and eighty feet. The whole area of the island is about sixteen square miles. Its shape approaches a trapezoid, with its shorter side, six miles in length, towards the sea, and its longer side extending eleven miles parallel to the main land. Between the two hilly ridges, which form these sides, there is a level plain, about two miles in width, now called the Flats. The greatest breadth of the Island is little more than three miles. Malabar Point is the name of that extremity which, to the south, faces the open sea, and at the northern extremity are the Hill and Fort of Warlí. The line which is parallel to the harbour and mainland has for its southern extremity the Light House and Burial ground of Colaba, and for its northern the tower called Riva Fort.

* Briggs' Ferishta, vol. iv. chapter 4.

† Paper by R. X. Murphy, Esq. in the "Transactions of the Bombay Geographical Society," vol. i.

‡ Baldæus, chapter 12.

Colaba was a separate island, until joined a few years ago by a causeway to Bombay. Between it and Malabar Hill is the Back Bay, to which we have already alluded. On the Colaba side the Bay is shallow and filled with dangerous rocks ; but under the opposite cliff is a channel, sufficiently deep for ships of considerable tonnage. To the north of Bombay is another Bay, with a beach called Mahim Sands, and on that side the island is separated from the mountainous island of Salsette by a small arm of the sea, which at one part is only a hundred and twenty-five yards wide, Salsette itself being separated from the main-land by another channel. To the South and East is the harbour, which contains several lofty, interesting islands, and is in one place six miles broad.* It extends a considerable distance inland, and, as it narrows, the shores on either side present various scenes of extraordinary beauty.

Observing the natural advantages of Bombay, the Company had hoped to gain possession of it so early as 1627. In that year a joint expedition of Dutch and English ships under the command of a Dutch General, Harman Van Speult, had sailed from Surat with the object of forming an establishment here, as well as attacking the Portuguese in the Red Sea. This plan was defeated by the death of Van Speult ; but in 1653 the President and Council of Surat again brought the subject under the consideration of the Directors, pointing out how convenient it would be to have some insular and fortified station, which might be defended in times of lawless violence, and giving it as their opinion that for a consideration the Portuguese would allow them to take possession of Bombay and Bassein. The following year the Directors drew the attention of Cromwell, the Protector, to this suggestion.†

It was the gratification, then, of a wish which had long been felt, when in 1661 Bombay formed part of the Infanta Catherina's dower, and was ceded to England on her marriage with Charles the Second. On the eighteenth of the following September a fleet of five ships, under the Earl of Marlborough, arrived in the harbour, and brought with them a Portuguese Viceroy to see that the articles of cession were strictly observed. But the Portuguese on the island had by that time discovered the value of the place, and were indisposed to resign their claims to such a favoured spot. They found an excuse in the demands which the English made. Lord Marlborough asserted, and they denied, that Salsette had been included in the cession. They also pretended that the patent or letter authorizing them to give up the place was informal, and finally they refused to arrange any terms or listen to any proposals.

Those were not days when the fortifications of refractory enemies could be ruined in a few hours by the fire of an English fleet, and the Commander was compelled to sail away. As the military part of his force were suffering from long confinement on shipboard, he landed them at Swally. There were four companies of a hundred men each, exclusive of officers ; and Sir Andrew Shipman, their Commanding Officer, immediately began to drill and prepare them for military operations. However, he

* Geology of the Island of Bombay; with a map and plates. By H. J. Carter, Esq., Assistant Surgeon, Bombay Establishment.

† Bruce's Annals, 1626-27 and 1652-53.

was soon interrupted by the President of the English Factory, who intreated him to depart, as the jealousy and fears of the Government were excited by such a display of force. Marlborough, therefore, having re-embarked Sir Andrew and his men, landed them on the small island of Anjídeva, twelve leagues to the south of Goa, where he left them. On this unhealthy spot they remained during the rains, without sufficient protection from the weather. The consequence was, that Sir Andrew Shipman and three hundred of his men perished. The Earl of Marlborough had sailed with his fleet to England.*

Previous to his departure, the Earl had offered to make over Bombay to the President and Council of Surat; but as their title would not be good without the sanction of royal authority, and even if it were good, they had not the means of enforcing it, this offer was declined. After Shipman's death, Cook had succeeded to the command of the wreck of an army, as the few English troops still surviving on Anjídeva might be called. Too glad to find an asylum at Bombay on any terms, he accepted such as the Portuguese were pleased to dictate, and the island was resigned to him on the following conditions, some of which were reasonable, others simply absurd :—He renounced all claim to the neighbouring islands, promised that the Portuguese should be exempted from all payment of customs; that private estates should be secured to their owners; that all deserters, run away slaves, Hindús in charge of property, Kunabí's or agriculturists, Bhandári's or toddy-drawers, and artificers who might escape from the Portuguese territories and place themselves under the protection of the British flag, should be immediately sent back to the Portuguese territory; that there should be no interference with the rites of the Roman Catholic religion, and not only that, but if any Portuguese should offer to embrace the Protestant faith, the English should not consent to receive him.† As these conditions were afterwards appealed to by the Portuguese, it is important to observe that the King of England refused to ratify them, and they were never ratified by the Crown of Portugal. The English Government indeed were so dissatisfied with Cooke's measures, that they deposed him, and demanded of the Portuguese Government satisfaction for damages sustained in consequence of the island not having been delivered over according to the original agreement.‡

The English were by no means charmed with their new possession, and to them it did not appear worth the precious lives and treasure which

* James Ley, third Earl Marlborough, an eminent mathematician and navigator, was afterwards Lord Admiral at Dartmouth. Commanding in 1665 "that huge ship, called the Old James, in that great fight at sea with the Dutch upon the 3d June, he was there slain by a cannon bullet." His honours reverted to his uncle, the fourth Earl, with whom the peerage became extinct. Burke's 'Extinct Peerage.' "He was a man of wonderful parts in all kinds of learning, which he took more delight in than his title; and having no great estate descended to him, he brought down his mind to his fortune, and lived very retired, but with more reputation than any fortune could have given him." Life of Clarendon, by himself.

† Translation from the ancient record in the archives of Goa, by Major T. B. Jervis, F.R.S. in the Transactions of the Bombay Geographical Society, Vol iii.

‡ So it is stated in a Letter from the Court, dated 1723. They appeal to the authority of the Records in the custody of the Lords Commissioners of Trade and Plantations, the Report of the Lords of Council, and the Letter of King Charles the Second.

it had cost. Indeed the place must have looked desolate enough. Large tracts of land which have since been recovered from the sea, were then overflowed. At high tides the waves flowed to the part called Umerkhádi, and covered the present Bhendi Bazaar. Near where the temple of Múmbádeví stands, a place still called Páydhuní, or " feet-washing," marks where a small stream of salt water was formerly left by the receding tide, and where persons might wash their feet before entering Bombay. Where Kámátápúr is now, there was then sufficient depth of water for the passage of boats. In fact during one part of every day, only a group of islets was to be seen. According to Fryer, forty thousand acres of good land were thus submerged.* The rest of the island seemed for the most part a barren rock, not being extensively wooded, as at present; but producing only some cocoa-palms, which covered the esplanade. The principal town was Mahim. On Dongarí Hill, adjoining the harbour, there was a small collection of fishermen's huts, and a few houses were seen interspersed amongst palm trees, where the Fort now stands. On various spots were built towers with small pieces of ordnance, as a protection against Málabár pirates, who had become peculiarly insolent, plundering villages, and either murdering the inhabitants, or carrying them into slavery.† The English also found, but soon removed, a Government House, which was slightly fortified, defended by four brass guns, and surrounded by one of the most delightful gardens. Portuguese society was depraved and corrupt. The population did not exceed ten thousand.

Besides his political failure, Cook was charged with fraud and embezzlement. The seat of Government, from which he was ejected, was then occupied by Sir Gervase Lucas, who had been well known in the Civil wars of England. A staunch royalist, he adhered to Charles the First's cause amidst it reverses, and when Governor of Belvoir Castle had, with a body of troops, escorted the King in his escape from the fatal field of Naseby.‡ He arrived in Bombay on the fifth of November 1666. Unhappily a misunderstanding sprang up between him and Sir George Oxenden, the President of Surat. It caused considerable irritation; but a reconciliation took place before the death of Sir Gervase, which occurred on the twenty first of the May following his arrival. Oxenden announced the melancholy event to Lord Arlington, and expressed his regret for the loss of an officer whose exertions and probity had been highly honourable.

Captain Gary was then appointed Deputy Governor. Hamilton calls him " an old Greek;" but he had been born in Venice of English parents. He was more merchant than soldier, and had gained some learning, being well acquainted with Latin, Greek, and Portuguese. He is even said to have been engaged in writing a treatise in Arabic, which he dedicated to the viceroy of Goa.§ Yet is he described as a proud, wasteful, and extravagant officer. His power was not undisputed.

* Mr. Murphy's paper as above. Fryer's account.
† Hamilton's East India Gazeteer.
‡ Clarendon's History of the Rebellion, Chapter 9.
§ Fryer, Letter iv. Chapter 2.

The Portuguese had in the time of his predecessor threatened a resort to arms, because a claim which the Jesuits' College of Bandora made for a considerable tract of land had not been allowed. This threat Sir Gervase Lucas had considered an act of treason, and declared all the Jesuits' lands forfeited to the Crown. Cook, therefore, who had yielded the reins of Government with reluctance, and retired in discontent to Goa, took this opportunity of asserting his right to succeed Lucas. Coming to Bandora he threatened to join the Portuguese in attacking Bombay. But his countrymen only treated him with contempt, and denounced him as a rebel and traitor.*

Such were the Governors of Bombay under the Crown. Either they were wanting in will or ability to discharge their trust efficiently. The King of England soon ceased to attach any value to this portion of his consort's dowry, and was only axious to get rid of his new and expensive acquisition.

On the first of September 1668 the ship *Constantinople* arrived at Surat, bringing the copy of a Royal Charter, according to which his Majesty agreed to bestow Bombay upon the Honorable Company, as the adventurers had for some time been styled. As the island had been found so burdensome, there was little difficulty in arranging the terms of transfer. It was to be held by the Company of the King "in free and common soccage, as of the manor of East Greenwich, on payment of the annual rent of £10 in gold on the 30th September in each year." At the same time were conveyed to the Company all the stores, arms and ammunition which were upon the island, together with such political powers as were necessary for its defence and government.†

On the receipt of this authority, the Right Honourable Sir George Oxenden, Kt., President of Surat, and his Council, held a consultation, at which they agreed to assume at once the Government of Bombay. But they felt that this would be an affair of some delicacy, as the royal officers might not be disposed to acknowledge the supremacy of a few mercantile agents, who were two hundred miles distant from them. They therefore resolved to proceed with caution, and before despatching any one to receive charge of the place, considered which of their number possessed the requisite tact and other qualifications. Their choice fell upon Mr. Goodyer, because he had lived on terms of intimacy with Gary, and whilst on a visit in Bombay had gained the affections of the officers, which, they remarked, "will very much conduce to their peaceable surrender, and our quiet possession of the place." With Goodyer were associated Streynham Master, and Cotes, members of Council at Surat, and Captain Young who was to be Deputy Governor.

Goodyer fulfilled his mission with judgment. On the twenty-third of

* The following have been the authorities consulted in addition to those before specified: Bruce's Annals; Fryer's account; Hamilton's "New Account"; Hamilton's Hindostan; Mill's History, Book i. Chap. iv.: Letter from the Deputy Governor and Council in the Surat Records, dated 2nd May 1677.

† Record of a consultation held in the Surat Factory on the 3rd September 1668. Treaties, Agreements and Engagements between the Honorable East India Company, and the Native Princes, Chiefs, and States in Western India; by R. Hughes Thomas. Bruce's Annals.

the month Gary drew up his troops in line, read to them the royal letters, and formally transferred the Island, its live and dead stock, and cash amounting to £4,879, 7s. 6d. to the Company's Commissioner. In reporting his proceedings to the Secretary of State, this last of Royal Governors declared, that "the unexpected change had much troubled him," and that he had performed his task with a heavy heart. His soldiers also manifested symptoms of resistance, but soon perceiving that they had only the alternative of being disbanded, they eventually submitted. Gary obtained a seat in Council, and afterwards was Judge of the Island. Young, the Deputy Governor, was soon dismissed for gross misconduct, which will be explained below.*

The next year the President himself visited Bombay, and, during a short stay, framed a set of regulations for its administration; but as he died soon afterwards, the island was left in a state of anarchy. Five commissioners were appointed for the management of affairs. One was Sterling, a Scotch minister; the others were Cotes, Captain Burgess, Lieut. Houghton, and James Adams, Chairman. The rest so little approved of this last functionary, that after two days they removed him from his situation.

Gerald Aungier having been appointed President of Surat, nominated Mathew Gray to the Deputy Governorship of Bombay. He was succeeded by Philip Gyfford, who had formerly been sent to open a trade at Tonquin. After his death in 1676, Henry Oxenden, Chief of the Factory at Carwar, became Deputy Governor. He enjoyed his honours but a short time, and dying was succeeded by Ward, whose term of power, as we shall see, was clouded by trouble and sedition.†

After the Company had obtained Bombay, a few years elapsed before they thought of turning it to their advantage. Gradually, however, they perceived that the place was appointed by nature to be an emporium of trade. Unlike the roads of Swally, which were exposed and dangerous, its harbour was safe and commodious.‡ Easy and direct communications could be opened with the English Factories in Persia, on the Málabár Coast, and the Spice Islands. They felt, moreover, that in case of a war with the Dutch, or if the Mogul Officers continued to heap upon them affronts which they had endured patiently, but which might soon be beyond endurance, they could only maintain their servants in India by holding Bombay with a firm grasp. There they had the great advantage, which was denied to the Factory at Surat, of a small territory, where the British were sole masters, where native officials could not meddle, nor native tyrants domineer. They therefore said :—"We are now much set upon the improvement of that our Island, and do esteem it a place of more consequence than we have formerly done." They thought that the best way of securing their little

* Consultation Book of the Surat Factory. Fryer's Account. Bruce's Annals.

† Fryer, Bruce, and other authorities differ a little as to the order of succession of these Deputy Governors. The above account I trust is quite correct.

‡ Letter from the Deputy Governor and Council of Bombay, dated 24th January 1676-7.

territory was, to increase its military strength, to encourage the growth of its population, and to develope its internal resources. The measures by which they hoped to attain these ends were enlightened and well deserving of success.

Their military arrangements included the establishment of a militia, and a re-organization of their regular force. Their plans for the former were in the main good, although some of the details appear ridiculous, and drawn up in ignorance of the native character. In 1677 the militia was composed of six hundred men, all owners of land. A hundred Brahmans and Banyás, who refused to bear arms, contributed money instead of service. The following instructions sent out by this trading Company to their agents in Bombay may induce a Military reader to smile :—

" We would have the inhabitants modelled into trained bands under English or other officers as there shall be cause, and make of them one or two regiments, or more, as your number will hold out, exercising them in arms one day in every two months, or as often as you shall think may be convenient, but you need not always waste powder at such exercise, but teach them to handle their arms, their facings, wheeling, marching, and counter marching, the first ranks to present, draw their triggers together at the beat of the drum, and fall into the rear for the second ranks to advance, as is often used with learners in our artillery ground, but sometimes they must be used to firing, lest in time of action they should start at the noise or the recoil of their arms."

The regular troops varied in number as the pecuniary circumstances of the Company led to augmentation at one time, or reduction at another. Sometimes their ranks were thinned to an alarming degree by the fatal inroads of disease. When the island was transferred to the Company, the garrison numbered two hundred and eighty-five men, ninety three of whom were English, and the rest French, Portuguese or Natives. These formed two Companies, each commanded by a Captain. The first Company comprehended two commissioned officers, sixty-six non-commissioned officers and privates, and twenty-eight topasses ; * the second, three commissioned officers, seventy-three non-commissioned officers and privates, and twenty-six topasses. This is said to have been the honourable Company's first European regiment, although many not Europeans found admission into its ranks.

Many of the recruits sent out were Germans, and more were applied for as they behaved with so much sobriety and regularity. When the Court directed that a militia should be raised, they also wished to have three companies of English and two of " Rashpouts" (Rájpúts). Each Company was to number a hundred men, and the Rájpúts were to have a

* I suppose that these were Indo Portuguese, but what was the meaning of the name ? Nieuhoff in his account of Batavia gives the following explanation :—" The Mardickers or Topassers are a mixture of divers Indian nations, called Topassers, accommodators, because they will accommodate themselves easily to the manners, customs, and religion of such as they live among : though some will have them derive their name from a precious stone called a Topaz." Nieuhoff's Voyages and Travels to the East-Indies.

commandant, with other officers of their own caste. In 1676 there were four hundred European soldiers, but, as these were supposed to be more than were required, it was ordered that the force should be reduced to three hundred, some of whom were to be sent to Surat, for a storm was gathering in that quarter. There were also forty troopers, mounted on such inferior horses as were reared in the country,* and able on an emergency to take up forty foot soldiers behind them. Their first commandant was Keigwin, and he drew a salary of a hundred and twenty pounds. In 1683 there were but a hundred and fifty English soldiers. A few extra files were usually kept to supply casualties, which were mournfully frequent. Keigwin afterwards commanded the first of the three companies of Infantry; the other two were commanded by Lieutenants Fletcher and Thornburn.

There was much difficulty in determining the exact position which the officers were to hold. When Shaxton was sent out in 1671 with the command of a Company, he was, in consideration of his high character, appointed a Factor, that so he might combine civil and military duties. He was also told, that if he continued to deserve well of the Company, he might become Deputy Governor. Captain Langford, the Chief Military Officer in 1676, was admitted to a seat in Council; but a caution was given that his case was not to form a precedent. The chief authority was to be held by Civilians, but they were also to study Military tactics, that when required they might hold commissions in the Army.

Making an unwise and odious distinction, the Court ordered that non-commissioned officers and privates should be punished with death for neglect or breach of duty, but that commissioned officers should only be reduced and deprived of rank. The regulations which they then made were for many years the martial law of India; but when royal troops were sent out, they disputed the authority of the Company's officers to administer martial law at all.

Fortifications with strong bastions were built at what was then thought a heavy expense. The ordnance consisted of twenty-one pieces of cannon, with the requisite stores. There were only two gunners, and the other soldiers served the guns as occasion required. At Mázagám, Sion, Sewri, Mahim, and Warlí were small forts also mounted with cannon. The Court were afraid to employ professional engineers as they would require large salaries, and they knew "the speculations into which men of this description usually lead their employers." So they at first directed, that Captains Smith and Tolderoy, two military officers, should act as engineers. But as in 1671 Herman Bake happened to be in Bombay, and made them an offer of his services, they appointed him their Engineer and Surveyor-General. Warwick Pett, a naval architect, was sent out to build ships for the Indian seas; but only British-built ships were at that time allowed to import Asiatic produce into England. *Pax quæsita bello,* wrote the Court, now suddenly blazing with martial ar-

* From the price which was fixed we learn, that then the value of a native horse was from sixty to a hundred rupees. But Fryer says, "£300 is an easy rate for a good Persian or Arab," Letter iii, Chap. iii.

dour, is an old maxim which must be observed in Bombay. They insisted that a strict guard should be kept, and that sentinels should watch day and night, as if an enemy were actually preparing to make an assault.*

Scarcely had the first measures been adopted for the defence of the Island, than an event shewed their wisdom. A Dutch fleet arrived on the 20th of February 1673 with the intention of taking it by surprise. Orme tells us, that Aungier, who happened to be at the time in Bombay, exerted himself on the occasion "with the calmness of a philosopher, and the courage of a centurion." Rickloffe Van Goen, the Dutch Commodore, found to his mortification, that he was likely to meet with a warmer reception than he had anticipated. Heavy ordnance were seen mounted on the fortifications, and sixty light field pieces were ready at hand. According to Fryer, the Fort was guarded by three hundred English troops, "four hundred topazes or Portugal firemen," "a militia out of Portugal," comprising five hundred men with English leaders, and three hundred Bhandáris armed with clubs.† There were also in the harbour three men of war, the largest carrying thirty guns, and five French ships which were ready to assist the English. Under these circumstances Rickloffe stood up to the Western side of the island, and threatened a descent in the Mahim Channel, but Aungier rapidly marched to that quarter, and ranged his troops in defiance along the shore. Doubtless the Bhandáris and their clubs appeared very formidable in the distance, otherwise the Hollanders with six thousand men on board their fleet would not have sheered off. They soon disappeared, and as in a short time peace was concluded between England and Holland, the people of Bombay were relieved from further apprehensions.‡

By way of increasing the population, and developing the resources of the island, attempts were made to establish manufactures. Directions were given for inviting spinners and weavers to settle, every legitimate influence was to be employed so as to attract them from the interior, and cotton was to be served out to them from the Company's stores, that they might convert it into cloth without any outlay of money. The Court, having heard that the manufacture of cotton stockings by knitting was successfully carried on at Goa, required that the same should be attempted in Bombay, and that four or five hundred pairs should be at once forwarded to England. Not only the poorer sort of artizans, but opulent tradesmen were also induced to settle by promises of liberal treatment and religious toleration. As a first step, a regular engagement was

* Bruce's Annals 1668-1676. Letters from the Deputy Governor and Council, dated 24th January 1676-7; from the Honorable Court, dated May 1682; 6th November 1683; 16th November 1683; February 1684, and 2nd July 1684; Letters from the President and Council of Surat to Bombay, dated 4th July and 14th August 1676. Hamilton's "New Account," chap. xvii. Hamilton's Hindostan. Fryer's Account, Letter iii. chap. 4, and Letter iv. chap. 3.

† The Governor's bodyguard was composed of Bhandáris. To this day men of this caste carry a union flag, and blow a large trumpet before the High Sheriff at the opening of the Quarter Sessions. Mr. Murphy's paper, as above.

‡ Fryer's account. Orme's Fragments, Sec. i.

entered into with Níma Párak, an eminent Banyá, residing in the city of Diu, and formal articles were agreed to on both sides. On the part of the Company it was promised, that all of the Banyá caste who might remove to the Island should enjoy the free exercise of their religion within their own houses, and should be secured from all molestation. It was stipulated that no Englishman, Portuguese, or other Christian, nor any Mussulman should be permitted to live within the private grounds of Banyás, to enter them for the purpose of slaughtering animals, or to offer their persons the slightest injury or indignity. If any should in opposition to these regulations offend them by intruding upon their privacy, the Governor or his Deputy should, on receiving a complaint to that effect, cause the offenders to be severely punished. The settlers were to be allowed to burn their dead, and to observe all such ceremonies as were customary at their weddings. Lastly it was engaged, that none who professed their religion, of whatever age, sex, or condition he might be, should be compelled to embrace Christianity, nor that any should be forced against their wills to carry burdens. These stipulations were in striking contrast, and probably it was intended that they should be so, with the harsh treatment which the natives had suffered from the fanaticism and injustice of the Portuguese.*

Other steps for the encouragement of trade were taken in accordance with the spirit of the age. Docks were to be constructed, and an armed vessel of a hundred and eighty tons to be stationed off the Island for the protection of shipping. The manufactures of the place were protected at first by exemption from duties, which were not demanded for calicoes made in Bombay, raw, wrought, and thrown silks, cotton yarn, gold and silver jewellery, bezoar stones, musk, amber and ambergrease.† But afterwards all exports were to pay a duty of three and a half per cent. Articles of food, such as cocoanuts, fish, salt, with other produce of the island or its waters, were subjected to the almost prohibitory duty of nine per cent, including one per cent for the expenses of the fortifications. Grain, timber, and all goods except Indian iron and tobacco, which were imported, paid two and a half per cent, and one per cent towards the fortifications ; Indian iron and tobacco paid nine per cent.‡

In 1670 the Court gave directions for the establishment of a Mint, and that it might have the countenance of royal authority, letters patent, dated fifth October 1676 and 28th of Charles the Second, were issued. In 1681 Mr. Smith was sent from England to be Assay Master and Mint Master on a salary of sixty pounds *per annum.*§

A Court House was erected in the most frequented part of the bazaar, not only that access to it might be convenient for all who were drawn into

* Letter from the President and Council of Surat to Bombay, dated 22nd March 1677.

† Bruce's Annals, 1668-69.

‡ Bruce's Annals 1674-75.

§ In 1697 the value of money coined at Surat and Bombay was fixed at 2s.-6d. the rupee ; the xeraphim of Bombay at twenty pence ; the Persian Shahí for Carwar at four shillings, and the Pagoda for Calicot at nine shillings. Persian characters were stamped on these coins, which offended the Emperor ; so for a time the practice was discontinued. Bruce's Annals, 1697-98.

litigation, but also that prisoners might be confined there, and, according to a custom still remembered in England, have opportunity to beg relief of passers by*. Two Courts of Judicature were established in 1670. The higher was a Court of Appeal presided over by the Deputy Governor and members of Council. Its decisions were to be final and without appeal, except in most urgent cases. The lower Court was presided over by one of the Factors, assisted by native officers, and took cognizance of all disputes regarding property under the value of two hundred xeraphims. The Deputy Governor and three Military Officers were also constituted a Court for the administration of martial law. Each Court was to meet once in the week. Allusion was made to trial by Jury ; but it was not considered practicable. About the same time also the Court of Directors recommended that a regular force of police should be established.†

In 1671 application was made to the Court for a Judge versed in Civil law ; but they declined compliance, fearing that he might be disposed to promote litigation, and probably would not obey the orders which the President and Council might find it for the Company's interest to give him. It is difficult to say what contingency the Court had in view ; but it seems very probable that they supposed no Judge who came out with the education and spirit of an English gentleman would prosecute interlopers to the death ; and the result shewed, that their fears were not groundless. As an experiment they resolved to send out some writers who had received a legal education, and who, if they conducted themselves well, might be called in as Assessors to the Courts of Justice.

At last by letters patent dated 9th August 1683, a Judge was authorized to preside over a Court of Admiralty for the trial of such interlopers as he could lay hands upon. Two merchants were to be joined with him, and it was particularly specified that the processes were to be in English not in Latin. The first who thus wielded the terrors of the law was John St. John, D.C.L. It was arranged that he should hold a commission both from His Majesty and the Company, the former bearing date 6th February 1684, the latter 7th April 1684. His salary was fixed at two hundred pounds per annum, with an allowance for two servants, and free commons at the Deputy Governor's table. Up to this time Englishmen accused of grave offences had been sent to their own country for trial ; but when Robert Johnson, a troublesome fellow, had thus been consigned to the Court, they desired that the practice should be discontinued, and that all criminals should be tried and punished in Bombay.‡

But when earnestly engaged in military and economical measures, the Company did not forget the care of their servants' bodies and souls. A cry of wailing for the dead seemed to cross the seas, which divide England from Bombay, and reach their ears. The many advantages of Bombay were counteracted by its pestilential climate. Of what use sending trusty Factors, and hardy soldiers there? They breathed the poisonous air but

* Letter from the Deputy Governor and Council to the Court, dated 24th January 1676-77.

† Bruce's Annals 1667-71. Kaye's Administration.

‡ Letters from the Court, dated February 1684 and 6th May 1685. Fryer's Account. Morley's Digest of Indian Law, vol. i.

a few short months, after which their services and lives were lost to their employers for ever. Three years was the average duration of European life. The catalogue of diseases and the records of deaths are, when read even at this distant day, truly saddening. In the months which intervened between October 1675 and February 1676, a hundred English soldiers perished ; and in the latter year Mr. Gyfford, the Deputy Governor, and Bake, Surveyor General. So strong was the dread of the climate, that when Child, who at other times was far too bold and blustering, had been appointed Accountant of Bombay, and second in council by the President and Council of Surat, he pleaded his apprehensions of disease, and positively refused to accept the office.* The natives indeed and naturalized Portuguese considered the island healthy ; but, wrote Fryer, fluxes, dropsy, scurvy, barbiers or loss of the use of hands and feet, gout, stone, malignant and putrid fevers, all combined to make it a charnel house of Europeans. Of every five hundred Europeans who came to live upon the island, not one hundred, in his opinion, ever left it.

The disease which was prevalent in the country and especially fatal in Bombay, was called by the Portuguese practitioners of medicine "the Chinese death," or cholic. It was divided, according to their system, into four kinds. The first kind was simple cholic, and its only symptom was severe griping. The second was attended with diarrhœa as well as pain ; the third with pain and vomiting. Purging, vomiting, and intense pain were symptoms of the last kind. This was supposed by Thevenot to be Cholera morbus, and it generally brought its victims' sufferings to a fatal termination within twenty-four hours. The remedy, upon which even Europeans relied, was of a painful and barbarous character. A hot iron was applied to the ball of the sufferer's foot. If he winced, it was expected that he would recover ; but if he shewed no signs of pain he was given over by his medical attendant.†

Various causes were assigned for the alarming mortality amongst Europeans in Bombay. The atmosphere was at first supposed to be polluted by the putrid fish, with which the trees were manured. A more reasonable conjecture was, that malaria arose from the low plains which were overflowed at high tides, and left in a swampy state when the sea receded. In 1675 a proposition for draining the swamps was submitted to the Court by the Government of Bombay. Several surveys were in

* Letter from the President and Council of Surat to the Factors of Rájapúr ; dated 16th November 1676.

† Fryer's Account. Voyages de Thevenot. Choix des lettres edifiantes et curieuses, tom. iv. Father Martin in these letters gives instances in which this treatment was completely successful. He adds that Signor Mancuchi, a Venetian Physician, had discovered another cure, by which he gained "vast reputation" at the Mogul Court, where he resided forty years. His infallible remedy was this :—"Take an iron ring about an inch and a half in diameter, and thick in proportion. Then heating it red hot in the fire, extend the patient on his back, and apply the ring to his navel, in such a manner that the navel may be as centre to the ring. As soon as the patient feels the heat (which must necessarily be in an instant) take away the ring as quick as possible, when so sudden a revolution will be wrought in his intestines, that his pains immediately cease." I have gone further into this subject than I otherwise should, because some have supposed that cholera is a new disease in India, and that it was not known two centuries ago.

consequence made, and in 1684 authority to commence the work was received.*

But without doubt many diseases were caused, and most were aggravated, by the intemperance which was so common. As long as the sick soldiers were attended by medical men at their own houses, there was no possibility of restraining them from the indulgence of their favourite vice. When death was staring them in the face they became more reckless. They cannot be kept from debauchery, wrote the Deputy Governor, " though never so sick, to the destruction of their bodies and souls." And again he remarks, that to persons labouring under the diseases of the country " strong drink and flesh is mortall, which to make an English soldier leave off is almost as difficlut as to make him divest his nature, nay though present death be laid before him, as the reward of the ill-gratifying his palate. This is the true cause our Bombay bills of mortality have swelled so high."

In order then that the sick might be provided with constant attendance and a regular diet, the plan of an hospital was forwarded to Bombay by the President and Council of Surat. The proposed building was to be capable of receiving seventy persons ; the cost was not to exceed four thousand rupees, and it was estimated that about a thousand rupees would cover the annual expenses of the establishment, which was to be under the superintendence of a resident surgeon. The President concluded by remarking :—" The lamentable loss of your men doth call on us for a speedy erecting the fabric, and doubt not but you will approve thereof." As a temporary measure the old Court of judicature was prepared for the reception of sick ; and the hospital itself was completed with an expedition which in India has been rarely equalled. A remarkable decrease of mortality in the following year was attributed to the success of the new arrangement.†

When so many works were in progress it occurred to the Government that a Church also was required. The project failed in execution ; but as it was a first attempt to establish openly a Protestant form of worship, it deserves consideration.

It would be interesting to ascertain whether during those first centuries when missionary zeal was so earnest and successful, the religion of Christ was ever preached in Bombay. There is one passage in history—and probably but one—which throws any light upon this part of the subject, and encourages us to amuse ourselves with guesses after truth. Bombay is said to have been anciently incorporated in the same province as the once famous port of Kalyán. Now there is no doubt that at this place a Christian Bishop resided so early as the beginning of the sixth century.‡ When Cosmas Indicopleustes sailed

* Letters from the President and Council of Surat, dated 11th January 1675-6 ; to the Court dated 17th January 1675-6 ; and from the Court dated February 1684. Description of Hindostan, by Walter Hamilton, Esq.

† Letters from the President and Council of Surat, dated 18th Dec. 1675, and 17th Jan. 1675-6: from the Deputy Governor and Council of Bombay, dated 24th Jan. 1676-7.

‡ General History of the Christian Religion and Church. By Dr. Augustus Neander, vol. iii. Sect. i. Neander was ignorant that there was such a place as Kalyán, and supposed that Calcutta was meant.

down the Western coast of India, he found at "Male where the pepper grows," or Málbár, a regularly ordained clergy, and at "Calliana" a Persian Bishop.* Do we not feel confident that the Bishop made some effort to propagate his religion, and may we not therefore suppose that the Gospel was then heard even in Bombay?

Sir John Mandeville declares, that when he wrote there were many Christians in parts of Western India, and brother Odoricus gives us such a circumstantial narrative that I must crave the reader's indulgence whilst I set before him the substance.

At the beginning of the fourteenth century, four Minorites, named Tolentinus of Marchia, James of Padua, Demetrius Laicus, and Peter of Senis, came to Thána, where they found fifteen Christian families. Although these were all Nestorians and schismatics, they received the Italian monks with cordial hospitality. Unfortunately the brethren took up their abode at the house of one who had a violent quarrel with his wife, and was summoned by her before the Kázi. The monks also had to appear as witnesses, and were drawn by the Mussulman Magistrate into a religious discussion. They maintained that Christ was very God, and being repeatedly asked for their opinion of Mahomed, at last plainly avowed, that he was the son of perdition, and all who followed him would infallibly be damned. This was too much for the other's patience, and the fathers were condemned to death. They were made to stand in the sun from nine in the morning until three in the afternoon, and as this had not the expected effect of destroying them, they were then beheaded.†

Sir Thomas Herbert found also Christians of St Thomas at Thána amongst other places. As many doubts have been cast upon the character of this interesting people, and it has been inferred from their present degeneracy that, such as they are, they have been for centuries, we are glad to ascertain how they appeared to an intelligent Englishman of the seventeenth century. He describes their forms and ceremonies as differing both from the Church of Rome and the Reformed Churches of Europe. Their Churches were low and badly furnished; but neat, carefully kept, matted, and without paintings or images. They came to them cheerfully, closed their eyes for contemplation after entering, and knelt towards the altar. They saluted their Priest with humble reverence; upon which he lifted up his hands and blessed them. Their service seldom occupied more than two hours. It commenced with a brief confession, not unlike that of the English liturgy, at the end of which all gave their assent with a unanimous Amen. Then followed an exposition of Scripture, which was listened to with attention and commendable decorum. Having sung a hymn they departed, first saluting again the Priest, who kept his hands elevated until all were gone. Herbert also states that they were in the habit of read-

* In the reign of the Emperor Constantine, Theophilus, a native of Diu (Διβοῦς) having been consecrated Bishop at Byzantium, returned to Diu by way of Arabia, and then travelling in India found Christianity existing.

† Itinerarium fratris Odorici; Hakluyt's Voyages, vol. ii.

ing at home a chapter from the Old or New Testament. They had few schools and little learning. On the first Sunday of every month the Priest read a homily, written, as they supposed, by one of the Apostles. Baptism was administered on the fortieth day after birth, unless the parent desired it sooner; the infant being wholly immersed, and the sign of the cross made on its forehead. Before Holy Communion two days were set apart for preparation. Both bread and wine were imparted, and received kneeling. The clergy were allowed to marry but once. In sickness a Priest was sent for both to pray and administer the Eucharist. At burials the corpse was placed with its head to the West. The writer adds that they observed Lent, and " Feast and Fast, as we accustome." " Laicks pay their *decimæ*, affect justice, profess truth, practise humility, and believe in Purgatory."*

But the first people who had numerous congregations for whom they raised solid structures in Bombay and its neighbourhood, were the Portuguese. Those zealous Roman Catholics induced a large number of natives to embrace their religion, and they built many Churches, a few of great magnificence. But the Portuguese attained their ends by unlawful means, and the carved stones of Bombay, Salsette, and Bassein, which they professedly raised to God's glory, are after all but records of fraud, rapine, and violence done to heathens' consciences.

The only place which the English had for the celebration of Divine service was a Hall in the Fort. The suggestion that a building should be raised and set apart for the purpose was first made by the Court of Directors. Sir George Oxenden, the President, eagerly took the hint, and was anxious that it should lead to some result. He declared that such an edifice was much to be desired, not only for the use of the English, but also that natives and foreigners who were unacquainted with our holy reformed religion might be so impressed with feelings of reverence for it, that haply they might wish to embrace it. Such persons could not witness the celebration of Divine service in the Hall, as there would be no accommodation for them, and in any case it would not be safe to admit them into the Fort. The President therefore submitted for the Court's approval the plan of a building, which would contain about a thousand people, and be of a " form proportionable to the small Churches in England," but plain and free from superfluous ornament. He had already proposed to the Company's servants that the expense should be defrayed by voluntary contributions, and they had come forward " freely and conscientiously," " some offering one year's wages, some half a year's, and the least a quarter." It was hoped that the Company would make good the balance. In order that no time might be lost, a certain sum had been raised already, which had been entrusted to the three Chaplains of Surat and Bombay, that they might purchase bricks, facing stones, lime and timber, so as to be ready for a commencement, when the Court should send the requisite authority. There was a difference of opinion regarding the site. Some proposed the burying ground at Mendaim's Point; but although that would be convenient for the Factors, it

* Sir Thomas Herbert's Travels, pages 355 and 358.

was removed from all places of native concourse, and therefore would not fulfil "the main design," which was, that the natives should repair to Church, "and observe the purity and gravity of our devotions." Others, therefore, suggested that the edifice should be raised near the Native Town, or between the town and the plot of ground set apart for European residences. It would then adjoin the high road leading to the Bazaar, and as it would be open and all might freely enter, some natives perchance might come from motives of curiosity to see the English way of devotion, and remain to pray. The President and Council stated these reasons, and confessed that on account of them they were disposed to adopt the latter opinion. All were agreed that the Church must for security be near the Fort, and that it should stand upon an open space, where it would be at a distance from other buildings. That the work might be performed with sufficient skill, the Court were requested to send out an experienced builder or surveyor, whose salary should be paid out of the sum collected by subscription.*

Such were the remarks of the President and Council. They display good feeling, and a degree of religious enthusiasm which is not supposed to have ordinarily prevailed amongst the merchants and politicians of that age. It was certainly an error to think that the natives would be enticed or their curiosity even excited by the cold and decorously dull worship which was then offered by the English in India, but it was remarkable that their conversion should be mentioned in official despatches as an object, the attainment of which was not only to be desired, but attempted, and, as they said, devoutly prayed for. However, all these pious intentions were frustrated. Five thousand pounds were collected, and they began to build, but the walls were never raised more than five yards. Further progress was interrupted by the Siddí's invasion, and it is said that Sir John Child, when Governor, appropriated the funds to his own use. But this must be accepted as the evidence of one who, being an interloper, was a victim of the Governor's monopolist zeal.†

The result of the Company's economical measures was soon visible in the growth of the revenues, and population, and the improved appearance of the island. The revenues had been slightly increased under the administration of Sir Gervase Lucas. They had been estimated at only £2,823 per annum, when the English got possession; but Gary shewed that in his day they had risen to £6,490, and in 1675 President Aungier calculated that the annual amount was £9,254.‡

* Letter from the President and Council of Surat to the Court, dated 17th January 1675-6.

† Hamilton's "New Account," Chapter xvii.

‡ Statement of the Revenues transmitted by Gary to the Secretary of State:—

	Xeraphins.					
Rent of Mazagon	9,300	0	40			
" Mahim	4,797	2	45			
" Parella	2,377	1	56			
" Vadela	1,738	0	40			
" Sion	790	0	60			
" Veroly	571	1	34			
" Bombaim	6,344	2	61			
				25,920	1	18

Within a few years the population had increased from ten to sixty thousand. The trade was rapidly becoming superior to that of the Factory at Surat, and the Court resolved that one half of all their shipping which left the port of London should load for Bombay direct, and not drop anchor first, as before, in Swally roads. Of course they were aware that the Governor of Surat would be annoyed by the diminution of trade at that place, and consequent loss of his dues. But they were beginning to have a sense of their own importance. So they merely instructed their servants to say—in case the Governor should raise objections—that if he would return some of the money which he had extorted from them, and discountenance pestilent interlopers, they might consider the question whether they should again resort only to Surat. In fact they were prematurely becoming a little arrogant. The experience of a few years only was required to teach them at a heavy cost that they were not sufficiently strong to stand in such an attitude.

We will now endeavour to take a dioramic view of Bombay in its improved condition. The population was composed of English, Portuguese, Hindús, Mussulmans, and native Roman Catholics, called "Cooly Christians," who were chiefly engaged in fishing. The dwellings of these different classes were not fixed in separate quarters of the town, but were placed indiscriminately. The town was a mile in length. The houses were low, and for the most part thatched ; a few only, which had been built by Portuguese or English, being of substantial construction. None of the windows were glazed ; but in many, oyster shells were used as a substitute for glass. There was a burial ground at a place called Mendaim's Point, from the name of the individual whose corpse was first interred there.* Within six hundred yards of the Fort the land was

	Xeraphins.		
Brought forward...	25,920	1	18
Rent of the Tobacco stank or farme	9,550	0	00
Rent of the Taverns	2,400	0	00
The account of Customes	18,000	0	00
The account of Coconutts	18,000	0	00
Xeraphins	73,870	1	18
More may be advanced	1,129	1	62
Total, Xeraphins	75,000	0	00

Which at thirteen Xeraphins for 22s. 6d. sterling amount to £6,490 17s. 9d.

Bruce's Annals 1667-78 and 1675-76.

In 1678 the Court were informed by Henry Oxenden that the Customs had risen to thirty thousand, and the duty on Tobacco to twenty thousand Xeraphins. About the same time also the Customs were farmed at £2,284 annually. (Letter from the Deputy Governor, dated 24th January 1676-7). With these figures the present values may be compared. Customs yield upwards of £275,000 ; Land Revenue £8,000 ; Abkarí, or tax on such palm trees as yield toddy, £9,000 ; Tax on Tobacco consumed on the island £8,000. Besides these the Municipal Fund receives from fees for liquor shops £2,500 ; Assessment on House and Grounds £20,000 ; Wheel Tax £8,000 ; Shop and Stall Tax £7,000. There are also some miscellaneous duties, such as stamps &c.

* Doubtless this was where the cooperage now stands, and where, not many years ago, tombs were still to be seen ; yet Hamilton, who was on the spot, describes it as a rocky point near the shipping, about five hundred paces South-ward of the old Fort, from which it was separated by a small Bay. But Hamilton is not always to be depended upon.—*New Account of the East Indies*, Chapter xvii.

being gradually cleared of trees and cottages.* There was one Church, a pretty object, belonging to the Portuguese. On Malabar Hill stood a Pársí tomb recently erected, and the ruins of a large Hindú temple. At Mahim was a Portuguese Church, with a house and other handsome buildings attached. There were also an English Guard-House and Custom-House. The Jesuits possessed a Church and extensive demesnes at Parell, and Sion was also their property. On the low ground to the South-east of Sion were salt pans, the Court having sent out directions that they should be constructed on the model of those at Rochelle in France, and Santavalli in Portugal.†

Colaba, or old Woman's Island, as it was called for long, had been taken possession of peaceably in 1674 after an arrangement made between Gerald Aungier and the Portuguese. For many years it was only used "to keep the Company's antelopes, and other beasts of delight." None of its land was appropriated to individuals, as from the first it was reserved to be a military cantonment.‡

In the Harbour, Butchers' Island—as it was then and still is called—was only used as a run for a few cattle, and a place where small vessels were hauled ashore and cleaned. Elephanta was also used only for cattle, and remained in the hands of the Portuguese. The figure of an elephant carved out of a black stone—from which the island received its name—was standing unmutilated, and so also was the figure of a horse.§ The tract on the main land extending from the South point of the Harbour to the river Penn was called "The Corlahs," and Bombay was dependent upon it for its supply of provisions, particularly at such times as the Portuguese prohibited all exportations from Salsette.||

At the other side of the small Strait which separates Salsette from Bombay were the Aquada Blockhouse, and on the hill a mile beyond Bandora the Portuguese Church, which so gracefully overlooks the sea. The Roman Catholic services were well performed. A new landing-place led to a College of Paulitines, as the Jesuits were then called. Before the College stood a large cross, and before that was a space, which, when the traveller from whose work this account is chiefly taken, visited it, was "thwack'd full of young blacks singing vespers." The collegiate establishment was defended, like a fortress, with seven cannon, besides small arms. Great hospitality prevailed, and distinguished guests were, on their arrival and departure, saluted with a roar of artillery. The Superior possessed such extensive influence that his mandates were respectfully attended to in the surrounding country, and the traveller who had the good fortune to be provided with his letters commendatory, was met by the people, wherever he halted, with presents of fruit and wine. The town of Bandora was large, with tiled houses. A view from mid-channel embracing the town, college, and Church of St. Andrew, was extremely picturesque. At a distance of four miles was another Church,

* But all the cadjan huts were not removed from the esplanade until 1802

† Letter dated February 1684.

‡ Fryer. Hamilton's Hindustan, and East India Gazetteer.

§ Hamilton's "New Account," Chapter xx.

|| Orme's Fragments.

described as magnificent; and the whole neighbourhood was studded with the villas of Portuguese gentlemen, many of whom lived in considerable state.

To the East of Salsette, the sail by way of Thána to Bassein, which is now so justly admired, must in those days have been of unrivalled beauty. Trombay was adorned with a neat Church and country seat. When Thána had been passed, the traveller's eye rested at every half mile on elegant mansions. Two of these deserve special mention. One, the property of John de Melos, was three miles from Thána. It stood on a sloping eminence, decorated with terraced walks and gardens, and terminating at the water side with a banquetting house, which was approached by a flight of stone steps. A mile further was Grebondel, the property of Martin Alphonso, said to be "the richest Don on this side Goa." Above rose his fortified mansion, and a Church of stately architecture. Within Bassein were six Churches, four convents, a College of Jesuits, another of Franciscans, and a library of historical, moral, and expository works. The Hidalgos' dwellings, with their balconies and lofty windows, presented an imposing appearance. Christians only were permitted to sleep within the walls of the town, and native tradesmen were compelled to leave at nightfall.

But whilst attempting to acquaint ourselves with the scenes amidst which the English lived, we have wandered from Bombay, and must retrace our steps. When we left it, several works of great importance had been completed, or were in progress. The expense of these was so great that at last the Company began to find themselves involved in difficulties. In 1684 they stated ;—"The island has stood us in first and last three hundred thousand pounds,"* and the debt upon their dead stock exactly amounted to that sum.† And when we remember the value of money at that period, and the Company's limited resources, we are not surprised at finding them exhausted by their efforts. They were compelled to recruit their finances by expedients, some of which were wise, some paltry, and others dangerous. In 1680 they sent out positive injunctions that all the expenses of the military and civil services in Bombay should be defrayed from the revenues. A house tax was to be imposed, the land surveyed, and portions to be let out on lease. It was hoped that by draining the Flats, considerable tracts might be reclaimed from inundation, and made profitable by cultivation. Other measures, which disgusted all classes and sowed the seeds of revolt, will be noticed when an account is given of home and personal affairs.

Yet the faults which the Court of Directors and their servants committed were chiefly the results of inexperience, and such as belong to a state of political infancy. But when we consider that they had sufficient penetration to discover the advantages of Bombay, which the royal Government seem never to have comprehended ; when we reflect upon the vigour, decision, prudence, and administrative skill which they displayed in constructing great works, fostering manufactures, adding to their military strength, and devising plans of economy, we must admit that the measures which they adopted for the improvement of this island illuminate the records of the East India Company.

* Letter from the Court to the President in Council. † Mill's History

CHAPTER V.

1662—1685.

CONTENTS.—*General and Mercantile affairs.*—Presidents Sir George Oxenden, Gerald Aungier, and Sir John Child.—The Company's investments and debts.—Factory at Amoy.—Articles of trade; indigo, pepper, &c.; Cotton; the first Cotton Screw; English Horses; slaves for labour; slaves for the fancy.—Hindrances to trade; bankers driven away; suspension of trade; vexations at the Custom-House, and meddling propensities of the officials.—Troubles of the Factors.—Question of keeping up Factories—Sivají plunders Surat; gallant conduct of the English—Second assault of Sivají; base conduct of the French—Losses at Carwar and Húblí—English interchange civilities with Sivají; Ustick's mission, and its results; Nichol's mission—Henry Oxenden and two Factors at Sivají's installation; settlement of a treaty; the butchers' friends—The Company's Navy—Sivají's Navy—The Siddí of Jinjíra—The Siddí enters the harbour of Bombay; awkward predicament—Frequent visits of the Siddí; cause disturbances—Contests for the possession of Haneri and Khaneri—The Court protests against war—Native opinion of English courage—The Court's crooked policy—Naval fight between the Maráthás and Siddís—Native Pirates; their contest with Europeans; cruel murder of an Englishman; fight at Vengurla; hazards of the coasting trade—The Portuguese; their futile threats; their priests expelled from Bombay; they murder an English Serjeant; vexatious interference; migrations from Bandora to Bombay—The Dutch; their war and intrigues—The French; their Factory; its failure—Capuchins at Surat; Father Ambrose—Prosecution of interlopers—Proposal for a new Company—James the Second proclaimed.

THE Company were fortunate in finding men of distinguished abilities to superintend their affairs at this period. On the nineteenth of March 1662 Sir George Oxenden, Knight, was appointed to be President and Chief Director of all the Company's affairs "at Surat, and all other their Factories from Zeilon to the Red Sea." His name is conspicuous above all others in the first pages of Anglo-Indian annals. In addition to his other titles, he had in 1669 that of Governor and Commander-in-Chief of Bombay. He was also empowered to select one of his Council for the office of Deputy Governor. Sir George died on the fourteenth of July 1669. Gerald Aungier, a zealous, bold, and highly honourable man, was his worthy successor, and died after a tedious illness in June 1677. Rolt, who had been appointed by the Company in 1669 Agent for Persia, then acted provisionally as President. He left India in January 1682, and John Child, who was created a baronet that same year, succeeded to the highest authority.* The characters of Oxenden, Aungier, and Child, will appear in the sequel.

Not only in Bombay, but at all their Factories, great efforts were made by the Company to extend their trade. We gain an idea of the business which was carried on by the Factors of Surat at this time, when we learn that in 1668 six ships arrived from England with goods and bullion to the value of a hundred and thirty thousand pounds. The next year twelve hundred tons of shipping arrived with stock valued at seventy-five thousand pounds. In 1670 came fifteen hundred tons of shipping; and in 1672 four ships with cargo and bullion valued at eighty-five thousand pounds. In 1673 stock and bullion were brought to the amount of a hundred thousand pounds. These sums appear trifling, when compared with the British Capital of eighty millions now supposed to be employed in India; but at that time they were considered large. The debt, for which the Factory was responsible in 1674, amounted to a hundred and thirty-five thousand pounds.

For the sake of forming a small link with the cotemporary history of another country, it may be mentioned here, that in 1681 there was an intention of despatching from Surat six small vessels to Tonquin and Amoy; but the plan was abandoned when information was received that the Tartars had driven the Chinese from Amoy, and the Company's Factory there had been destroyed.

With regard to particular articles of trade, it may be remarked, that indigo or anile was more in demand than ever. Pepper, Saltpetre, raw and wrought Silks to the value of thirty thousand pounds in a year, calicoes to the value of a hundred and sixty thousand pounds, and various drugs, were exported to England. A trade in diamonds was chiefly confined to private dealers, who frequently made large profits.†

Considerable attention was already paid to the exportation of raw Cotton, and so early as 1684 attempts were made to save freight by compressing it into bales with the aid of machinery. For this purpose the Company sent out "a screw or engine," and at the same time wrote thus:—"We would the more encourage the affair of Cotton, and press you to pursue the method we have proposed of contracting a considerable weight into a little room, because, if we can bring it home to save the freight, we shall do a considerable service to our country by the noble addition it will cause to our English, and so remote navigation." Here is a strange jumble of Cotton screws and patriotism, and the probability is, that the Court were not so disinterested as they pretended. It is a fact worthy of notice, that the introduction of Screws into India must be assigned to this early date, and not to a much later one, as Mr. Royle has done in his valuable work upon Cotton.

Several attempts were made to introduce a breed of English horses, but it was found very difficult to preserve them alive during the long voyages which were then usually made.‡

* Fryer, Letter viii. chapter i. Bruce's Annals. Letter from the Council at Surat to Bombay; dated 30th June 1677.

† Bruce's Annals. Fryer, Letter ii. chapter v.

‡ Letters from the Court to the President and Council of Surat; dated July 1683 and February 1684. Colquhoun's Treatise; Appendix.

Slaves were amongst the exports of the English Factory at this time. The Island of Saint Helena had been bestowed by the Crown upon the Company, and they wanted labourers for their plantations. So they desired their President at Surat to send them cargoes of negroes, with as little concern as if they had been any other kind of live or dead stock, and mentioned twenty pounds per head as the purchase-money. At first only males were exported, and these desolate beings remained at St. Helena without any of those domestic enjoyments by which even the life of a slave may be solaced. However, there is a point at which oppression defeats its own projects. Like many other animals when deprived of their mates, the slaves became troublesome. So wives were demanded for them. The Honourable Company do not indeed hint that their commercial minds were susceptible of pity, but their interests were in this case promoted by shewing kindness to their human cattle. "It may be convenient," they wrote, "you should send near as many female slaves as male to St. Helena, because the male will not live so contented, except they have wives."*

The market at Surat was supposed to be stocked with such a large assortment of live goods, that all fancies might be suited there. The next order which the Court sent, shewed that they relied upon it for a supply of their minutest wants. They were on the look-out for a leash of slaves, and such slaves as only the most whimsical of men could have thought of. As the contents of their singular despatch will be imagined scarcely credible, it will be advisable to quote the exact words. They form a postscript, but are evidently the most important part of the letter :—

"His Majesty hath required of us to send to India to provide for him there one male and two female blacks, but they must be dwarfs of the least size that you can procure, the male to be about seventeen years of age, and the females about fourteen. We would have you, next to their littleness, to chuse such as may have the best features, and to send them home upon any of our ships, giving the commander great charge to take care of their accommodation, and in particular of the females, that they be in no way abused in the voyage by any of the seamen; for their provision and clothes you must take care to lay it in, and let them be set out with such ear and nose rings, and shackles for ornaments about their legs (of false stones, and brass, but not with gold) as is usual to wear in the country, but let them not be used by them in the voyage, but sent to us apart."†

Whether three unhappy creatures of precisely such ages, sizes, and features as were required, or whether indeed any, were ever procured and forwarded, we are not informed. The Court seemed as if they did not feel that they were seeking to traffic in human beings. They write not of men and women, boys and girls, but only use the words male and female, as they might in reference to any strange animals.

The reason why this order was sent is obvious. It was in the year 1683, when the Company were seriously alarmed lest their exclusive

* Letters as above.

† Letter from the Court to the President and Council of Surat; dated May 1683.

privileges should be lost. A rival Company were strenuously endeavouring to obtain a Royal Charter, and it was said that the people favoured their attempt. Even the King and Council had taken the matter into consideration. The old Company, therefore, strained every nerve to conciliate the monarch, and were anxious to indulge all the caprices of the royal and effete debauchee. They not only listened to his puerile request for toys with souls in them*, but also would have them ornamented in such a manner, as they supposed would satisfy the most fastidious taste.

The English trade at Surat was so hampered by native interference, that we cannot wonder at the Company's desire to remove it to Bombay. One year the Shráffs and Banyá's, with whom the Factors transacted business, were banished from Surat, on account of a religious dispute. The consequence was, that these important auxiliaries of trade called in their money that they might bury it, or conceal it, till the return of better times, refusing to advance any for the Company's investments, or to take such goods, as were imported, off the Factors' hands.

At another time not only was the trade, but the lives of Europeans were in danger. Some Dutch seamen had, in a drunken frolic, insulted a native officer, and, fearing chastisement, they took refuge in the English Factory. The Governor, having had this represented to him by designing persons as a hostile combination against him of French, Dutch, and English, issued a proclamation, ordering all natives to withdraw from the service of Europeans, and declaring that any European wearing arms might be put to death with impunity. The Chiefs of the three nations were this time so wise as to act in unison, and as all made a feint of abandoning their Factories and quitting Surat, the Governor was brought to reason. They were invited to return, and, after a negotiation of six weeks' duration, their privileges were restored.†

Obstructions at the Custom House were particularly vexatious, especially to those who had incurred the Governor's displeasure, or had not gained his favour by an unsparing use of bribes. Thevenot has given us a minute account of the way in which travellers, and merchants in particular, were tormented. When he arrived at the bar of the river, he was taken in a small boat up the stream to the Custom House. Although he searched that place at eight o'clock in the evening, he was not permitted to land until the next morning at ten. His person was then so strictly reached, and the conduct of the officers was so offensive, that his patience was put to a sore trial. And he was treated less severely than many others. As soon as a ship cast anchor at the bar, her commander was rowed up to the Custom House, where he was obliged to give notice of his arrival. A guard was then placed over the vessel to prevent the removal of any article. From each passenger a fee of half a rupee was demanded, and he was charged another half rupee for his passage in the boat. As the Custom House was only open from ten o'clock until noon, the traveller was compelled to wait until the next day, if he did not happen to arrive in the intervening time. A body of Peons armed with thick bámbús were drawn

* Aristotle calls a slave ἔμψυχον ὄργανον—a tool with a soul.

† Bruce's Annals, 1669-1672.

up at the landing place, and it was their business to prevent all who came on shore from holding any communication with the bystanders. After passing through a large court the travellers were ushered one at a time into an apartment where the chief officer sat in state. Their names were first registered, and often they were then required to strip themselves. If gold or silver were found upon their persons, two and a half per cent of the value were claimed. Native ingenuity was taxed to discover articles on which duty might be levied, so that even gilt buttons were included, and the Purser of the Company's marine had to pay for these appendages to his coat, as often as he crossed the river. After this scrutiny they were dismissed ; but were obliged to return another day for their baggage, which was completely rummaged. Clothes were unfolded, pistol-barrels sounded, the smallest articles examined, and it was sometimes a month before those who had merchandize could get it passed. Christians paid a duty of four,* and native tradesmen of five per cent on their goods.

European tourists often complain of the petty annoyances inflicted upon them by the preventive officers of Austria and Italy : native merchants sometimes grumble at the treatment to which they are subjected in the Custom House of Bombay. If they could only have visited Surat in the olden time, they might have indeed been indignant at the meddling propensities of native rulers. The Governor himself searched the baggage of Sir Thomas Roe, and appropriated to himself such articles as pleased him.† On another occasion, the Governor was found seated in the Custom House. His sharp eye fell upon a bracelet and diamond in the midst of a traveller's baggage, and immediately he signified to the owner that it was his pleasure to purchase the ornaments. The poor fellow did not wish to sell. But what matter? His Highness wished to buy. The other protested earnestly that they were presents from dear friends. His remonstrances saved the diamond, but the Governor detained the bracelet, until, as he said, the stranger should honour him with a visit. It is almost needless to add that the bracelet was never recovered.

It is not to be concluded that the English were always subjected to the vexations here described, but they were ever liable to them, and if they happened to offend the Governor of the city, they were oppressed whenever occasion offered. Sometimes they were indulged to a great degree, and permitted to introduce contraband articles without being questioned. At other times their property was seized, and taken at any valuation which the native officers chose to determine.‡ The President and all European women were suffered to pass without examination.

The history of the English Factors at Surat throughout this whole period is a record of troublous years with a few bright days of joy and

* But according to a firmán issued by Aurangzíb, and dated 25th June 1667, the English and Dutch Companies only paid an *ad valorem* duty of two per cent on all merchandize. Treaties, Agreements, &c.

† Sir Thomas Roe's Journal.

‡ Voyages de Thevenot ; Liv. i. chap. 1 & 15. A Voyage to Surat by Oleef Foreen, Chaplain of the Gothic Lion. A Voyage to Surat by J. Ovington M.A. Baldæus. Fryer, Letter ii. Chap. v.

hope. Interlopers were as wasps to them; the Dutch could outbid them in the markets; the Portuguese intrigued against them; the Maráthás tried to plunder them; and the Moguls to crush them. In 1662 and following years the Factors, in compliance with directions which they received from home, sought to ruin interlopers by selling their own goods at low rates. But here the Dutch stepped in, and by means of their superior capital, competed with them successfully. The English had reduced their prices so low that the strain upon their commercial strength was too great. They were compelled to contract their operations, and suppress some of their small Factories.*

On account of these difficulties it was for long an open question whether Factories, when established on an adequate scale, were not a useless expense, and whether it would not be prudent to give them up altogether. In many places the Dutch carried on trade without them, and entered into contracts with native merchants. Why then should the English Company lavish such large sums upon houses, lands, fortifications, and equipments? So late as 1666 a native merchant was employed at Surat to obtain the investment of the season, and for some time this expedient succeeded. Probably the Factory would have been given up, if the Directors had not clung to the patronage which they enjoyed by its means, and which was wholly theirs, whilst their share in the profits of the trade was insignificant.† A Factory which had been established at Ahmedábád was closed, but another one opened at Nandrabád.

Sivají was for long a cause of anxiety to the English Factors. They closely watched all his movements, dreading lest they themselves might be the objects of his next expedition. They declared that "he seemed to be every where and prepared for every emergency." At length, on the fifth of January 1664, he entered Surat. Such of the inhabitants as were able made their escape; the helpless Governor shutting himself in the castle which was protected by English cannon,‡ and leaving the Maráthá robber to plunder the city at his convenience. An Englishman named Smith was seized by Sivají's troops, and carried into his presence. He afterwards described him as seated in a tent, and ordering his executioners to chop off the heads or hands of such unfortunate inhabitants as he suspected were concealing their wealth. Both the Dutch and English Factors stood upon the defensive; the conduct of the latter was so gallant that they not only held their own, but saved the property of many natives. So highly did the Emperor Aurangzíb appreciate their courage and resolution, that he sent to the President, Sir George Oxenden, a robe of honour, and granted the Factory exemption from a portion of customs duties. The Company also shewed their approval of the President's conduct by presenting him with a gold medal,§ together with a gratuity of two hundred pounds for himself, and four hundred pounds to be distributed amongst the Council and subordinate servants. They also ex-

* Mill's History.
† Mill's History, Book i. Chap. 4. Bruce's Annals, 1670-71.
‡ Obtained from the wreck of the ship Middleburgh. Baldæus.
§ Bearing the motto—"Non minor est virtus, quam quærere, parta tueri."

pressed a wish that he would continue in the administration for three years longer.

Again, on the third of October 1670, Surat suffered under this scourge. At the head of fifteen thousand men Sivají pillaged the city. This time several lives and some property were lost in detached warehouses belonging to the English, but, as before, their Factory was gallantly defended, Streynsham Master having in the President's absence come with a party of seamen from Swally and taken the command. The Dutch Factory being in a retired quarter of the city was unmolested; but the French, who had lately established themselves here, saved themselves by ignominiously agreeing that the plunderer should pass through their Factory to attack and rob an unfortunate Tartar, styled by our Factors, "The King of Kaskar," who, having been deposed by his son, had made a pilgrimage to Mecca, and was returning with his suite in fancied security. By this base and cruel robbery Sivají obtained "a vast treasure in gold, silver and plate, a gold bed and other rich furniture."* Laden with booty he soon withdrew his army from the city; but roving bands of his followers for long infested the neighbourhood and terrified the inhabitants; in some instances actually presenting themselves before the Governor, and boldly demanding a contribution.†

In February 1665 Sivají had attacked Carwar, a town in the province of Canara, where, as we have seen, the English had established a small Factory; but the place being well defended, he contented himself with levying a contribution, of which the Factors' share amounted to a hundred and twelve pounds. In 1673 he attacked and plundered Húblí, where also was a Factory. The English lost on this occasion property to the value of 7,894 pagodas. Some time afterwards they demanded of Sivají an indemnity for their losses, but he steadily refused any, maintaining that his troops had not molested the Factory. A little furniture, he said, and a few trifles might have been taken; but he would not admit that their value exceeded two hundred rupees.‡

Although the English had thus suffered much from the hostility of the Maráthá usurper, they were constrained to treat him with consideration and respect. Even when he was actually engaged in assailing Surat, the Factors of Bombay felt so dependent upon his country for their grain and firewood, that they addressed him in conciliatory language, and interchanged civilities with him. During the monsoon of 1672 they were so terrified by an ineffectual attempt which he made to take the Portuguese settlement of Ghorabandar, that they endeavoured to secure themselves by a treaty, and for that purpose sent Mr. Ustick to wait upon him. Happily Sivají's interests corresponded with their wishes. So long as they were his friends the value of his conquests was increased by their trade: if they had been his enemies, they might have permitted the Moguls to pass through the harbour of Bombay, and make a descent upon his defenceless

* History of the Marathas. By James Grant Duff, Esq. vol. i. Chap. vi and viii. Fryer's Account. Bruce's Annals.

† Letter from the President and Council of Surat to the Court; dated 26th May 1677.

‡ Grant Duff's History, Chapters vi and viii. Hamilton's East India Gazetteer. Orme's Fragments.

coast. He therefore agreed to an alliance. Mr. Ustick was also instructed to demand thirty-two thousand pagodas for damages sustained, but of course the hope of obtaining such a sum was visionary. However, Sivají readily consented to respect for the future all possessions of the English, and to indemnify them for such injuries as he admitted that he had inflicted upon them ; if only they would join him in an expedition against Jinjíra, and re-establish their Factory at Rájapúr. The reply of the English was to the effect, that being mere merchants they never took up arms except in self-defence, and that they could not venture upon a return to Rájapúr, unless provided with some security for their safety.*

The Factors still indulged the hope of obtaining compensation from Sivají, and in May 1673 Mr. Nichols went to him as their Envoy. He was first introduced to Sambhají, the son, and afterwards to the Rájá himself; but he had no more success than his predecessor.

When Sivají's victories had justified his actions in the minds of his followers ; when successful rebellion, treachery, robberies, and assassinations combined with acts which had been suggested by a certain generosity, a love of enterprize and singular daring had exalted him to the position of a hero in the estimation of Maráthás, they cheerfully gratified his ambition by permitting him to occupy a throne. The ceremonial of his installation was in part witnessed by Henry Oxenden, afterwards Deputy Governor of Bombay. With a view of concluding a treaty on the Company's behalf, he and two other English Factors travelled to meet Sivají at Rerí or Ráigarh. After some difficulties had been removed, twenty preliminary articles—most of them favourable to the Company—were signed on the sixth of April 1674. Sivají engaged to allow ten thousand pagodas as an indemnity for the losses sustained at Rájapúr. He did not indeed consent to pay this sum in cash ; but it was obtained in the native manner by a little intricate arrangement. According to this the English were permitted to purchase annually for three years goods to the value of five thousand pagodas, for which they were only to pay two thousand five hundred pagodas. They would thus recover seven thousand five hundred pagodas, and the remaining two thousand five hundred were to be made up by a temporary exemption of the Rájapúr Factory from the usual customs. It was further agreed that the English should establish Factories at Rájapúr, Dábhol, Chaul, and Kalyán ; that they should trade wherever they pleased in the Maráthá territories, and fix their own prices without being subjected to any arbitrary rules. For all goods which they should import, a duty of not more than two and a half per cent *ad valorem* was to be paid ; the current coins of the Company and Maráthás were to be exchanged according to their specific values ; and lastly, it was engaged that all the Company's property which might be wrecked on the Maráthá coasts, should be restored to its owners. Sivají manifested great reluctance in consenting to this last article. He was at once ready to promise that protection should be secured to the crews of shipwrecked vessels ; but he considered it his privilege to claim for himself the vessels and their cargoes. Finally, all difficulties were overcome, and the unlucky Factory of

* Bruce's Annals, 1671-72. Grant Duff's History, vol. i. Chap. viii.

Rájapúr was re-established. But Fortune never favoured it with her smiles.*

A cotemporary writer has left a graphic account of this Embassy, in which with the spirit of a true Briton he incorporates some curious tales of the larder. With a sneer at the unchristian appetite of a Maráthá, he says that "the diet of this sort of people admits not of great variety or cost, their delightfullest food being only *cutcherry*, a sort of pulse and rice mixed together and boiled in butter, with which they grow fat." On the other hand the English Factors, being in danger of growing lean, hankered after the flesh pots of Bombay. It was some time before they could make an application to the Rájá, and a Mussulman butcher "was ordered to supply them with what goat they should expend." He only provided them with half a goat each day ; but this was more flesh meat than he had sold for some years before ; and the old man was so well pleased with his customers, that with great labour he dragged his tottering limbs up the hill to catch a glimpse of *the butcher's friends.* For the information of those who study "the art of dining" in India, our author concludes thus :—

"So rare a thing is it to eat flesh among them ; for the gentiles eat none, and the Moors and Portugals eat it well stew'd, bak'd, or made into pottage ; no nation eating it roasted so commonly as we do. And in this point I doubt we err in these hot countries, where our spirits being always upon the flight, are not so intent on the business of concoction ; so that those things that are easiest digested, and that create the least trouble to the stomach, we find by experience to agree best here."†

Although on shore the military preparations of the English at that time were strictly defensive, and in that respect similar to those which in ancient days a feudal baron of Europe found it necessary to adopt for his protection, yet they were not always unwilling to take an offensive position at sea. They had three men-of-war—the *Revenge*, mounting twenty-two guns, the *Mayboon*, of two hundred and twenty tons, which had been taken from the Dutch, and the *Hunter* of fourteen guns ; besides smaller vessels confusedly styled by English writers manchuas, gallivats, grabs, shybars, balloons, prows, hoys and ketches.‡ With this fleet the Factors were becoming sensible of their power, and although their masters insisted upon abstaining from all hostile aggressions, they themselves were disposed to venture with timid and uncertain steps into the dangerous field of war. There were two Native powers, whose ships they always watched with

* Grant Duff's History.

† Fryer's Account.

‡ *Manchua* for *Machava*, a small vessel of ten or twelve candies ; *gallivat* for *galabat*, is described by Hamilton as a large row boat with two masts, rarely exceeding seventy tons ; by Vaupell it is said to be of from a hundred to a hundred and fifty candies, to carry two lateen sails, and to have been ordinarily used for piratical purposes ; Grab, Arabicè *ghuráb*, Maráthí *guráb*, had rarely more than two masts, and was then of a hundred and fifty tons ; some with three masts were of three hundred tons. *Shybar* or *Shebar* for *s'ibád*, a large vessel. *Balloon* for *balyánv*, a state barge. *Prow* for *Parav*, a small botella seldom exceeding thirty candies. *Hoy* is an English name. *Ketch* or *dorioh*, meaning one and a half, from having a main and mizen masts—Hamilton's History of Hindostan, vol i. Paper by J. Vaupell, Esq., in the seventh volume of the Bombay Geographical Society's Transactions.

suspicion. Sivají's fleet, if estimated by numbers, would appear formidable indeed. The Factors of Carwar, giving an account of it in 1665, state that it consisted of eighty-five frigates and three great ships. Such a force, when only seen upon paper, might have been viewed even by the great powers of Europe with apprehension; but probably its actual strength was trifling. The "great ships" may indeed have carried three masts; but by the term "frigate" was signified, we may suppose, the small coasting vessels, which vary in burthen from thirty to a hundred and fifty tons.*

The other marine power upon the coast was commanded by Siddís.† This people were originally natives of Abyssinia, but having been for generations in the Mogul Emperor's pay, their families had received grants of forts and lands on condition of equipping vessels and rendering naval service. One, whose descendant still holds the town and port of Jaffrábád on the coast of Kátiwár, possessed at that time the Fort of Jinjíra, and when attacked in 1668 by a powerful force of Sivají, applied to the English for assistance. The authorities of Bombay were anxious that the President should comply with his request, and the reason which they gave is worthy of notice, as showing that they had not yet learnt to estimate the true value of their insular possession. Those cunning intriguers and short-sighted politicians hoped that, if they were permitted to interpose, Jinjíra might eventually fall into their hands; and they suggested that its advantages as a settlement would be superior to those of Bombay.‡ Jinjíra! Where and what is Jinjíra? You may still find its place on a map; but it is no port nor resort of trade; it has fallen into merited obscurity.

These Siddís were troublesome, dangerous neighbours, and it is difficult to say whether their enmity or friendship was most to be dreaded. In 1672 they anchored with a fleet off Bombay, and requested the President's permission to enter the Harbour, and ravage the districts which belonged to Sivají. Their application was refused; but having afterwards relieved Jinjíra, which was besieged by Sivají, and routed the Maráthá troops, they returned to Bombay so inflated by success that they entered the Harbour without thinking it necessary to ask any one's consent. The President received them with constrained civility, for he was in an awkward predicament. On the one side the Siddí urged him to form a league against Sivají, on the other side Sivají vowed, that if this were done he would instantly invade Bombay. It was lucky that the Siddí was reasonable enough to take this dilemma into consideration. He promised to abstain from hostilities against the Maráthá districts which lay along the Harbour, and prepared to take his departure. His followers, however, gave proofs of their savage intentions by burning several houses at Mazagám.

* Grant Duff's History, vol. i chap 6.

† What is the origin of this word? A friend suggests 'Saiyid.' It was certainly used as a title or complimentary name; not as we now use the word 'Seedy' for an African seaman.

‡ Grant Duff's History, vol. i. chap. 7.

The next year the Siddí again came and craved permission to "winter" in the Harbour. By "winter" we may observe in passing, the English denoted that wet and boisterous, but hot and steamy season between June and October. President Aungier, being afraid that the great Mogul might resent upon the Factors at Surat any inhospitable treatment of his admiral, permitted the unwelcome visitors to haul four of their vessels ashore, on condition that their crews should withdraw and leave them under the garrison's protection. In October these ships put to sea, and having joined a considerable fleet, ravaged Sivají's district, shed much blood, and carried away men, women, and children to be sold into slavery.

In 1674 a fleet of the Siddí's again made its appearance. Several of the men landing at the village of Sion scared away the inhabitants, and would have occupied their houses during the monsoon, if they had not been expelled by the English troops. It was then agreed that no more than three hundred of the Siddí's men should remain on shore at one time, and that those should bring no other weapon but their swords.*

In 1677 the English were nearly involved in a quarrel with these people, because a certain Ensign Thorpe chose to insult and injure the crew of one of their small vessels.† This incident will be mentioned in another place; it is enough to remark now, that a wound was left which time alone could heal. Yet Siddí Sambhol again applied for leave "to winter on the island." This was a proof of confidence, which the Deputy Governor received like a bear's hug. He was by no means hospitably disposed; but, as the crafty African contrived to prolong the negotiation until the monsoon had fairly set in, it was not then possible for his fleet to leave the Harbour. He and his people resided for a month or two at Mazagám without creating any disturbance; although their intrigues were unfailing sources of anxiety to the British Government. A threatening message from Sivají was the first intimation which the English received of an injury which the Siddi had inflicted on the inhabitants of the opposite shore. A Brahman, with money procured from Sambhol, hired a boat and party of men, who kidnapped four other Brahmans and transported them to the Siddí's ships, where they were kept in close confinement. Sivají's menace aroused the President to discover and punish the men stealers. Eleven were apprehended, three of whom were executed, and the remainder sent as slaves to St. Helena.‡

In October the restless propensities of these people gave rise to fresh alarms. Ali Kossim had been appointed by the Emperor to supersede Sambhol, and that month he arrived to take command of the fleet. Whether the old commander was willing to obey the august mandate for his degradation, we know not; but certainly his officers and sailors were determined that he should not. The followers of the two Siddís were divided into factions, and commenced a regular fight. The Deputy Governor immediately commanded his little army to interfere, and only when

* Orme's Fragments.

† Letter to the Court from the Deputy Governor and Council of Bombay; dated 24th January 1676-7.

‡ Orme's Fragments.

all the followers of Ali Kossim had been disarmed, and four horses of English troopers killed, was the broken peace restored.*

The next year, at the earnest intercession of the Native Governor of Surat, the Siddí was again permitted to reside at Bombay. His small vessels were hauled ashore, and the large ones moored near Mazagám. Many of his men took up their abode in the town, and daily committed acts of violence against the Hindús. Brahmans, being the objects of their especial aversion, were sometimes seized by them and subjected to impurities which no penances could expiate. The sufferers urged Sivají to avenge them by entering the Harbour, and burning the Siddí's fleet. Some Maráthá troops actually threatened to invade Bombay, but as the Portuguese were alarmed for the safety of Bassein and resolved to oppose their march, the expedition was recalled.

Once more, on the twenty-eighth of April 1680, we find the Deputy Governor and Council subjected to annoyance by these people. With the greatest effrontery they brought some prisoners which had been seized in Sivají's districts, and offered them for sale in Bombay. The English Government discovered twenty-one such unfortunate beings and immediately released them. A few days afterwards the Siddís attempted to introduce contraband goods, and attacked the guards at the Custom House. Their leader Kossim sailed with his fleet into the harbour, and anchored off the Fort. The discharge of a few guns brought him to reason : but Sambhají, who had succeeded his father Sivají,—the death of the latter having occurred at the beginning of this month—was so annoyed at the protection which the English had unwillingly afforded the Siddís, that he also threatened an assault and invasion.

Sambhají's fleet actually did attack the Siddís at the little island of Haneri, and this led to a fresh annoyance. Having defeated Sambhají's men with great slaughter, the triumphant Siddís brought eighty heads in baskets to Mazagám, and were proceeding, as a matter of course, to range them on poles along the shore; but the English Government, feeling what the others thought a silly squeamishness, positively prohibited the ghastly exhibition.†

This little Island Haneri, and its twin sister Khaneri, commanding to a certain extent the entrance of the Harbour, were eagerly coveted by the English Government, who saw in them a strong temptation to commence an aggressive war. As Khaneri was supposed to have no fresh water, it was neglected by all parties until 1679, but in October of that year Sivají, enraged at the Siddís' predatory excursions, and being prevented from retaliating by attacking them at Bombay, took possession of Khaneri. This measure placed him in such a position that he could not only pounce upon his African foes, but also, when they were protected by the English, make reprisals on the latter's shipping.

Under these circumstances the English, in conjunction with their new allies the Siddís, attempted to eject the Maráthás. Their first step was to send an aged Captain, or—as another writer states with more proba-

* Letters from the Deputy Governor and Council of Bombay in October 1677.
† Orme's Fragments.

bility—a drunken Lieutenant* in a small vessel, with instructions to demand why the intruders had come to Khaneri. This Officer being induced to land, he and his crew were treacherously cut off. The *Revenge*, a Pink, and seven native craft were then ordered to lie at anchor so as to block up all the avenues to the rock. Upon this challenge the Maráthás, with forty vessels, attacked the English fleet, took one grab, and put to flight all except the *Revenge*. The little man-of-war was commanded by Captain Minchin, and the gallant Captain Keigwin, who was Commodore for the occasion, was with him. These officers coolly permitted the Maráthás to board, and then sweeping the deck fore and aft with their great guns, destroyed some hundreds, sunk four of the enemy's vessels, and compelled the rest to seek refuge in flight. Yet, signal as was this success, they did not recover Khaneri.

As a counter movement against Sivají, Siddí Kossim proceeded to entrench himself at Haneri, and in 1680 Sambhají in vain attempted to drive him out. Although guns planted on these rocks could never have such a long range as to prevent ingress to, and egress from, the Harbour, yet when they were in possession of uncertain friends, like the Siddis and Maráthás, the annoyance must have been almost insupportable. The Deputy Governor in Council therefore earnestly asked the Court's permission to expel these occupants. But prudence was the order of the day. The Court in reply declared that they were quite opposed to any such undertaking, and then expounded a policy which they soon found reason to change in reality, although not in profession. They say :—"Although we have formerly wrote you that we will have no war for Hendry Kendry, yet all war is so contrary to our constitution, as well as our interest, that we cannot too often inculcate to you our aversion thereunto." The same injunction is repeated only in still stronger terms the following year, although the inconvenience of allowing these islands to be occupied by the sailors of another nation is fully acknowledged.†

This excessive caution of the English was, as may be supposed, called timidity by the Natives, who rather mortified the Factors by taunting them in some such language as the following :—"Why vaunts your nation ? What victories have you achieved ? What has your sword done? Who ever felt your power ? What do you possess ? We see the Dutch outdo you ; the Portugals have behaved themselves like men ; every one runs you down ; you can scarce keep Bombaim, which you got (as we know) not by your valour but compact ; and will you pretend to be men of war, or cope with our princes ? It's fitter for you to live on merchandize and submit to us."‡ Reading these taunts in the nineteenth century, we almost look at them as prophecy under the garb of satire. At that time, however, a prophet could only have said ; 'O thou sword of the English, how long wilt thou be quiet ? Put up thyself into the scabbard, rest and be still. Thou hast not yet received thy charge against the nations of India. For the English, submission and patience are now appointed.'§

* Bruce says "an aged Captain," Orme "a Lieutenant in a fit of drunkenness."

† Letters from the Court ; dated 22nd April 1681, and May 1682. Grant Duff's History, vol. i. chapter 10. Hamilton's Hindustan.

‡ Fryer, Letter vii. chapter 1.

§ See Jeremiah, chapter xlvii, 6 and 7.

Although the pacific instructions of the Court seem plain and decisive, their policy was in truth mean and crooked. They recommended their servants to temporize with the great and semi-barbarous powers by which they were surrounded ; but yet encouraged them to enforce an observance of treaties by the employment of armed vessels. They thus hoped, that if their military enterprizes should fail, and they should be blamed in England, they might shift all responsibility from their own shoulders to those of their servants in India. So much, be it remarked, is admitted even by their apologists.*

The Siddís continued to visit Mazagám frequently, to annoy the English, and plunder the opposite districts of the Maráthás. They even purchased houses, and established their families in Bombay. One Maráthá vessel, which they seized in 1681, was rescued by the guard-boats of the English. In 1682 continual skirmishes took place between their fleet and Sambhají's, both sides being guilty of gross outrages. At last Sambhají prohibited the exportation of grain from his territories to Bombay, and, as the Portuguese, glad of an opportunity to distress the English, did the same, the price of provisions was tripled. A sanguinary conflict ensued between the fleet of Sambhají, commanded by Siddí Misrí, a relation of that Sambhol, who had been dismissed the Emperor's service, and the regular fleet of the Siddí, commanded by Yákút Khán. Victory declared for the latter, and Misrí being mortally wounded was brought to die at Mazagám.†

Another evil, which in time grew to enormous magnitude, had always been a serious hindrance to English trade. The Western Coasts of India had been notorious for pirates even when visited by the Romans in the days of their power, and their fleets which came annually from the Red Sea carried a number of archers for protection against these rovers.‡ Ptolemy wrote of them, as if he respected their heroism. § Marco Polo in 1269 said, that with their wives and children they passed all the months of fair weather at sea, that each of their fleets comprised twenty ships, which being ranged at a distance of five miles from each other, made a line of a hundred miles, and that as soon as one descried a merchant ship, she made a signal to the rest, so that it was scarcely possible for their victim to escape.||

These pirates of Málabár were at first considered formidable to English vessels even when well armed. Sir Thomas Herbert fell in with a piratical craft, to which chase was given by two of the ship's boats, each containing fifty musqueteers. A hand-to-hand engagement followed. The pirates used their weapons with such desperate courage, and plied so well what Herbert calls " a sort of hand-granado with a volley of invenomous shafts," but which, probably, was nothing more than a " stink pot," that the English were constrained to retreat, with half of their men either

* Bruce's Annals 1677-8. Mill's History, Book i. chap. 4.
† Orme's Fragments. Grant Duff's History, vol. i. chap. 10.
‡ Plin. Hist. Nat. Lib. vi. c. 23.
§ Writing of them as ἀνδρων πειράτων.
|| Pennant, vol. i.

killed or scalded. The same English ship came upon forty boats of pirates at Mangalore; but all made good their escape.

During the whole period which this narrative embraces, the coast was infested with these marine thieves and others called Sanganians or Sindanians.* The latter yielded in courage but not in cruelty to the pirates of Málabár.

In 1677 some of these wretches seized an Englishman near Cotárra, whilst he was sailing in a Portuguese vessel from Damán. They demanded a ransom; but in conformity with a principle which has been generally adopted by the British Government in India, Mr. Bourchier, who was acting for the Deputy Governor of Bombay, refused to give any. He well knew that such a payment would only lead to more seizures, and believed that his determination was prudent and humane, although apparently cruel. The disappointed pirates bound their unhappy prisoner to a tree, and lanced him to death.†

Fryer, when passing up the river to Vengurla, met a Málabár pirate, which had made prize of a grab in open day. The English vessel in which he sailed immediately attacked her, although she had sixty fighting men who defended themselves with small guns, stones, and stink pots. As the gunner of the English vessel had been left in the slums of Goa, one of the Factors was obliged to serve the single gun. He performed this duty so clumsily that he set his own clothes on fire with a cartridge, and leaped over board to quench the flames. Taking advantage of the confusion caused by this mishap, the pirates attempted to board, but were repelled by a discharge of blunderbusses. They then sheered off. The English were warmly congratulated and complimented for their gallantry by the Chief of the Dutch Factory at Vengurla, and others who had been spectators of the combat. They afterwards heard that the Captain of the pirate vessel and several men had been killed, and that numerous other vessels of the same class were lying in wait for them with a view of taking their revenge.‡

As for the Native vessels engaged in the coasting trade they were as mice, for which the Málabárese and Sanganians contended like dogs and cats. The superior courage and strength of the former generally obtained the prey. Or, perhaps, the native traders might be better compared to rabbits, skipping from one burrow to another. During the day they lay concealed in some hiding place, and towards evening a sailor would ascend an eminence to make a survey. Not until they were satisfied that no pirates were in the neighbourhood, and their movements were screened by the darkness, did they venture forth. In short, the paths of the ocean were fully as dangerous for defenceless travellers as those of the land.§

Secure as the present position of the English in India appears, it is difficult to imagine the constant alarms and anxieties amidst which they

* Sangadians are mentioned by Arrian. Todd says that the proper name would be Sangam-dhárians, from *Sangam* an embouchure, because they frequented such places, Travels in Western India by Lieut. Colonel James Todd chapter 20.

† Letter from the Deputy Governor and Council; dated 3rd April 1677.

‡ Fryer, Letter iv. chapter 2.

§ Thevenot. Liv. i. chapter 6. Fryer, Letter v. chap. 1.

must have formerly lived. We cannot say whether they had most cause to fear the hostility of native powers, freebooters by sea and land, or their European rivals. The Portuguese continued to insult and injure them, nor was it at once discovered how much more audacious were the words than the acts of that decaying race. They had lately exposed themselves to contempt, by suffering a force of six hundred Arabs from Muscat to invade the territory and plunder the churches and houses of Bassein, although the garrison outnumbered their assailants.* Yet recreant as was this behaviour of their troops, President Aungier wrote soon after that they had "grown very prodigiously bold." They chased a Málabár vessel into the harbour of Bombay, and then insisted that the Deputy Governor should give her up as their lawful prize. The reply was a peremptory refusal. So Manoel de Saldanha, their General, arose in his fury, levied an army of twelve hundred men, and vowed that if the vessel were not surrendered peaceably, he would invade Bombay, and take it by force. He actually began to march, but then found that the English Chief was not to be frightened into submission by threats. His opponent's calm resolution induced the General to alter his plans and beat a retreat, whilst the English chuckled and laughed. He was also, they said, "very much reproached by the Hidolgoos and Padrees for his rash folly."†

The high tone with which the English addressed their neighbours in this affair was new, and in remarkable contrast with their style at other times. The Deputy's firmness met with the full approbation of his superior, who was only afraid that there were spies within the camp. Some Roman Catholic priests had been more busy than became them in this matter. The President therefore directed that a strict account should be taken of such persons, "and particularly of that Jesuit Padree at Parell, and the Padrees in Mahim."‡ The refuse of the Goanese clergy were continually resorting to Bombay, and remaining there without having a cure of souls, or any regular appointment, and it was difficult to ascertain whether they were engaged in political intrigues, or merely escaping from the irksome discipline of a monastic life. In the one case they were likely to prove dangerous; in the other only troublesome; but that their object was either to make the Portuguese on the island ill affected towards the Government, or else to free themselves from all restraint, and lead licentious lives, appears to have been undoubted. An order was therefore issued, requiring "all such vagabond Padrees" to repair to Chaul, or wherever else they pleased. It bore a semblance of intolerance, but was in reality a protective ordinance.§

When menaces had failed to obtain any satisfaction, some Portuguese of Salsette resorted to baser means of indulging an impotent revenge, and foully murdered a Serjeant Southerland, who had strayed beyond the English boundary. The President declared "such bloody violences cannot

* Orme's Fragments. This was in 1674.

† Letter from the President and Council of Surat to Fort St. George; dated 25th March 1676.

‡ Letter from the President and Council of Surat to Bombay; dated 28th March 1676.

§ Letter from the same to the same; dated 17th October 1676.

be put up without satisfaction," and ordered that the Superior of the College at Bandora should be called to account for this assassination, as it was perpetrated within the limits of his jurisdiction. We are not told whether this reasonable demand met with due attention.*

Envy was the mainspring of Portuguese hostility. The English Factors said ;—" They are ever exquisite seekers of all ways imaginable to do us mischief, envying us, we suppose, the sudden prosperity this place is rose to." Holding, as they did, Karinjá and Salsette, they had it in their power to fetter English trade with the interior, and they were far from backward in making use of their opportunities. For all goods passing inland they exacted a duty of ten per cent, but their heaviest impost was upon timber brought to Bombay from Kalyán and Brimsley.† For this they demanded a duty of thirty-three per cent, in addition to a charge of twenty per cent made by their officer who commanded at Bassein, as a premium for permission to let it pass through his district. At one time they forbad all transportation of Rice from Bandora to Bombay, and, although their own supplies were abundant, placed a duty, which was so heavy as to be almost prohibitory, on the exportation of fruits, vegetables, and fowls from all parts of their territory. However, the English steadily resisted the demand for custom-duties at Thána and Karinjá, and threatened an appeal to arms in case an attempt was made to enforce payment.

From one part of their illiberal system the Government of Bombay reaped considerable benefit. That intolerance by which the Portuguese have earned an unenviable celebrity, was as ruinous to their settlements as it was advantageous to their neighbours. Brahmans, whose services were of much value, lived at Bandora in constant fear that when they died their children would be seized by the Priests and baptized. Many of them, therefore, escaped to Bombay, and of those who remained some built on that Island houses, where they left their wives and children as in places of security.‡

The Dutch Factory at Surat was now on a grand scale,§ yet the affairs of that nation were conducted with such economy and skill that they were held up by the Court of Directors as models to which they expected their Factors to conform themselves.|| As the Portuguese were the most troublesome rivals of the English on land, so the Dutch were their most formidable enemies at sea. After the war had broken out between the two nations in 1664, the cupidity of each was instigated by the desire of excluding the other from the Indian trade. In England avarice hoped to profit by national indignation, and even poetry condescended to swell the stream of popular fury, taking for its themes " delenda est Carthago," and

* Letter as above.

† So written in the Records.

‡ Letters from the Deputy Governor and Council of Bombay to the Court, dated 24th January 1676-7 ; and from the Court to the Deputy Governor &c., dated December 1683.

§ Voyages de Thevenot, Liv. i. chap. 7.

|| Letter from the Court to the President and Council of Surat ; dated 16th November 1683. Fryer's Account, page 63.

the tempting prizes of the Lowlanders' commerce.* But probably the expectations of the Dutch had a better foundation, as the armaments which they sent to the Indian seas were far superior to those of the English. When the avaricious designs of the two nations were frustrated by the peace, the Dutch still endeavoured to attain their object by intriguing with Native merchants. The English Company also was almost ruined by the expenses of a fleet which they had equipped to revenge upon the Dutch their expulsion from Bantam, but which was prevented from sailing by Charles the Second. They were unable to remit the usual sums of money to India for the purchase of cargoes, and their Factories having to supply the deficiency, became involved in debt.†

At this period the French made their first appearance at Surat as traders. Colbert, their Minister of Finance, had contrived the establishment of an East India Company in 1664, and their agents settled at Surat in 1668 under Caron, a man of French extraction, but who had grown old in the service of the Dutch Company at Japan. Having been banished from that country on account of his intrigues, and not well received by the Dutch at Java, he placed himself at the disposal of the French, by whom he was sent to Surat; but he appears to have soon become convinced that his countrymen were incapable of competing with the English and Dutch.‡ In 1671-2 a French fleet of twelve ships arrived, bringing stock which was valued at a hundred and thirty thousand pounds. Their purchases and sales were made with such rashness, that for a time they reduced the price of European, and raised the price of Indian goods. But the English Factors perceived that they were poor men of business, and not likely to prove successful rivals in commerce.§ As for their Factory, Fryer dismissed the consideration by merely saying, that "it is better stored with monsieurs than with cash; they live well, borrow money, and make a show." The conclusion of the French speculation was, that they ran away from Surat without paying their debts, and when they sought permission to return, were positively refused.‖

Some French Capuchins had also established themselves at Surat, and having used the name of an Aleppo merchant to purchase land, had built a monastery and elegant church. Important services which they rendered to the English when in trouble were many years afterwards acknowledged with gratitude by the President and Council.¶ The intrepid and disinterested conduct of Father Ambrose, their Superior, deserves to be recorded. When Sivají was approaching the city, the good father appeared before him and implored him to spare all Christians. Even this Hindú had

* Thus Dryden in his "Satire upon the Dutch";—

> "As Cato did in Afric fruits display,
> Let us before our eyes their Indies lay.
> All loyal English will like him conclude,
> Let Cæsar live, and Carthage be subdued."

† Raynal, vol. i. Book 3.

‡ Raynal, Book 4.

§ Mill's History, Book i. Chap 4.

‖ Fryer's Account. Raynal, Book 4.

¶ Letter from the President and Council to the Hon. Thomas Pitt; dated 13th April 1700. Voyages de Tavernier, Tome iii.

sufficient respect for his character to grant his request. The Convent was left unassailed, and all who took refuge in it escaped without injury.*

Not the least of the anxieties with which the English Factors were harassed, arose from a constant expectation of having their trade shared by interlopers. Strict injunctions were received from home that such should be seized; if possible, by surprise, in order to avoid bloodshed; but at any rate they were to be seized. When taken, their ships with the cargoes were to be confiscated. One-half of the value was appropriated to his Britannic Majesty's use, and the other half, according to their charter, to the Company.† Against some who had evaded the Factors' vigilance, successful actions were brought in the Courts of England.‡ At the same time the Company declared publicly that Free Trade was permitted—but this was a quibble, or rather an unblushing falsehood.§

To men hedged in and protected by exclusive privileges, it seemed as preposterous that any regularly organized body should be authorized by Government to enter their field of commerce, as that the trade should be altogether opened. Several propositions for establishing a new Company had been made, received favourably by the people of England, and even listened to by the King. These the old Company affected to treat with contempt, although there is no doubt that in secret they were really alarmed. At last, in 1682, they had so far succeeded in propitiating the King and his Council, that they flattered themselves the threatened storm had altogether passed away.

"We suppose you may have heard the noise of the new subscriptions," they wrote, "or a new East India Stock,—a thing in itself frivolous, and serving only to amuse idle and ignorant people, not Princes nor Councils of State, or any wise man. But, however, to lay that matter for ever asleep, it had lately a great debate before his Majesty and Council to the Company's great honour and reputation, which is enough for us to say to you upon this occasion."||

Deluded Court! When they wrote in this triumphant and self-gratulatory style, they little knew what rivalry was in store for them. They leaned upon the King and Council—a reed which broke and pierced them. They had confidence in a bad cause, and such usually leads to shame and discomfiture.

In October 1685 accounts reached Bombay that Charles the Second was dead. On the twenty-fifth James the Second was proclaimed at Surat with all possible solemnity, and a congratulatory address forwarded to him by the President and Council.¶

* Raynal as above. Voyages de Thevenot, Liv i. chap. 16.

† Letter from the Court to the Deputy Governor and Council of Bombay; dated May 1682.

‡ Letter as above; dated February 1684.

§ Fryer's Account.

|| Letter from the Court to the President and Council; dated 22nd May 1682.

¶ Bruce's Annals, 1685-86.

CHAPTER VI.

1662—1685.

CONTENTS.—*Home and personal Affairs.*—Swally, and the ride to Surat—The Factory—Rank and pay of the Factors; the rest of the Establishment; idleness—The President's style—Sepulchral monuments—The Court remonstrates —Characters—Fryer; his history; his Travels into the interior, ascent of the Ghâts and other adventures—Sir George Oxenden; his family; character; descendants—Gerald Aungier; his religion; death—Religious phrases in ordinary use—Contrast in the immorality of the times—Governors Cook and Gary—Deputy Governor Young; his outrageous conduct—A Naval Ensign—A Drunkard's broadside—A Military quill-driver—Gentleman Jones the Serjeant—A Corporal's freak—Official peculation—Bombay punch and its effects; duelling and gambling; Clive's opinion of the Military—The Court's opinion of their servants—A cargo of Ladies; bad investment; their cruel treatment—Children of mixed marriages—Mutinies at Bombay; causes; spirit of the times; retrenchment; first mutiny; Shaxton sent home; the Court disgusts all classes; Keigwin raises the standard of revolt; Statesmanlike conduct—The President fails to establish order—Officers sent from England—Sir Thomas Grantham arrives, and gains possession of Bombay—Treatment of the rebels—Factories at Dharamgám, Honáwar, Carwar, Rattera and Brinjan—Anecdotes of the Factors.

THE Factors of Surat were making themselves extremely comfortable, and indeed gradually imitating that style and grandeur which distinguish the corporate societies of England. Some of them resided at Swally where at first they had been contented to pitch tents, but in the days of President Andrews convenient bungalows were erected. The scene here was interesting, particularly after the periodical arrivals of ships from Europe. A suitable landing-place led to the English dwellings. English, Dutch, and French colours were hoisted on their respective flagstaffs; and at the sea-side were the tombs of several Europeans.

When the residents of Swally visited Surat, they generally maintained their dignity by travelling in some state. Horses were not used for draft; but their ordinary conveyances were two-wheeled carts or four-wheeled waggons, drawn by bullocks, and styled by courtesy chariots or coaches. With few exceptions these were made after the native fashion, and the rider was compelled to sit cross-legged in them. Fryer says, "they were covered with scarlet and ill hung, being much like those sold at London to please little children with, only larger and lined with velvet." They were escorted by a company of peons, such a troop, remarks the same graphic author, as may be seen "in old pictures of our Lord's apprehension."

The English Factory was a handsome and solid building of stone. It supported an upper and lower gallery, was ornamented by some good carving, and contained private apartments, with "a neat oratory," and common dining-room. Strangers were pleased with the numerous curiosities which were exhibited in it. There were various specimens of zoology, then considered novelties; amongst them a good collection of tumbler, fantail, and other pigeons, fighting-cocks from Siam, milk-white turtle doves from Bussora, cockatoes and newries from Bantam, a cassiowary which had the power of digesting iron, and diminutive Ahmadavats.

The hours for transacting business with natives were from ten to twelve, and again from four until night. At such times the Factory was a scene of extraordinary noise and bustle.

There were not more than twenty-eight Factors and Writers.* Their apartments seemed to a visitor extremely elegant, when compared with others in India. The higher grades of rank were attained by a regular system of seniority, and an order of precedence was strictly observed. First came the President and eight members of Council, five only of whom were obliged to reside at Surat. Next to the President ranked the Accountant, who acted as Treasurer, and prepared the accounts for audit. After him came the Warehouse-keeper, who registered the sales of European, and the purchases of Oriental goods. Fourth was the Purser Marine, who was required to give an account of all exports and imports, to pay seamen's wages, provide stores, and discharge other duties connected with the shipping. The fifth was the Secretary, who regulated the general affairs. These five were members of Council.

When a young man first arrived in India he was styled an Apprentice; but after a time this term seems to have been thought vulgar, and given up.† When he had served his apprenticeship, he became a Writer; his salary was ten pounds *per annum*, and he was held under a bond of five hundred pounds to serve for five years. At the expiration of that time he became a Factor; his salary was raised to twenty pounds, and he was bound in the sum of a thousand pounds. After three years he became a Senior Factor; and after another three years, a merchant with forty pounds *per annum*. The chiefs of minor Factories, Bombay, Bantam, Persia, Ahmedábád, Agra, Húblí, Rájapúr, Carwar, and Cálicot, were taken from this class of servants, but many preferred remaining in Council at Surat, as they were enabled to make such large profits there on consignments. The Accountant's salary was seventy-two pounds, fifty-two of which were paid in India, and the rest in England. The President's

* Lists were periodically sent home to the Court. The above is the average after a comparison of numerous lists.

† The following is the Court's regulation:—"For the advancement of our Apprentices we direct that, after they have served the first five yeares, they shall have £10 per annum, for the two last yeares; and having served those two yeares, to be entertayned one yeare longer, as Writers, and have Writer's sallary: and having served that yeare, to enter into the degree of Factors, which otherwise would have been ten yeares. And knowing that a distinction of titles is in many respects necessary, we do order, that when the Apprentices have served their times, they be stiled *Writers*; and when the Writers have served their times, they be stiled *Factors*; and Factors, having served their times, to be stiled *Merchants*; and Merchants having served their times, to be stiled *Senior Merchants*."—Bruce's Annals, 1775-6.

salary was five hundred, a gratuity of two hundred having been added to the former salary of three hundred pounds, "for the purpose of removing all temptation to engage in private trade;" and in President Aungier's case this gratuity was increased to five hundred pounds on account of special services. The President was obliged to sign a bond for five thousand pounds. In 1679 the salary of the Deputy Governor of Bombay was reduced to a hundred and twenty pounds. Half of all salaries, with the exception of the Accountants and Writers, was paid in England, and was considered a security that, in case of any misdemeanour, the offending party might be fined by the Court. Writers received their ten pounds in India. A Chaplain, who received fifty pounds salary, and—significant condition—fifty pounds more "during good behaviour," a Physician and Surgeon, whose incomes corresponded with the Senior Factors', completed the European part of the establishment. A Múnshí was also attached to the Factory in order that the young men might be instructed in native languages, but few made any effort to learn them. The Court complained that they were an idle set. Indeed their betters often set them but a poor example. Some who ranked next to members of Council, and others who had been sent out as Chiefs of subordinate Factories, were severely reprimanded for indifference, idleness, and gross neglect of their official duties. Many had quite a schoolboy's dislike of the pen, and so their masters directed that a school-boy's punishment should be inflicted upon them. For every day their work was neglected they were to be fined one dollar, which was to be deducted from the portion of their salaries paid in India. But lest the Company should be suspected of any mercenary motive in taking these dollars, they were to be added to the fund which was raised for defraying the expenses of public buildings and the decorations of Bombay!*

That an impression might be made upon the natives, the President indulged to a considerable extent in pomp and state—even more than the Dutch President. He had a standard-bearer and bodyguard composed of a serjeant and double file of English soldiers. Forty natives also attended him. At dinner each course was ushered in by the sound of trumpets, and his ears were regaled by a band of music. Whenever he left his private rooms he was preceded by attendants with silver wands. On great occasions, when he issued from the Factory, he appeared on horseback, or in a palanquin, or a coach drawn by milk-white oxen—doubtless of that large and beautiful breed for which Gujarát is celebrated.† Led horses

* Letter from the Court to the President and Council; dated 16th November 1683. Bruce's Annals.

† Fryer's sketch from nature of "a coach" is so fresh and accurate that the reader shall have a copy:—"Two large milk-white oxen are put in to draw it, with circling horns as black as a coal, each point tipped with brass, from whence come brass chains across to the headstall, which is all of scarlet, and a scarlet collar to each, of brass bells, about their necks, their flapping ears snipped with art, and from their nostrils bridles covered with scarlet. The chariot itself is not swinging like ours, but fastened to the main axles by neat arches, which support a four-square seat, which is inlaid with ivory, or enriched as they please; at every corner are turned pillars, which make (by twisted silk or cotton cords) the sides, and support the roof, covered with English scarlet cloth, and lined with silk, with party-coloured borders; in these they spread carpets, and lay bolsters to ride cross-legged, sometimes three or four in one. It is borne on two wheels only, such little ones as our fore wheels are, and

with silver bridles followed, and an umbrella of state was carried before him. The equipages of the other Merchants and Factors came behind in procession, and corresponded with the President's.*

These accounts of the President's grandeur are confirmed by tombs which still remain standing at Surat. What was the style of the living may be inferred from the houses of the dead ; and, moreover, Fancy may see in these sepulchral ruins the continuance of an undying rivalry between the agents of England and Holland. Van Reede, the old Dutch Chief, has a brave charnel-house. His mouldering bones lie beneath a double cupola of great dimensions, formerly adorned with frescoes, escutcheons, and elegant wood-work. Its original cost may be supposed to have been enormous, when we read that to repair it cost the Dutch Company six thousand rupees. It is not indeed to be compared with the Mohammedan tombs of Delhi, Agra and Bíjapúr, but no European structures of the kind, except the tomb of Adrian at Rome and a few others, equal it. Doubtless the intention of its builders was to eclipse the noble mausoleum which covers the remains of Sir George and Christopher Oxenden, who died a few years earlier than Van Reede. Christopher is commemorated by a cupola within the loftier and more expansive cupola raised in honour of his more distinguished brother, the President. The height of this monument is forty feet, the diameter twenty-five. Massive pillars support the cupolas, and round their interiors are galleries reached by a flight of many steps. The body of an Indian Viceroy might have found here a worthy resting place ; it is far too superb for the Chief of a Factory, and his brother who was only a subordinate.†

The fact is, that the President's pomp and extravagance were in advance of the times, and the Court of Directors strove to check them. A Company of "adventurers" could ill afford to support a kind of royal state, and however much they might have desired that their representatives should present an imposing appearance to the natives of India, they complained bitterly of the heavy charge, at a time when they were expending large sums upon the fortifications of Bombay. They plainly told their President that they would be better pleased, if he could suppress his rising vanity, and mortify his inordinate love of display.‡ Two years later also they ordered that he should only be styled Agent ; and his salary be reduced to three hundred pounds a year.§

pinned on with a wooden arch, which serves to mount them. The charioteer rides before, a-straddle on the beam that makes the yoke for the oxen, which is covered with scarlet, and finely carved underneath. He carries a goad instead of a whip. In winter (when they rarely stir) they have a *mumjuma*, or waxcloth to throw over it. Those for journeying are something stronger than those for the merchants to ride about the city, or to take the air on ; which with their nimble oxen they will, when they meet in the fields, run races on, and contend for the garland as much as for an Olympick prize ; which is a diversion, *To see a cow gallop*, as we say in scorn ; but these not only pluck up their heels apace, but are taught to amble, they often riding on them." Letter vi chapter i.

* Letter from the President and Council to the Court, dated 28th January 1663-4. Fryer's Account. Thevenot, Liv i. Chapter 7. Gautier Schouten, Tome i.

† Olof Foreen's Voyage. Thevenot.

‡ Letter from the President and Council, in reply to the Court ; dated 17th January 1675-76.

§ Kaye's Administration.

The reader is now invited to come behind the scenes at Surat and Bombay, and see what after all was the state of society, when its fine dress and ceremony were thrown aside.

And first, he shall be introduced to a gentleman whose book is, next to official records, the best authority we have for a knowledge of men and manners at that time. Fryer had graduated as Doctor of Medicine at the University of Cambridge, and having given abundant proofs of his learning, penetration, and sagacity, was elected a Fellow of the Royal Society. On the ninth of December 1672 he left England in the ship *Unity*, accompanied by ten other East Indiamen, and, after visiting the Coromandel Coast, arrived the following December at Bombay, where he was received by President Aungier. There his medical services were in constant requisition, not only for his countrymen, but also for distinguished Portuguese and natives. "John de Mendos," of Bassein, sent for him to attend his only daughter, a handsome girl, on the point of marriage with the Portuguese Admiral of the North. He then went to Junar at the request of the Mogul general, and was attended by a Brahman, who acted as interpreter, his servants, and numerous peons. Travelling in a palanquin with eight bearers—the usual number, we may observe, in those days—he passed Thána, and reached Kalyán, where he gazed with astonishment on ruins of stately fabrics, and many traces of departed magnificence. As he progressed, he noticed with the eye of a close observer, the habits of the natives and condition of the country. Governors and other officers were not a little troublesome. "A hungry look hung upon them all;" and Fryer, who was never satisfied with any one so well as himself, thought that he escaped their exactions, only by his singular courtesy, good humour, and adroitness. Leaving behind him Múrbár and Desír, he ascended the Gháts to Appagám. This seemed to him—if we may judge from his statement—an enterprise little inferior to Hannibal's passage over the Alps. There was no road, but stones forming broken steps, and the breathless porters threaded their way amidst hanging trees, the roots of which had been left bare by the falling earth. Wearied as they were, even the promise of "nectar in the skies" was but a faint encouragement to them. Hands and feet were all called into requisition. "To look down made my brains turn round," writes the traveller; "over my head pendulous rocks threatened to entomb me." Intense labour extorted tears of anguish from his servants' eyes; but when at last, by a narrow cavern cut through the rock, they reached the summit, a little arak distributed amongst them, according to promise, made them hasten cheerfully to the nearest village.

On reaching his destination, Fryer attended the darbár, respectfully presented a letter from the English President, and met with a courteous reception; but after being told who his patients were, was desired to wait for the occurrence of a fortunate day. At length being summoned to the harem, he found a bed hung with silk curtains, and was desired to place his hand under the curtains, in order that he might feel an invalid's pulse. At first his conductors played him a trick, and let him touch the wrist of a healthy slave; but when he declared that the owner was in robust health, there was extended to him an arm which gave signs of a weak constitution, and left him no doubt as to what should be his prescription. The following day the Khán sent for him to bleed another of his wives. Across the apartment into which he was ushered a large curtain extended, through a hole of which an arm was stretched. As good luck would have it, there was behind this screen a number of inquisitive ladies, who, as they peeped through, so pressed upon it, that suddenly it gave way, and revealed the whole bevy fluttering like so many birds over which a net has been spread. None endeavoured to escape, but there they stood, pretending to be excessively modest, and peering at the Doctor through the open lattices of their fingers. As for him, he found himself holding by the arm "a plump russet dame," who summoned the blood to her cheeks, and commanded that the curtain should be replaced. No offence was given or taken. The Doctor was rewarded with a golden shower of pagodas poured into the basin, over which his patient had been bled, and his servants, to his infinite satisfaction, drew them out of the extravasated gore.

But Fryer had the Company's interests in view, as well as his own. He did his utmost to open a trade between Junar and Bombay, suggesting that the Mogul General might in this way provide his army with horses from Bussora and Mocha, in exchange for which he could give the ordinary merchandize of his country. However, the Maráthá army, possessing the intervening districts, were an obstruction in this route, which probably was not overcome.

As Fryer was returning, the bearers of his palanquin must have tried to enjoy a joke at his expense; but it was in the end no joking matter for them. Drawing near a small grove, they saw such a blaze of light created by fireflies that they really were, or pretended to be, terrified. The learned Doctor, not being milder and gentler than the rest of his countrymen, drew his sword, and, as he said, by opening a vein or two, let out the shaitán, who had crept into their fancies. Yet the perpetrator of such a wanton and tyrannical act could listen with the most tender compassion to tales of misery, which the natives told, and which probably were at that time as harrowing themes as the people of any country have ever dilated on.

Two men amongst the English, who resided in India, and as far as we know, only two, deserve particular and honourable mention. Sir George Oxenden, and his successor, Gerald Aungier, would have done credit to any age or nation. When the detestable licentiousness and political baseness which degraded Charles the Second's reign, were leavening Anglo-Indian society, these two men remained uncorrupt. They were professedly religious characters, and their behaviour was in the main consistent with their profession.

Sir George Oxenden's family is said to have derived its origin from Oxendenden in the parish of Nonington, Kent, and to have resided in that country since the reign of Edward the Third. Their arms may, I believe, be seen in a window of Denton Church, impaling the heraldic shields of Twitham, Barton, Ratlinga, Yonge, Wenderton and Broadnax. Sir George's elder brother, Sir Henry, was the first baronet.

In the inscription on the monument at Surat, which is designed to commemorate Sir George and his brother Christopher, the former is styled

" a great man," and the affection by which the brothers were bound to the last, is simply and touchingly recorded. Sir George was both good and great. In his official correspondence there is a strikingly religious tone. When after long delay a Chaplain had been sent to Swally, he and his Council " most humbly thanked" the Company for showing " such spiritual care for their souls." They added that their minister was a great comfort to them, that his comportment was " sober, and becoming his function and call to holy orders," and that they felt sure of deriving " future comfort and happiness from his piety and sober behaviour." Even Alexander Hamilton, who had rarely a good word for Indian officials, said that " when Sir George died, piety grew sick, and the building of Churches was grown unfashionable." The zeal which made him so anxious to have a Church built in Bombay, extended its liberality to England. In 1660 he gave a velvet cushion and pulpit cloth to the Church of Wingham, and in 1682 five hundred pounds for repairs of the same Church and Chancel. He also bequeathed three hundred pounds for the repairs of Adisham Church. In the accounts of his demise which the Factors forwarded to the Company, they express the general regret felt at Surat and Bombay for his loss, feelingly describe the probity and talents with which he had guarded the Company's privileges and managed their commerce, clear his character from unjust aspersions, and finally declare that he had gained the respect, not only of the English, but of the Dutch, French, Native Government, and Merchants of Surat.

Sir George Oxenden had accumulated considerable wealth. The bulk he left, together with his noble example, to the line of baronets, who, from that day to this, have possessed Brome, and other valuable estates in Kent.*

Gerald Aungier was also a man of high character, although perhaps inferior in goodness of heart to Oxenden. He was too fond of religious phrases, and sometimes used them in excess. When accused by the Court of vanity, he warmly defended himself, and endeavoured to strengthen his arguments with quotations from Scripture, adding, that he had done all things in season, and with a constant remembrance of the account which he must render to Almighty God.† In writing about the Church which they were proposing to build at Bombay, he shewed that he was actuated by missionary zeal. He trusts that it will have an influence for good upon the natives, so that " when the merciful pleasure of God shall think good to touch them with a sense of the eternal welfare of their souls, they may be convinced of their error, sensible of their present dangerous, uncertain wanderings, and desirous to render themselves happy in a more sure way of salvation, which we pray God grant in His good time." ‡

Another document seems to us peculiarly to disclose his feelings, and admits us to view in one regard his way of life. On his departure for

* Letter to the Court from the President and Council at Swally, dated 28th January 1663-4. Bruce's Annals 1669-70. Hamilton's " New Account," chap. xvii. The History and Topographical Survey of the County of Kent ; by Edward Hasted, Esq.

† Letter as above ; date, 17th January 1675-6.

‡ Letter as above.

Bombay he instructed Mr. Streynsham Master,* the Deputy, as to the management of affairs during his absence, and commenced thus :—

"Firstly, that a blessing may attend you in all your proceedings, we recommend to you the pious order observed in our family, to wit, morning and evening prayer, the strict observance of the Lord's day, the preventing all disorder, profaneness, and debauchery, the preservation of the peace, and good government among our fellow servants ; in all which we shall not doubt your careful observance, being well acquainted with your own inclination thereunto, and therefore need not mind you thereof, but as it is one of the most essential parts of your charge."†

Worn out with his exertions, Aungier solicited the Court's permission to return to England, as soon as a duly qualified person should be appointed to succeed him ; but he did not live to see his wish fulfilled, and expired in India. Of him also Hamilton writes most favourably and says, that when he resided in India thirty years afterwards Aungier's name was even then revered by the inhabitants of Surat and Bombay. So highly had the President been esteemed for his love of justice and dexterity in the management of affairs, that in commercial questions the natives were accustomed to refer their differences to his arbitration, and in no single instance had any been known to dispute the equity of his award.‡

Other official papers were of the same stamp as Oxenden's and Aungier's despatches, above quoted.§ Were the President and Council concerned to hear of the Deputy Governor's ill-health, they regretted that at that distance they could do nothing "more than by their prayers to God for him." Their President, they said, had been ill, but "praised be to God, he is now in a way of recovery." Did Aungier and his Council comment with grief on Colonel Bake's death in February 1677, they devoutly added, "We desire Almighty God to prepare us all for our last change." Had their ships arrived in safety, they blessed God for it, or piously ejaculated, "Thanks be to Almighty God." Did they make the melancholy announcement that an epidemic disease was raging, they wrote in these words :—"It hath pleased God to let us see what we are, by the frequent mortalities which have happened amongst us." And their despatches ordinarily concluded with the devout formula, "We commend you to the Almighty's protection," or some similar words of valediction.||

But what are the conclusions to which these passages lead us? Words and phrases may ordinarily be received as just exponents of an individual's mind ; when first adopted also in official communications, religious expressions shew that the writers are anxious to have their

* Streynsham Master was afterwards Chief at Madras, and in 1680 laid there the first stone of the first English Church in India, carried on the work at his own charge, and never halted till he had brought it to a conclusion. He was dismissed the service by the Court's order in 1681 ; but his offence is not stated. He was then knighted, and elected a Director of the New Company, which derived great benefit from his experience. His family was afterwards connected by marriage with that of Oxenden. It had been endowed with the manor of East Langdon in Kent by Henry the Eighth after the dissolution of monasteries. Bruce's Annals 1681 and 1700. Mill's History, vol. iii. Hasted's Kent.

† Diary of the Surat Factory ; 10th January 1669.

‡ Bruce's Annals 1676-77. Hamilton's "New Account," chap. xvii.

§ Diary of the Surat Factory, 10th January 1669.

|| Letters from the President and Council to Bombay, Fort St. George, &c. &c.

faith publicly recognised; but the frequent repetition of them by others only proves, that they were forms to which men had become habituated. When a Frenchman first took leave of his friend with the words á Dieu, or a Maráthá first saluted another with the invocation 'Rám, Rám,' a religious sentiment was expressed; but such is not usually the case when these words are used now. And so, when Oxenden and Aungier wrote religiously, their sincerity might be trusted; but the other religious phrases used in despatches prove nothing respecting the state of public feeling.

A religion without a morality was every year gradually becoming a disgrace of the English people. Charles the Second quartering Nell Gwynn in Dr. Ken's prebendal house, that facetious mistress proclaiming in the streets that she was His Majesty's "Protestant whore," His Majesty and the Duke of Buckingham sleeping over South's profound discourse, until aroused by the preacher's witticism,—these were straws which shewed how the wind was blowing in England, and, of course, how it would blow in India. At Surat and Bombay the grossest immorality prevailed in both high and low places, although the lives of the Presidents were irreproachable.

Cook, the first royal Governor of Bombay, was charged with extorting twelve thousand xeraphims from the inhabitants; and his own accounts proved that he had applied them to his own use; also with dishonest management of Sir Abraham Shipman's estate, and deducting from it fifteen per cent, which he pretended to claim for his commission. Gary, who governed the following year, is represented to have been a vain, intriguing, headstrong and overbearing, but plausible man. He was afterwards appointed to be one of the Company's judges, and it is said that he summoned a man to appear before his Court on Friday, although he had been executed, according to the judge's own sentence, on the previous Tuesday. The Court waited, but death was guilty of contempt, and no prisoner appeared in spite of the fuddled judge's mandate.* Then we come to Young, the Company's first Deputy Governor, who was a drunkard, scoffer, and avowed despiser of the Christian religion. No fewer than twenty charges were brought against him on the twenty-second of January 1669, before the President in Council. In the first charge he was accused of tyranny when discharging his official duties, and illegally imprisoning his subordinates. In the second he was accused of openly throwing contempt upon religion, and declaring that it "was but a State policy to keep men in hand." The third and fourth charges were so extraordinary that they are here given in the prosecutor's words:—

"3rd, That he hath on the Sabbath day hindered the performance of public duty to God Almighty at the accustomary hour, continuing in drinking of healths, detaining others with him against their wills; and while he drank, in false devotions upon his knee, a health to the Union, in the time appointed for the service belonging to the Lord's Day, the unhappy sequel shewed it to be but his projection of a further disunion.

"4th. That to the great scandal of the inhabitants of the Island, of

* Hamilton's "New Account," chap. xvii.

all the neighbours round about, both papists and others that are idolaters, in dishonour of the sobriety of the Protestant religion, he hath made frequent and long drinking meetings, continuing sometimes till two or three of the clock in the morning, to the neglecting of the service of God in the morning prayers, and the service of the Company in the meantime hath stood still while he slept, thus perverting, and converting to an ill private use those refreshments intended for the Factory in general."

The last charge accuses this infatuated man of crowning all his acts of sin and folly by threatening to hang the President. The trial ended with an order that he should be taken on ship board and sent to England, but that at the same time be treated with as much respect as possible.*

Such were their honors, the Governor and Deputy Governor of Bombay. It occurs to us that they could scarcely have held others with a very tight rein, so we will turn to persons under their authority, and first summon Mr. Thorpe to appear. This officer, who was an Ensign in the Company's Navy, having quitted the harbour of Bombay in his manchua, was one day taking a cruize off Danda Rájapúr, and there descried a boat belonging to the Siddí's fleet making towards him. The Siddí's people had taken him for a Málabár pirate, and he did not choose to undeceive them until they came pretty near. Then his colours were run up to the mast head, and they, perceiving their mistake, began to sheer off. But Thorpe being in a rakish mood, was disposed to turn rover in reality, and take the opportunity of making a little money. So he invited some of the Siddí's crew to pay him a visit. In simple confidence they came; but no sooner were they on board than the dashing Ensign charged them with a design of seizing the Honorable Company's manchua. They stoutly declared that they had no such intentions, but their earnest protestations were in vain. He ordered the hands of two coolies who had come on board to be fastened behind their backs, and in this condition they were hoisted up to the vessel's yard. The pain soon drove them to say whatever he required, and they admitted that their Captain had intended to make the manchua his prize. Thorpe had then gained his point. Pretending that they were pirates, he took the Captain and two of his men prisoners, and with their arms, money, and papers, sailed away down the Coast. This affair involved the English in no little trouble. The Siddí demanded satisfaction, and of course sent in an exaggerated statement of losses sustained. He maintained that he had been robbed of two thousand six hundred rupees; but the Bombay Government declared that only forty rupees were in his boat, and excited his indignation by offering to restore that sum. The offending Ensign was deprived of his commission, but afterwards reinstated.†

After this, in 1683, the peace existing between the English and Siddí was again in danger of being interrupted by the wild frolic of an English Captain. This officer having just arrived from England, had entertained on board his ship a party of friends from shore. Heated with wine the whole company paid a visit to Siddí Kossim's ship, where the English

* Consultation held at Surat 22nd January 1669.

† Letter to the Court from the Deputy Governor and Council of Bombay; dated 24th January 1676-7.

captain addressed in abusive language all whom he saw, and then drew his sword. He was disarmed, slightly wounded, and placed with his companions in a boat. Returning to his ship the drunkard fired a broadside on the Siddí, who did not return a shot. Happily no one was killed, and only two or three persons were slightly wounded, when further outrage was stopped by signals and messengers from the shore. An express was sent to Surat, where, as had been anticipated, the English were thrown into the greatest alarm, expecting that the Mussulman population would demand revenge.*

Another officer, named Pitts, was a most troublesome subject. He had entered the service as a Clerk, but preferring a sword to a pen, had been appointed supernumerary Lieutenant; however, he proved as useless on parade as he had been at his desk, being addicted to intemperance, and particularly fond of bespattering his brother officers with foul language. The indulgent Directors, when referred to, lamented that he had ever been employed, but were indisposed to ruin him by dismissing him from their service. They therefore adopted an ordinary expedient of the time, and continued to recognize his military title, whilst they required him to follow his avocations at the desk. They perhaps hoped that he would march from his office to a field of war with as much ardour and intuitive knowledge, as did afterwards the wondrous Clive.†

A young gentleman named Jones was an instance of a fall in life which has since had many parallels amongst the Company's European troops. His father was a Justice of the King's Bench, but the son having ran a career of folly and crime enlisted in the Company's service, and was sent out to Bombay as a Serjeant. The Court of Directors consented that their President and Council should be rough-riders of this wild colt. Through them the Judge forwarded forty pounds, which were to be his sole allowance for two years, and were to be doled out to him in six or eight dollars at a time. On no account was he to return home unless by his father's express desire.‡

We next descend to a Corporal—a fellow who by his recklessness greatly damaged the new fortifications of Bombay, and threw all the inhabitants into consternation. He had filled with wild fire an old bandoleer, intending to fasten it to a dog's tail, and when the dog was not to be caught, had thrown the bandoleer into the air. The wind was high and bore the combustibles to a neighbouring bastion, where the contents of thirty-five barrels of gunpowder were spread out to dry. A tremendous explosion followed. Eight natives who were working on the bastion, and a sentry, were killed, some of their limbs being blown over the Fort. The doors of the magazine, which had been securely fastened, were burst open, and the whole town felt the shock. The Corporal's punishment was peculiar to the times. He was sentenced to run the gauntlet thrice, and then be cashiered.§

* Orme's Fragments.

† Letter from the Court to the President and Council, dated December 1683. So Captain Shaxton was made a Factor as soon as he came out, "that he might combine his military with his civil duties."

‡ Letter from the Court to the Depy. Govr. and Council of Bombay, dated May 1683.

§ Letter from the Deputy Governor and Council to the Court; dated 3rd April 1677.

We should observe that these examples are not selected from a very large number of Europeans, but that there were only a few at Surat and Bombay. Consequently they must be held to exhibit in themselves a discreditable state of society. But we must produce further evidence of this. The Factors were bent upon attending to their own interests, and the public service suffered much. In vain did the Company attempt to suppress private trade. On the other side of India resistance to their orders had ended in open rebellion. They had added, as we have seen, to the three hundred pounds, which was the salary of their Presidents, two hundred more, as a compensation for the loss of private trade. But of course these ambitious Chiefs could not remain contented with a paltry five hundred pounds per annum. The other Factors contrived to increase their gains by peculation, and had fallen into the "sinful practice," as the Company justly styled it, of employing on their private ships the soldiers who were maintained at their masters' expense.*

Continual squabbles occurred when men's passions were inflamed by intoxicating liquors. A duel fought between Mr. Hornigold and Captain Minchin had its origin at some wild orgies, and, as President Aungier remarked, was "the usual effect of that accursed Bombay punch, to the shame, scandal, and ruin of the nation and religion." The combatants were confined to their quarters and suspended from the service, pending a reference to Surat; but as the Deputy Governor interceded for them, they were pardoned after paying a fine of fifty xeraphims, which were added to the fund raised for building an hospital.† After every arrival of recruits from England a fearful mortality prevailed at Bombay, chiefly occasioned by their immoderate use of punch and toddy.‡ Gambling also occupied the time of both officers and men, who all felt much aggrieved when an order was issued, that no play for any sum higher than five rupees should be permitted.§ In fact, the account which the great Clive gave of this period is perfectly correct:—"Formerly the Company's troops consisted of the refuse of our gaols, commanded by an officer seldom above the rank of Lieutenant, and but in one or two instances with that of Major; without order, discipline, or military ardour."||

The Court of Directors must be called as witnesses to shew the prevalence of vice. Morals had become so corrupt that they were obliged to interfere, and in 1682 sent out most stringent orders that reformatory measures should immediately be enforced by authority. They remark with severe reprobation the "riot, prodigality, carelessness and folly," which were so common. They were determined to check "expensive and vicious habits." "All incorrigible lumber" was to be removed out of the way, and such persons as were unfit for the service were to be dismissed "in a summary way, without formality of tedious, impertinent, chargeable examinations, attestations, certificates, letters, or other trumpery."

* Letter from the Court to the President and Council; dated May 1682.

† Letter from the President and Council to the Deputy Governor and Council, dated 24th January 1675-6. Mill's History, Book i. chap 4.

‡ Letter from the same to the same, dated 14th August 1676.

§ Letter from the Deputy Governor and Council to Surat; dated 6th December 1686.

|| M. S. quoted by Bruce in his "Plans for the Government of British India." Part II. Chap. i. Sec. 4.

Their rating instructions are concluded thus :—" If there be any in Bombay in our service that are riotous, unfaithful, or negligent, fail not without favour or affection, anger or prejudice, to give impartial notice of them to our President and Council at Surat, who we doubt not but will ease you of such burdens."*

Nor, we are sorry to add, were these vicious propensities indulged only by men. A great many females on the island were far from exhibiting the gentler virtues which usually adorn their sex, but in this instance the Company themselves were chiefly to be blamed. As Rome in her young days sat desolate until cheered by the ravished Sabines ; as the poor slaves of St. Helena would not take kindly to their toil until the Company brought a cargo of sable maidens to brighten their dreary hours ; so also it was thought that the exiled soldiers of England must have a similar solace in Bombay. Gerald Aungier first suggested that they ought to be encouraged and assisted in contracting marriages with their countrywomen. Consistently with his character he took a religious view of the question, and pointed out that the men being Protestants were in the habit of marrying native Portuguese women, the consequence of which was that their offspring were, " through their father's neglect, brought up in the Roman Catholic principles to the great dishonour and weakening of the Protestant religion and interest." He therefore recommended that a supply of women should be sent out from England. This proposal was acceded to by the Court of Directors, and apparently improved upon, for they not only induced such persons as were adapted to be wives of private soldiers to come, but " gentlewomen and other women." Unhappily " the gentlewomen," as they still continued to be styled, had not learned before they left England to behave themselves ; therefore their countrymen at Bombay were not very forward in offering them their hearts and hands. Some, however, married ; but a judicious observer, who visited the island soon after, was shocked to see how sickly their children were in consequence of the free and easy way in which the mothers lived, and their inveterate habit of taking strong liquors.†

But what was to become of those who remained single and unnoticed ? Of course they supposed that the Company were their honorable guardians, and that if they could not find husbands, they would at least have the protection of Government. Not so the Company. To the first party indeed a guarantee was given that they should be supported for the first year, and if, at the expiration of that time, they were still unmarried, they should be allowed their diet for another year. This engagement was faithfully kept. But then came out a second party, fondly expecting that they would be treated like their predecessors ; indeed they affirmed " that so much was declared to them at the East India House by Mr. Lewis." Nevertheless their claims were not recognized. After considerable agitation on their part, and reluctance on the President's part, six or eight pagodas a-month were allowed to *such as were actually in distress.* The

* Letter from the Court to the Deputy Governor and Council of Bombay ; dated May 1682.

† Proposals touching Bombay island, recommended to the Honorable Company by their President and Council at Surat, regarding taxes, defences, &c, 3rd February 1671. Government Records. Fryer's Account.

President and Council in writing to the Court made a merit of this base and cruel economy. "We have refused to put you to this charge," they write, "declaring we have no order from you, which hath caused some discontent among them ; only we have thought fit to assist those who are more objects of charity, to keep them from perishing for want of sustenance." To keep them from what ? The poor creatures had clearly been deluded and almost left to starve. What was the result ? They must have been tempted, if not actually driven, to sell their charms to the first bidder. The small stock of virtue which they had brought with them was of course soon expended. Then, and not till then—when they had been led into temptation—the voice of authority, and erring, mocking piety assumed a threatening tone. "And whereas," wrote the President and Council, "you give us notice that some of the women are grown scandalous to our nation, religion, and Government interest, we require you in the Honorable Company's name to give them all faire warning that they do apply themselves to a more sober and Christian conversation ; otherwise the sentence is this, that they shall be confined totally of their liberty to go abroad, and fed with bread and water, till they are embarqued on board ship for England."* O ! Gerald Aungier ! In all this affair you had much Protestant zeal, but little Christian love.

The reader will have remarked that a jealousy of the Roman Catholic religion led to this introduction of English women, and the same feeling suggested a proposition that all children of Protestant fathers should be brought up carefully in the reformed Religion. The President and Council wished to promulgate a standing order to this effect, and to enforce it under severe penalties. Particularly would they visit with their resentment "the Padrees" who would "endeavour to baptize the said children, or entice them away from the Protestant faith."† But no provision was made for the religious education of children, nor was the establishment of a school contemplated.

This period closed with one of the most formidable and successful revolts that have ever shaken the British Government in India. It was a time when men's minds were every year becoming more agitated, and there was a disposition to resist all absolute power, particularly that of monopolies. In England, the decisions even of Courts of law were becoming more and more liberal upon questions of exclusive privileges, and there was a hope, which had extended itself to India, that the claims and authority of the Company would soon be overthrown.

It was unfortunate that the Government were obliged to select such a time for enforcing measures of retrenchment, and that thus they gave offence not only to natives, but also to the best of their European servants, both civil and military. It must be admitted that the military especially were treated most shabbily by them, and had many just causes of complaint. Not only was their pay trifling, but repeated efforts were made to pare that down as much as possible, and the rate of exchange, on

* Letters from the President and Council to the Deputy Governor and Council, dated 18th December 1675 ; and from the same to the Court, dated 17th January 1675-6.

† Letter to the Court from the President and Council at Swally, dated 28th Jan. 1663-4.

which it depended, was lowered. Captains were expected to be satisfied with Lieutenants' allowances, Lieutenants with Ensigns', and a surplus which had been actually received by them before the reforms were made, and to which they considered that they had a just claim, was ordered to be refunded.*

Could any Government expect that their troops would return such ungenerous treatment with steadfast attachment and unshaken fidelity? In 1674 the Court of Directors received a most solemn warning that such would not be the case. The soldiers affirmed that the Court had promised them a month's pay, with a free discharge, after they should have served three years; and when this was not accorded to them, they broke out into a mutiny, which was only subdued after concessions had been made. Three of the ringleaders were condemned to be shot, and on one—a Corporal Fake—the sentence was executed. The other two were pardoned by the President. Shaxton, the Officer in command, was suspected of abetting the revolt, and was accused of remissness in checking his men's insubordination. Fryer, who was on the spot at the time, thought that a foolish rivalry divided the civil or mercantile, and military branches of the service, and that Shaxton's real offence was similar to one which excited Romulus to commit fratricide, for that he had only mortified the Factors' vanity by treating their engineering efforts with contempt, and ridiculing some palisades with which they had fortified Bombay. Whatever the nature of his crime, he was obliged to give up his sword, and was placed in confinement. A Court of Judicature was then formed for his trial, in which a pompous attorney impeached him and compared him to Cataline. But the soldier defended himself with ability, and the Court decided that they could do nothing, but refer his case to the Court of Directors. He was therefore sent to England, where he died at the termination of his voyage.†

A few years later, retrenchments led to more alarming results, and ended in revolution. The great expense of placing Bombay in a posture of defence had, as before stated, been so inadequately met by the revenue, and the Company were becoming so burdened with debt, that they resorted to both the unhappy expedients of raising the taxation, and still further reducing their officers' pay. It was ordered that the annual expenses of the island should be limited to seven thousand pounds. The military establishment was to be reduced to two Lieutenants, two Ensigns, four Serjeants, four Corporals, and a hundred and eighty privates. No batta or extra allowance was to be paid, as before, to the detachment of thirty soldiers at Surat. The troop of horse was to be disbanded, and Keigwin, its Commandant, dismissed the service. The Government had no choice, but to comply with these impolitic orders. Keigwin went to England; but returned in 1681 with the rank of Captain-Lieutenant and Third in Council, which was the highest position to which for the future any military officer was to be capable of rising. With singular capriciousness, the order that he should have a seat in Council was revoked the following year,

* Letter from the Deputy Governor and Council to the Court; dated 24th January 1676-7. Orme's Fragments.

† Fryer, Letter iii. chapter iv., and Letter iv. chapter iii. Bruce's Annals, 1675-79.

and it was mentioned that his pay was to be only six shillings a day. As the Company's public table had been discontinued, he applied also for subsistence money, and, after much altercation with the Deputy Governor, was allowed twenty-five rupees a month, subject to the Court's approval. This approval was withheld, and Keigwin ordered to repay the extra allowance which he had received. Thus the minds of their troops and ablest officers were embittered against the Company. They disgusted the natives also by levying a duty of half a dollar upon all ships anchoring in the harbour, one rupee a-year on each fishing boat, and the same on each shopkeeper.* Lastly, with what in our times seems unparalleled meanness, they ordered that only one-half of their native labourers' wages should be paid in money, and the other half in rice, valued "at the Company's price," which was explained to mean such a price as would give ten per cent clear interest after all expenses had been defrayed.†

Keigwin had formerly been Governor of St. Helena, and was a disappointed and discontented man. At the same time he was distinguished for firmness and resolution, so that the Company were unwise as well as ungenerous in trifling with his feelings. He was now in command of the Garrison, and having received promises of support from Thorburn, Alderton and Fletcher, officers under his authority, he raised the standard of rebellion. All the troops, the inhabitants, and one at least of the Chaplains soon joined him.‡ Following Cromwell's example, he used his sovereign's name, when deliberately acting in opposition to all constituted authority, and in a proclamation, dated the twenty-seventh of December, declared that Bombay was subject only to the King of England.

Being chosen Governor by the unanimous voice of his followers, Keigwin held the reins with a strong hand, and successfully maintained order. He seized and confined Ward, the Deputy Governor, with such members of council as adhered to him. He also took possession of the Company's Ship *Return*, and the *Hunter* Frigate, which was commanded by Alderton, and had on board fifty or sixty thousand rupees for investment at Carwar. But he appropriated to himself none of the Company's treasure, and only applied for the expenses of Government the ordinary revenues, which he raised by such a judicious imposition of taxes, that his system was continued after the revolt was suppressed. In brief, during his enjoyment of power, he acted as honestly, wisely, and judiciously as any lawful Governor. The sole control of military affairs he reserved for himself; but permitted Thorburn to superintend the Civil departments.

In his relations with Native powers, Keigwin especially shewed prudence, and really benefited the Company. Sambhají had made some difficulty about confirming a treaty with the English, which his father Sivají had arranged; and he requested that Gary, whose shrewdness had established him in the Maráthá's favour, might be sent to confer with him.

* Bruce's Annals.

† Letter from the Court to the President and Council.

‡ There were ordinarily two Chaplains at Bombay, and one at Surat or Swally. Church, Polwhell, Badham, and Watson, are mentioned in the lists as Chaplains about this time. Yet a few years ago a Secretary to Government put on record that Mr. Cobbe (A. D. 1720) was the first Chaplain in Bombay. See a Report on the Landed Tenures of Bombay; by F. Warden, Esq.

Through this diplomatist, Keigwin induced Sambhají not only to permit the establishment of Factories at Caddalor and Thevenapatam, but also to grant the English exemption from duties in the Carnatic, and allow them twelve thousand pagodas, as compensation for losses sustained at places which the Maráthás had plundered. As for the Siddí, Keigwin repressed his insulting conduct with decision, and would neither suffer him to keep his fleet at Mazagám, nor even to come there except for water. Knowing these facts, we are the more inclined to believe a declaration, which he made in his own defence, to the effect that unless he had taken possession of Bombay, it would have been seized either by Sambhají or the Siddí, both of whom were anxious to gain a footing there, and each was jealous lest the other should anticipate him in its acquisition.*

In the meanwhile Sir John Child, now President of Surat, and his Council, found that as they had no troops, any attempt to force the rebels into submission would be hopeless. Yet they tried what threats would do, and when they had used these to no purpose, conciliatory measures had no better result. At first three Commissioners, Zinzan, Day, and Gosfright, were sent to Bombay. The President then went there himself, and reached the harbour on the thirty-first of January 1684, but he and his officers were no friends with any party, and were compelled to return without effecting their purpose. The crews of their ships could not be depended upon, and refused to act against the mutineers, so that they hastily despatched three vessels with valuable cargoes to England, and stationed two confidential persons at Khaneri and two at Versova, with directions to warn any ships which might appear in the offing that they were not to enter the harbour of Bombay, but sail at once to Swally.

When the intelligence reached England that Bombay had revolted, and the President had not been able to reduce it to order, the King commanded the Court of Directors to appoint a secret committee of inquiry. This was composed of their Governor,—as the chairman was then styled—Deputy Governor, Sir Benjamin Bathurst, Sir Jeremy Sambrooke, and Mr. Joseph Herne. Upon their report his Majesty sent a mandate under his sign manual to Keigwin, requiring him to deliver up the island, and offering a general pardon to all, except the ringleaders. That the President might have additional authority, he was declared Admiral and Captain General of the Company's sea and land forces. Sir Thomas Grantham, who had left in a sixty-gun ship before the revolt was known in England, was appointed Vice Admiral, and Captain Tyrrel was sent with the *Phœnix* Frigate to assist Grantham, and then to cruize against interlopers. It was further declared that if Keigwin and his followers offered any resistance, all should be denounced as rebels and traitors, that a reward of four thousand rupees should be paid to any one who would seize Keigwin, two thousand for seizing Alderton, and two thousand for Fletcher. Supposing it possible, however, that a general pardon might have been already proclaimed, it was decided that in that case the ringleaders should be kept under surveillance, and if guilty of any further treasonable acts, apprehended and executed.

* Grant Duff's History, vol. i. chapter x. Hamilton's Hindostan. Orme's Fragments. Orme only says that Keigwin recovered 2,600 pagodas from Sambhají.

Sir Thomas Grantham arrived at Bombay on the tenth of November 1684, and showed remarkable promptitude and courage by landing immediately without attendants. This coolness and confidence in the generosity of Englishmen made a due impression, and Keigwin having invited him to a conference, agreed to deliver up the Fort to him on the twelfth. A few dissentients raised a tumult on the following day, and even threatened his life, so that the island was not formally surrendered until the nineteenth, when Sir Thomas delivered it to three commissioners who had come from Surat—English, St. John, and Zinzan, afterwards Deputy Governor. Keigwin having obtained the promise of a free pardon for himself and adherents, took his departure as soon as possible for England, where he arrived in July 1685. Thorburn being a married man with a family, and having a small estate upon the island, was compelled to remain; but he believed that protection was secured for himself and property.

Such was a revolt which happily began and ended without bloodshed—if we except a wound inflicted at table by Thorburn on Keigwin in a drunken quarrel. Alarming as it was, and dangerous, to the existence of Anglo-Indian power, it forms an episode in our history, of which we are not ashamed. Keigwin emerges from the troubled sea of rebellion with a reputation for courage, honour, and administrative capacity. His crime of treason was in a measure atoned for by his moderation and shining qualities, and found some palliation in the provocation which he received, and which the President—as we infer from his subsequent conduct—must have aggravated. On the other hand, the clemency of the Crown and Company is worthy of all admiration, and leads us to ask, Where is the nation that can, like the English, vindicate the authority of its Government, bring down the haughty front of successful rebellion, and at the same time not suffer justice to inflict a single pang on mercy?

It is true that accounts differ as to the manner in which the terms of surrender were observed; but if it should be shewn that they were infringed, an imputation could not be cast upon the English Government, nor—save indirectly—upon the Company, but only upon their President. Writers who were favourable to the Company, simply state that they acted in good faith; their opponents accuse their servants of treachery, but with such obvious malice, that we suspect their veracity. Fletcher, who had joined the rebels, but whose conduct was, in other respects, unblemished, retained the command of his company. But Thorburn is said to have fallen a victim to Sir John Child's malignity, and there is every reason to believe that he was treated with singular harshness. It is possible that he was justly committed to prison, in consequence of his inability to satisfy the demands of his creditors; but when there, we are told, not a slave was permitted to attend upon him, nor his own wife to visit him. Hard treatment brought on a fever, and his life was in danger. The jailor conveyed this mournful intelligence to his wife, who hastened, together with her two small children, to the General's presence, and entreated that her husband might be provided with a medical attendant. The boon was denied, but she was permitted to share his sufferings. She soothed his pain one day and part of a night, after which he breathed his last. Shuddering humanity turns with distrust from the remainder of the narrative; and therefore we abridge it. On returning home she found the doors of her own house closed against her, and was obliged to take up her abode with her slaves and children in a small outhouse. Her relatives ventured to give her succour only at night, and by stealth. The widow of Thorburn was a proscribed outcast, till her beauty and sufferings attracted the love and compassion of an officer who commanded an East Indiaman, and imagined that he was independent of Sir John Child. He wedded her, and also her misfortunes. At the General's request he was deprived of his appointment. Grief soon put an end to his troubles and his life. The lady was again left a widow, with a thousand pounds of East India stock for the support of herself and family.

According to their own records, the Company intended that some who had shared in the late rebellion should be dealt with as severely as the terms of the treaty would permit. Their instructions to this effect were repeated. As for Watson, "that scandalous Chaplain at Bombay," as he is styled, they wanted words to express their detestation of his conduct. "Let him have no salary from us," they wrote, "from the time of his rebellion, nor any other officers there, as near as you can, without incurring a new hazard, until you are firmly settled in your Government. And let Mr. Watson know he is no more our servant; banish him the island; and let him take care to pay for his own passage home, and provide yourselves of another Chaplain for Bombay out of some of our ships, if you can meet with any so much to your satisfaction as you have at Surat in the room of Mr. Badham deceased."*

A few words regarding some minor Factories will bring this period of our history to a close.

In 1674 there was a Factory so far inland as Dharamgám in Khandesh—at least we conceive that place must be intended, although it is variously styled Dongong, Drongom, and Dorongom. It is described as a hundred and thirty coss from Surat, and the road to it passed through Sálér, and Mulér. There was also a route through Nandrabár, at which place a káfila with merchandize for the Company was plundered in January 1681 by a band of robbers, who are only said to have not been Maráthás, and probably were Bhils.†

On account of the pepper grown in the surrounding country, a small Factory containing eighteen persons had been established at Honáwar, but after a short time it came to a melancholy end. About the year 1670, the Chief procured a fine bull dog from the Captain of an English vessel which had come there to take in cargo. This animal when accompanying the Factors on an excursion seized a sacred cow in the neighbourhood of a Hindú temple, and killed her. Instigated by the Brahmans, the natives were resolved to revenge this injury to their prejudices, and in a fury of fanaticism murdered every Englishman. Some natives, more friendly than the rest, caused a large grave to be dug, and in it the eighteen

* Letters from the Court to the President and Council; dated February 1684, October 1684, and 17th January 1685. Bruce's Annals. Mill's History. Hamilton's "New Account, &c." Chapter xvii.

† Orme's Fragments.

victims were interred. The Chief of the Factory at Carwar sent a monumental stone, on which was engraved the story of their wretched fate. There the traveller read the names of John Best and seventeen other Englishmen, who, according to the epitaph, "were sacrificed to the fury of a mad priesthood, and an enraged mob."*

Another interference with native prejudices, accompanied this time by dishonesty, nearly led to the destruction also of the Factory at Carwar, and all its inmates. Two small vessels having arrived there from Surat to load with pepper, an English sailor from one of them stole and slaughtered a cow. A mob of Hindús was speedily collected, and being fired upon by the English Factors in self-defence, two children of rank were killed. The people then attacked and destroyed the carts on which the pepper was being conveyed to the sea shore. They were only restrained from further violence by the expectation of a battle between the Moguls and Maráthás, which fortunately kept them in a state of suspense and anxiety.†

The English possessed two small Factories named Rattera and Brinjan to the south of Ponáni; but they were afterwards abandoned when the Factory of Anjengo was established. Sterne has given Anjengo a place in the sentimental literature of England, and at this early period sentiment seemed to haunt its neighbourhood. It was in the country of the Rání of Attinga, to whom the English paid their court by sending an annual present. In 1685 this offering was conveyed to the princess by a young Englishman of remarkably prepossessing appearance. Sable royalty was smitten with his charms, and compelled to admit that she was under the influence of love. She offered the comely youth her hand, but he modestly declined so great an honour. However, he remained with her Highness a month or two, and then withdrew, laden with valuable testimonies of her affection.‡

* Hamilton's "New Account," Chapter xxiii.
† Bruce's Annals, 1684-85.
‡ Hamilton's "New Account," Chapter xxvi.

CHAPTER VII.

1685—1697.

CONTENTS.—Sir Josiah Child; his character and influence with the Company; new designs of the Court—Sir John Child; his early history; becomes General; his character discussed—Sir John Wyburn, Deputy Governor; his career and death—The Court prepares for war; recruit their forces; secrecy—Preliminary steps to war—Child's disinterestedness—The Company's policy discussed—Child begins to capture native ships—The Court's approval—Aurangzíb's anger—Factors imprisoned—Child insults the Siddí; his first misgivings—Desertion of the militia and of Europeans—The Siddí invades Bombay; his success—Child negotiates; his abject submission—The Siddí withdraws—Review of Child's proceedings—Child prosecutes Petit and Bourchier—His death—Bartholomew Harris, President—Vaux, Deputy Governor; his History: suspension and death—Hard times for interlopers—Seizure of three interloping vessels—Successful resistance and escape of others—European pirates; their settlements at Bab-el—mandel and Madagascar—Sawbridge's cruel fate—Captain Avory plunders native vessels—Fury of the mob at Surat—The Company's ships, the *Mocha* and *Josiah*, engaged in piracy—Native rovers—Fight with a Frigate—The Factors placed in irons—Sir John Goldesborough—Cook and Weldon, Deputy Governors—Annesley, President; his conduct and dismissal—Sir John Gayer, General.

IN order that the continuity of our history might not be interrupted, we have kept the President in the background. He shall now, however, hold that prominence to which he is fairly entitled.

Sir Josiah Child was Governor of the Company, and Chairman of the Court of Directors. He had become known in 1677 as the writer of a pamphlet against free trade, and being a man of large capacity, unwearied vigour in thought and action, prolonged experience in commercial affairs, and regardless of any moral principles which might stand in the way of his ambitious designs, he exercised over the other Directors an influence amounting to despotic power.*

Under his guidance the Company began for the first time to rush impetuously after political importance and power. The example of the Dutch, which Sir Thomas Roe had formerly warned them not to follow,

* Burnet gives this account of him:—"This summer Sir Josiah Child died; he was a man of great notions as to merchandize, which was his education, and in which he succeeded beyond any man of his time; he applied himself chiefly to the East India trade, which by his management was raised so high, that it drew much envy and jealousy both upon himself and upon the Company; he had a compass of knoweldge and apprehension beyond any merchant I ever knew; he was vain and covetous, and thought too cunning, though to me he seemed always sincere." History of his Own Times, Book vi.

now filled them with ambitious desires. That which he had raised as a beacon to caution them against danger, was now the light which attracted them. "The wise Dutch," they remarked, "took ten times more interest in administrative functions and military preparations than in the affairs of commerce." The Honorable Company must increase its revenues—that was their object. "'Tis that must make us a nation in India," they wrote. Without revenues they were merely, they said, "a great number of interlopers," and persons of little mark or consideration.*

Sir Josiah found in his brother an excellent agent to carry out these projects. John Child had lived between the ages of ten and eighteen years at Rájapúr under the charge of Goodshaw, his uncle. Having afterwards been the means of bringing this uncle's dishonesty to light, and thus getting him dismissed, he himself when not twenty-four years of age succeeded him as Superintendent of the Factory,† and in due course of time became President for the affairs of the East, and Governor of Bombay. He was usually addressed by the title of General. When in 1687 Bombay was made superior to all the Company's settlements in the East, his government was also styled a Regency in imitation of the Dutch and Portuguese, and that his dignity might be properly supported it was ordered that he should be attended by a body guard of fifty Grenadiers.‡

It is extremely difficult to form a correct opinion of his character. Bruce, the Company's annalist, will not admit a word to be said in his disparagement. No individual's name stands higher on the Company's records. There he only appears as deserving the highest honour. But witnesses on the other side maintain that he was a consummate villain. Raynal styles him "avaricious, turbulent and savage," and, apparently with justice, traces to his acts the calamities in which the English were involved. But probably Raynal's authority was Hamilton, who accuses him of fraud as well as excessive and wanton tyranny, and Hamilton was unduly biassed against him ; for he was one of those interlopers to whom the General was ever a bitter and uncompromising enemy.§

The truth of the matter seems to be this. Sir John was really anxious to promote the Company's interests, and as their policy was unprincipled, he was quite ready to make it his. They had become deeply involved in debt. They owed £281,250 to natives of Surat, and it had become inconvenient to discharge even the interest of such a sum. Instead therefore of following the old-fashioned way and paying, they were resolved to discover some other means of escaping from their obligations. The two Childs were the men to devise and execute such a plan. We do not see any ground for accusing Sir John Child of that selfishness and peculation in which many of the Company's servants indulged to their lasting disgrace. Not that he neglected his own interests, only he identified them with the Company's. He was a deceiver and oppressor for their sakes. His system of administration, as well as that of his brother the Chairman, was

* Bruce's Annals, 1666-1690.

† Hamilton's "New Account," chapter xx.

‡ Bruce's Annals. Letter from the Court to the President and Council of Surat, dated 6th May 1685.

§ In addition to Bruce, Hamilton, and Raynal, we read of him in Letters from the Court to the President and Council of Surat; dated May 1682, and 6th May 1685.

essentially dishonest. We may rejoice now that it met with just retribution, and that his backers in England were involved by it in temporary ruin. He is said indeed to have acted upon his brother's sole authority, without the sanction of other Directors. If that was the case, the Court deserved to suffer the losses which were in store for them, on account of a negligence and incapacity which in them amounted to actual crime.

As soon as the Directors heard that Keigwin's rebellion was suppressed, and their authority again acknowledged in Bombay, they sent Sir John Wyburn to be Deputy Governor, vice admiral, and second in Council, holding the rank of Lieutenant Colonel and Captain of the second Company of British infantry. His salary was fixed at a hundred pounds per annum, in addition to Captain's pay of eight shillings per diem, and an allowance for diet, which was to be only a hundred and fifty pounds per annum, when the Governor was on the island, but two hundred and fifty pounds during the Governor's absence. He owed his appointment to the favour of James the Second, who when Duke of York had been shipwrecked on his passage to Scotland, and rescued by him from a watery grave. For this service Wyburn was knighted, and although a political opponent he still preserved the monarch's regard. As neither he nor Zinzan was sufficiently submissive to the General, the Court ordered that both should be dismissed; but Wyburn did not live to hear of this disgrace. He died in 1688, much regretted.

The Directors were now prepared to assume the offensive in war, whenever a good opportunity should offer. They were puffed up with mistaken ideas of their power. The Company was but a child, and seeing a giant rather old and infirm squared its little fists, as though ready to fight him. The Court pompously announced that they were determined to levy war, not only on the Nawáb of Bengal, but in the sequel on the Emperor himself. Nor was that even sufficient to satisfy their pugnacity. They actually directed their General to seize the goods of the Kings of Siam, Bantam, and Jambi, as reparation for injuries received. And since the change of Government in England had left them nothing to fear from Priests or Jesuits, they also contemplated possessing themselves of the Portuguese territories, which were contiguous to Bombay. At the same time they ordered, that Bombay should be "as strong as money and art could make it," in order that they might have a fortress to serve as a basis of operations.

By way of increasing their military strength, the Court applied to the King for a Company of regular infantry, and one of the Marquis of Worcester's companies was ordered to be sent out under the command of Captain Clifton, the Adjutant, who was to have a salary of thirty pounds in addition to Captain's pay, and was to be junior member of Council. The star of the military was on the ascendant. All Captains of infantry were for the future to have seats in Council.

Yet the Court thought that they were proceeding with great caution, and used their utmost endeavours to keep their designs secret. Their General was the sole repository of their confidence, and greatly annoyed was he to find, that during his absence from Bombay, their despatches had been opened by Sir John Wyburn, and the contents made known to his Council. He feared at first that his measures might be prematurely brought to light; but hoped to prevent any ill effects by a continuance of that duplicity, for which he has been so greatly commended by the Directors and their apologists.

The preliminary steps which gradually led to the crisis were these. The Emperor Aurangzíb had been justly offended with some violent and piratical acts of English officers on the coast of Bengal, and his indignation was excited to the highest pitch when he heard that his Governor of Surat had been insulted by the English authorities. Child was in this case the real offender. Having long since made up his mind for war, he proposed to throw all the odium of it upon interlopers. He therefore maintained that these intruders had inflicted serious injury upon the Company, and that the native authorities were responsible for having aided and abetted them. Bruce admits that he "had determined to act on this principle." This was the pretext on which the question of peace or war was to hinge. Of the Governor of Surat, therefore, Child proceeded to make numerous demands, some of which were reasonable, others extravagant. As he must have anticipated, they were received with contempt, and then assuming that justice was on his side he waited until he had a fair opportunity of resorting to violence.

As the Mogul's ships had returned from Mocha and Bussora, for the season, he could not seize any of their property at sea, and therefore found it convenient to postpone a declaration of hostilities. In the meanwhile, with a disinterested zeal for the Company, which is deserving of some credit, he assured them that he would take all the responsibility of the war upon himself, so that if fortune shook her wings and left them, they might disclaim his measures, and thus find an opening for negotiations with their enemies.

And here let us venture to unfold the view which we think ought to be taken of these proceedings. The Company's conduct must be stigmatized as rash and disingenuous, impolitic and unjust; but some excuse for it may be found in the caprice and dishonesty of the native powers. It is a fact beyond dispute, and one which the natives of India should mark well, that *the moral as well as the physical weakness of the Indian nations first suggested to the Company their ideas of conquest.* When English trade had been fairly established, it was continually threatened with ruin by the caprices of a despot, the cupidity of his officers, or the lawless violence of regular armies and plundering tribes, scrambling for the pieces into which the empire was falling. The Company could place no dependence upon firmáns or grants, upon the friendly disposition of a native Governor, or the forbearance of any conquering horde. To-morrow the Mogul's necessities might drive him to annul the firmán, and impose upon them new and hard conditions, the friendly Governor might be withdrawn, and a new horde come with an unslaked thirst for rapine. Under these circumstances the Company felt that they could only place dependence on themselves. Where might was right, they must hasten to put in their claim, or consent to have it for ever disallowed. There is no doubt that if they could have reposed any faith in treaties, have believed the friendly assurances of natives, and have respected the word of an Indian potentate, they would have been content to live under his shadow. As it was, they found it necessary to create a power of their own, to build their hopes upon war and aggression.*

Resuming our narrative, we observe that on the second of May 1687, Child and his Council went to Bombay, leaving Harris as Agent at Surat. As so many English still remained at that place, the General thought it would be imprudent to act on the offensive near India, and therefore sent his two largest ships, the *Charles the Second* and *Modena*, to seize all Mogul or Siamese vessels which they might find at Mocha and Bussora. Two ships were also despatched to China with similar instructions. Piracy had been so profitable in the hands of private speculators, that the jealous Company now entered into the business.

It was hoped that the Factors might be removed from Surat, before intelligence of these transactions could reach there, and Capt. Wright was sent with the *Cæsar* to lie off the mouth of the river. His orders were to release the Agent and Factors by negotiation, if possible ; but in case that failed, and the aggressions in the Persian Gulf had been discovered, he was to seize all vessels belonging to the Mogul or King of Siam, and detain the principal persons found on board as hostages for the Factors' safety.

This cunning plot was disarranged by an alarm given to the authorities at Surat, in consequence of the commander of the *Dragon* having seized a vessel whilst on her passage from that port to Siam. No violence was yet offered to the Agent and Factors, but they were carefully watched. Child pretending that by this a fresh insult was offered to the English, took possession of all ships belonging to Surat which were then at Bombay. Upon this the Governor of Surat seemed disposed to make terms, and permitted Bonnell, one of the Factors, to visit Bombay with a complimentary note from him to the General, in which he expressed a desire to accommodate matters, and to know what arrangement would be considered satisfactory. He afterwards sent two merchants, to whom Child delivered a statement of grievances in thirty-nine articles.

That he might have at least one ally, the General then entered into a treaty with Sambhají, who agreed to give the English fifty thousand rupees, and two thousand candies of rice, on condition that they should protect the creeks and mouths of the rivers along the Western Coast.

At this time Captain Andrews, who commanded the *Charles the Second*, returned with one interloping and six Mogul ships as his prizes. Hostilities, therefore, could no longer be concealed, and Andrews was sent to act with the *Cæsar* at Surat in seizing all Mogul vessels, and watching the Siddí's fleet, or destroying it, if it should attempt to put to sea.

The appointment of a new Governor to Surat held out a faint hope that some pacific arrangement might yet be made. This functionary had been previously known as friendly disposed towards the English, and that he still continued so was inferred from the fact that he immediately opened a conference with the Agent, Harris.

It is worthy of note that at this stage of the proceedings the Court so

* Bruce's Annals, 1687-88.

highly approved of the ability and spirit with which Sir John Child had acted, that they resolved to present him with a thousand guineas.

The new Governor of Surat was not found so yielding and gentle as had been expected. On the contrary, his tone was threatening, and he soon began to treat the English as enemies. On the twenty-sixth of December 1688, he seized and imprisoned the Factors Harris and Gladman, ordered all the goods of the Company to be sold, and offered a large reward to any who would take Sir John Child, dead or alive. The General, who had up to this moment been trying to hold a mask before himself, now threw it aside altogether. Finding that all his efforts to release Harris and Gladman were fruitless, he took several richly freighted ships of native merchants, attacked a fleet laden with provisions for the Mogul army, and captured forty of their vessels.

Still this crafty ruler wrote to Aurangzíb, and professed that his intentions were pacific. But the Emperor was not now to be blinded by a little dust. He was exasperated in the highest degree, and sent an order for the confiscation of all property belonging to the English at Surat. The Factors were detained in prison, and at times made to gratify the mob by parading the streets with chains suspended from their necks. Although they were afterwards liberated from Jail, they were closely confined to their Factory until the seventeenth of October 1691. During the intervening years their condition was wretched in the extreme. In their letters they appeal piteously for relief, " which," say they, " we think our poor dejected spirits can't have more occasion for than at this juncture."*

Although Child had written courteously to the Emperor, he treated his Admiral, the Siddí, with arrogance, and told him plainly that if his fleet ventured to sea, he would assume that their intentions were hostile, and deal with them as enemies. At the same time he addressed a letter to the Court, in which he expressed his resolution to continue the war, and by no means to purchase a dishonorable peace. However, we now for the first time catch some glimpses of misgivings ; for he admitted that the Mogul's power had been increased by the conquest of Golconda and Bíjapúr, and his successes over Sambhají. For the first time also he seemed to think that aggression must find its limits. He thought it would be hazardous to provoke the Portuguese by attacking and occupying Salsette ; for the very good reason that he had not sufficient troops to defend Bombay. As for the militia, they had already began to desert, so soon as they apprehended an attack from the Siddí ; an example, we may add, which was followed by Europeans, and as he remarked, " the loss of one European was of more consequence to him than the death of one hundred blacks."

After a few convulsive struggles Child's pride received its death blow ; his blustering tones were silenced ; his turbulent spirit and trenchant energies crushed. Instead of attacking the Siddí, as he had threatened, and thus adopting the only measure which could have secured the safety of Bombay, he simply acted on the defensive. He tried to justify this vacillation by pleading the inactivity of the English Presidents in Bengal and Madras ; but

* Bruce's Annals. Hamilton's "New Account," chapter xix. Letters from the Chief at Surat ; October 1691.

they were in a predicament similar to his own. Although he once seemed to have drawn his sword and thrown away the scabbard, he now tried negotiations, and when he heard that a new Governor had arrived at Surat, fondly hoped that he should gain his point by a change of conduct, which his cunning enemies attributed to the true causes—irresolution and conscious weakness.

But it was too late. Child's arrogance, and his seizure of the provisions intended for the army of Yákút Khán, the Siddí, had made that officer a willing agent to execute the Emperor's wrath. With an unaccountable infatuation the English Governor had neglected to strengthen the fortifications of Bombay, although the Court of Directors had so urgently reminded him that this was necessary ; and on the fourteenth of February 1689, the Siddí landed at Sewri with twenty or twenty-five thousand men. Although there were several small vessels in the harbour, which might have prevented the disembarkation of his troops, no effort of the sort was made, and the soldiers of a redoubt where he landed, after firing a gun to give the alarm, retired with precipitation. At one o'clock in the morning three guns from the Castle apprized the inhabitants of their danger. Then might be seen European and Native women rushing with their children from their houses, and seeking a refuge within the Fort. Next morning the Siddí marched to Mazagám, where was a small fort mounting fourteen guns, which the English abandoned with such haste, that they left behind them eight or ten chests of treasure, besides arms and ammunition. Here the Siddí established his head quarters, and despatched a small force to take possession of Mahim Fort, which also was found to be deserted.

The following day the enemy advanced. The General ordered Captain Pean with two companies to drive them back ; but he and his little party were defeated. Thus the Siddí became master of the whole island, with the exception of the Castle, and a small tract extending about half a mile to the southward of it. He raised batteries on Dongarí Hill, and placed one within two hundred yards of the Fort. All persons on whom the English authorities could lay hands were pressed into their service, and amongst them Hamilton, who has given us details of these transactions. Thus passed the months from April to September.

During the monsoon the Siddí obtained supplies from the interior and from the Jesuits of Bandora, who paid a heavy reckoning for thus assisting the enemy, as at the close of the war their property was seized. Provisions were extremely scarce in the English quarters until the monsoon was over, but then the Company's cruizers being able to put to sea, were so successful in capturing vessels and supplies belonging to the Mogul's subjects that distress was alleviated. Still the danger was imminent. The Siddí's army was increased to forty thousand fighting men, and the English troops, which never amounted to more than two thousand five hundred, dared not venture to meet them in the field.

Under these circumstances Sir John Child saw that negotiation was his only resource, and soon he also discovered that nothing short of abject submission could appease the Emperor. He tried the effects of bribery upon the Imperial officers, and endeavoured to atone for his past insolence by submitting to the meanest degradation. He despatched two envoys, George Weldon and Abraham Navaar or Navarre a Jew, to Court, where they arrived in fifteen days. After being subjected to the indignity of having their hands tied behind them, they were permitted to prostrate themselves as culprits in the Emperor's presence. The great sovereign was puffed up with the pride of victory, having just taken Rerí, and seized Sambhají's family and treasure. He sternly reprimanded the envoys, but being fully aware how important it was for the welfare of his Empire that the English trade should be retained, and that his devout subjects should have the protection of their fleet, without which they would not venture on their pilgrimages,* he listened to their entreaties, and consented to an accommodation, on condition that all monies due from them to his subjects should be paid, that recompense should be made for such losses as the Moguls had sustained, and that the hateful Sir John Child should leave India before the expiration of nine months.

On these terms the Emperor granted the English a new firmán. The conditions which had been required by Sir John Child before the war were unnoticed, and the language of the document was more humiliating and contemptuous than any which had been addressed to the English from the first settlement of their Factory in India. The Company were treated, not as the subjects of an independent power, but as criminals, who having been mercifully pardoned, were again admitted to live in a state of slavery.†

Harris and the other Factors were released from prison on the fourth of April 1690 ; but the Siddí, who had already remained more than a year at Bombay, did not withdraw his army until the twenty-second of June, when the property captured by the English had been restored, and the fine paid to the Mogul. He then departed, having first set fire to the Fort of Mazagám, and the same day William and Mary were proclaimed in Bombay King and Queen of England. The Mogul troops left behind them a pestilence, which in four months destroyed more than had perished in the war, so that only thirty-five English soldiers were left on the island. No fewer than sixty Europeans had deserted to the Siddí, but all returned to their allegiance on receiving a promise of pardon.

* President Harris afterward said, that the real cause why the Mogul had granted peace was, that a free passage might be allowed to the Pilgrim Ships between Surat and Judda. Bruce's Annals, 1692-93.

† Translation of the firmán of Aurangzíb to the Company, dated February 27th 1689-90, " in the 33rd year of a most glorious reign."

" All the English having made a most humble submissive petition, that the crimes they have done may be pardoned, and requested another Phirmaund, to make their being forgiven manifest, and sent their Vakkeels to the heavenly palace, the most illustrious in the world, to get the royal favor ; and Ettimaund Caun, the Governor of Suratt's petition to the famous Court, equal to the skie, being arrived, that they would present the great King with a fine of 150,000 rupees, to his most noble treasury, resembling the sun, and would restore the merchants' goods they had taken away, to the owners of them, and would walk by the ancient customs of the port, and behave themselves for the future no more in such a shameful manner ; therefore his Majesty, according to his favor due to all the people of the world, hath pardoned their faults, mercifully forgiven them, and out of his princely condescension agrees, that the present be put into the treasury of the port, the merchants' goods be returned, the town flourish, and they follow their trade as in former time, and Mr. Child, who did the disgrace, be turned out and expelled. This order is irreversible." Bruce's Annals.

The Company are said to have lost four hundred and sixteen thousand pounds by this first throw in the game of war. And this was not all. Their interests suffered even more in England than in India. The British nation felt that a disgrace had been inflicted upon them, which they attributed to the Company's misconduct. Hence all those who hoped to get into the Indian market gained confidence. This Company, they argued, is clearly unfit to represent English interests in India ; try another Company. The public approved, and, what was more to the point, the House of Commons also approved the suggestion.

When these memorable transactions are reviewed, the reader should be requested to keep in mind that we have two contemporaneous authorities—the records of Government, and the narrative of Alexander Hamilton. For facts we have mainly relied upon the former, since we acknowledge their accuracy ; but yet we find our opinion coincide in many respects with the latter. According to the former, all the measures of Sir John Child were unexceptionable. The Court pronouced his conduct "faithful and honorable." They afforded him a consistent and unfailing support, which says much for their generosity and constancy, but also, we conceive, proves the obliquity of their moral vision. It must always be remembered that Child was fortunate in having a brother at head quarters, and living during times which did not encourage severe scrutiny into political delinquencies. Opposed to the Court's testimony in his favour is the condemnation of Hamilton, according to whom Child's actions were from first to last reprehensible. And without surrendering our judgment to this interloper's prejudices, we must yet maintain that the view taken by Government is, on their own showing, perverted and unreasonable.

It is admitted on all sides that the results of Child's measures were disastrous in the extreme. And although we are far from asserting that in political affairs failure always proves the incapacity of the agents, we yet think that in this case it was a necessary consequence of defects, both moral and intellectual.

For a mercantile Company which received but little support from the Crown, and was ten thousand miles distant from the scene of operations, to wage a war with an Emperor and several other princes at the same time, was *an error* ; for it to dissemble, and without issuing any declaration of war to seize ships belonging to the subjects of those princes, was *a crime.* Persons who professed to be honest traders became pirates. Consequently, they were both bad traders and bad pirates.

When Child had once violated natural law and incensed the Emperor, his hopes of success depended upon two measures, neither of which did he adopt. Bombay might easily have been made impregnable to native forces by strengthening the fortifications, and unassailable by destroying the Siddi's fleet. But Child neither made it one nor the other. Although warned that he must look to the walls and bastions, he neglected to do so; although he had threatened to destroy the Siddi's fleet, he permitted it to land an army on the island without let or hindrance.

Weldon, when afterwards he was Deputy Governor of Bombay, drew up an able report, in which he pointed out some of these errors. He himself was the first to propose that a wall should be built round the town, and he observed that if the fortifications had been stronger, the Siddí would never have invaded the island, or if he had been prevented from landing, a more favorable firmán might have been obtained. Weldon also gave it as his opinion that the entire subjugation of Bombay was prevented, not by the opposition of the English, but by the jealousy of Mukhtar Khán, who was afraid of the credit and influence which the Siddí would gain by its reduction.*

During Child's tenure of office there was as much discord at home as abroad. He brought charges before the Court against two members of Council, Petit and Bourchier, for alleged encouragement offered to interlopers. They were said to have held a correspondence with the Governor of Surat, and to have gained his favour by giving out that they were employed by a new Company, which would soon trade at Surat on a large capital, and pay customs without reserve. Child also accused them generally of malversation, but with such secrecy that they were only kept aware of his proceedings by the communications of vigilant friends in England. Suspecting that his representations would readily find credit with the Court, and that he would receive authority to seize their property, they had it privately removed from the Factory into a house, hired for the purpose. As soon as the ships had arrived from England, and the Directors' packet had been opened before the assembled Council, it was found to contain orders for the dismissal of the two gentlemen. They immediately withdrew from the board ; but Child sent an injunction that they should not be permitted to leave the Factory. The reply was, that they had already left, and the doors of their apartment were locked. He ordered that the locks should be wrenched, and their papers examined ; when to his mortification nothing but their beds and empty trunks was discovered. He then endeavoured to apprehend them ; but was unsuccessful in this also. They willingly severed their connexions with the Company, and embarked in trade on their own account, doing their utmost to injure the Factory, and representing to the native authorities that the King of England had transferred his protection from the old to a new Company.

The remaining history of these two men was eventful. Bourchier, fearing Child's revenge, endeavoured to procure a special firmán, which should place him under the Emperor's protection, and with that object visited Delhi. His application was not rejected, but compliance was delayed for fourteen months, when a drunken Englishman effected that in which sobriety and prudence had failed. Bourchier's interpreter, Swan, having been inspired with artificial courage by potations of arak, rushed towards Aurangzíb as he was taking his ride, and placing his petition on his head clamoured in the Persian language for justice. Attracted by his European garb, the Emperor invited him to make his complaint known ; on which Swan declared that his master desired to become a subject of the great monarch, that he might be freed from the English Company's intolerable oppression. The request was granted. The next day

* Bruce's Annals, 1687-1691. Grant Duff's History, vol i. chap. x. Hamilton's "New Account," chap. xix. Raynal, vol. i. Book iii. A Voyage to Suratt in the year 1689 ; by J. Ovington, M. A , Chaplain to His Majesty.

Bourchier obtained his firmân, and traded securely in defiance of Child and his myrmidons.

Poor Petit was not so fortunate. After his dismissal, he was a warm supporter of Keigwin, and engaged to supply the rebels with grain from Surat. He also visited them in his own vessels, and was welcomed as one of their most valued counsellors. But when trading in the Persian Gulf, his ship was assailed by pirates, and was blown up whilst he was bravely defending her. He was not killed on the spot, but in his haste to escape from the flames, jumped into the long boat, fell, and received such a severe blow on the head that concussion of the brain ensued. The pirates carried him to Gujarát, and as they in vain demanded a ransom for him, he there perished miserably on the twenty-second of October 1684. Sir John Child, when in an official letter announcing his death to the Governor of Surat, declared also that he had "gone to the devil"; but we may remain satisfied with knowing that on this head even the active President had no correct information.*

The above accounts may be relied upon as being confirmed by grave and accurate writers. Other imputations which Hamilton makes against Sir John Child in these affairs of fraud, cruelty, bribery, and subornation, of attempting to poison Bourchier, and persuading the pirates to treat Petit so harshly that he died under the effect of their barbarity—all these are so incredible, and so palpably set down in malice, that they claim no further notice at our hands.†

Sir John Child did not long survive the humiliation caused by an utter failure of his ambitious designs. He died on the fourth of February 1690, whilst the negotiations with the Emperor were pending. "The death of wolves is the safety of the sheep," and the removal of this obnoxious man much facilitated the restoration of the English to Aurangzíb's favour. He left behind him considerable wealth—some said at least a hundred thousand pounds. His widow afterwards married George Weldon, the Deputy Governor.‡

Bartholomew Harris succeeded as President of Surat and Governor of Bombay, the more imposing title of General being for the present discontinued.§ Harris had been one of the Factors who were placed in confinement, and, as it was contrary to the etiquette of the Imperial Court that any one who had been convicted of a capital offence should without special permission be honoured with marks of the Emperor's esteem, he was unable to attend in order that the usual firmán and official gifts might be presented to him. This duty therefore was delegated to the Deputy Governor. Harris was a man of feeble mind and indolent disposition, so that the management of affairs fell into the hands of Samuel Annesley, who himself succeeded in due time to the Presidentship.

Vaux was appointed Deputy Governor. He had formerly been book-

* The above expression is quoted by Hamilton from thirty-five printed articles of grievances forwarded by Sir John Child to the Governor of Surat. Hamilton represents Child's language as habitually gross and obscene.

† Hamilton's "New Account," chap. xvii. Bruce's Annals, 1683-84. Orme's Fragments.

‡ Hamilton's "New Account." Ovington's Voyage.

§ Bruce's Annals, 1690-91.

keeper for Sir Josiah Child in England, and, on account of his good behaviour, had been made by his master supercargo of a ship employed in the China trade, now beginning to be the most profitable of all the Company's speculations. Eventually he found his way to Bombay, where he was entertained as a Factor.

Dr. St. John not having been found sufficiently tractable and forward in persecuting private traders, Vaux was nominated Second Judge. St. John bitterly complained that a man ignorant of law, and utterly unqualified for the duties of the bench, was thus thrust into his office. But the excuse offered was, that it was intended the lawyer should devote himself exclusively to maritime cases. However, it is certain that Vaux also sat in judgment upon interlopers, and it is beyond a doubt that the two Childs hoped he would wage a war of extermination against them. To their great disappointment he did not prove such an unscrupulous agent as they wished.* He was perfectly willing to enforce *the law* with the utmost rigour, but he was so cautious as not to proceed further. 'What a timid fool,' thought his patron. In a letter which Hamilton read and copied, Sir Josiah pleasantly observed that the laws were "a heap of nonsense, compiled by a few ignorant country gentlemen"; but utterly unfit for the regulation of commerce and the guidance of the Honorable East India Company. 'My orders, Sir,' he wrote in other words, 'are to be your rules, and not the laws of England.'

In spite of his lingering regard for an antiquated code, Vaux was thought worthy of the Deputy Governorship. But after two years he was suspended from the Company's service, and remained unemployed until 1697, when he and his wife, whilst enjoying a sail on the Taptí, were upset and drowned. His tomb is still a landmark for ships as they approach the river's mouth to Surat.

It was a hard time for interlopers at the beginning of this period; but before the close of it they derived advantages from the political liberty with which England was blessed. The legal powers with which the Court of Admiralty at Bombay was vested, were sufficient to satisfy the most avaricious and cruel disposition. Interlopers could be seized as pirates, and when convicted, sentence of death was passed upon them. Execution of the sentence was indeed stayed until the King's pleasure could be known, but meanwhile the offender languished in imprisonment, and when at last pardoned by an exercise of the royal prerogative, his property having been already confiscated, he was reduced to beggary. Yet the Directors were still fearful that an appeal to a higher Court might gain him redress, and therefore sent out orders that when their Judge Advocate in India had passed sentence, there should be no inquiry into the legality of his proceedings.†

When the *Phœnix* frigate was on her passage from England, she captured three interloping vessels. One was a small craft which she discovered off the coast of Madagascar. Another was the *Bristol*, which Sir Thomas Grantham had seen at Surat, but did not think himself au-

* Bruce's Annals, 1685-86.

† Bruce's Annals, 1685-86. Mill's History. Hamilton's History of Hindostan, vol. i. page 232.

thorized to interfere with. She was now on her return voyage, and had put into Johanna for repairs. The Captain of the *Phœnix* made no scruple about seizing her; and the third day after she sank. Mewse, her supercargo, being tried in Bombay, was, in addition to the loss of his property, condemned by the General to pay a fine of a thousand pounds, and to be imprisoned until such time as the money should be forthcoming. However, on the remonstrance of Vaux, he was set at liberty, and the Company was afterwards compelled to pay in England sixty thousand pounds to the owners of the two vessels. The third, the *Little Betty*, belonged to a Quaker, named Hastewell, whose spirited conduct obtained him satisfaction. He arrested Tyrrel, the commander of the Frigate, as he was leaving the Exchange, and, although that officer claimed King James' protection, the resolute Quaker recovered twelve thousand pounds, which were much more than the value of the vessel and cargo.*

At one time the Court wrote out to their President that they had resolved to prosecute forty-eight of the principal interlopers; at another they ordered him to dismiss any of their servants who should be convicted of corresponding with such persons.† However, their desire to do mischief generally exceeded their ability. When the *Success*, private trader, arrived at Surat, the President ordered the Captain of the *Benjamin* to attack her, but his crew positively refused to fight in such a cause. The Commander of the interloper traded as he pleased, and all that his enemy could do was, to express his chagrin to the Court, and request the Dutch Governor of the Cape of Good Hope to do for him what he could not do for himself, and detain the *Success* on her homeward passage.‡ Another attempt to interfere with a certain Captain White failed still more signally. Having in vain begged the Governor of Surat to prevent this interloper from trading, the President offered to grant him permission on certain conditions, which he specified; but this offer was rejected. The conclusion was amusing. White attained his object and sailed away, when the Governor, fearing that he might after all be a pirate, actually compelled the President to become security for his good behaviour. At last the Company's applications in England to have the voyages of free traders stopped, were decisively negatived.§

It may be pleaded in extenuation of the active malice with which the Company's servants persecuted interlopers, that it was often impossible to distinguish private and honest traders from pirates. Great numbers of adventurers had been attracted from all countries to the Indian coasts, and some resorted to robbery on the high seas, as a more expeditious way of making money than ordinary commerce. Such reckless Captains created a terrible sensation. Native piracy, with its hole and corner business, was completely eclipsed. Instead of small boats from Málabár and Sind, which took by surprise boats smaller than themselves, there were now in the Indian seas stately vessels with tiers of guns, and manned by the stout seamen of Europe. These without any resistance pillaged native craft, and often treated the crews with great barbarity, whilst for all such acts the Company were held responsible. It is not easy to see how the

* Hamilton's "New Account," chap. xvii. and xviii.
† Bruce's Annals, 1691-92.
‡ Bruce's Annals, 1692-93.
§ Ib. 1694-95.

distinction between these pirates and independent traders could be always determined. Both were acting illegally, and to attack both was not only the Company's interest, but was generally required of them by the Mogul as a condition on which he extended to them his protection.

A few examples will serve to illustrate the truth of these remarks. The mouth of the Red Sea was infested by European pirates. At first they attempted to command its entrance, by building regular fortifications on the island of Prim, near the straits of Bab-el-Mandel, where they found a good and convenient bay for their shipping. But the difficulty here was, to obtain water. After digging through fifteen fathoms of hard rock, they only came to such as was brackish. They therefore abandoned Prim, and removed to St. Mary's Island, at the East of Madagascar. Finally they settled on the main island, and intermarried with families of the native chiefs. Their cruizing ground was in the Indian seas. In 1696 a ship which was conveying Arabian horses from Bombay to Surat was seized by them, and when the commander, named Sawbridge, pertinaciously expostulated with them, they sewed his lips together with a sail-maker's needle and twine. For several hours he was thus kept, his hands being fastened behind him. They then plundered his ship, burned her and the horses, and set Sawbridge and his crew ashore near Aden, where he expired.

The most notorious of the rovers was Captain Avory, who, although a most daring robber, had not like others a character for brutal ferocity. Having fitted out in the West Indies a ship called the *Fanny*, mounting forty-six guns, and manned by a hundred and thirty sailors, fifty-two of whom were French, and the rest Danes, English, Scotch and Irish, he spread terror amongst the native seamen and merchants of Surat. From one large ship he obtained in 1695 booty valued at three hundred and twenty-five thousand pounds sterling, and a young Mohammedan lady, who was returning from Mecca. He was satisfied with securing these prizes, and did not, as formerly was done, torture, or in any way injure the crew, but allowed the vessel to proceed on her voyage. Great was the commotion when she reached Surat. The populace was in arms, and the Governor was compelled to place a guard over the Factory, lest it should be plundered, and the inhabitants massacred.

At length matters were brought to a crisis. In 1696 Avory seized and plundered the *Ganjsavái*, the largest of the Mogul ships, as she was on her passage from Surat to Mocha with pilgrims. This was sacrilege. Popular resentment was carried to the highest pitch of fury, and the Governor was compelled to act decisively. The English President, Vaux, and others, amounting to fifty-three Englishmen at Surat, and ten at Swally, together with the Factors at Baroch, were all placed in irons and imprisoned. Afterwards they were confined within the walls of the Factory.*

The following year pirates, sailing under British colours, plundered, burned, and sank three English vessels.† Avory at last gained such

* Hamilton's "New Account," chapters v. xiii. and xix. Bruce's Annals, 1695-97, Grant Duff's History, chap. xi.

† Letter from the President and Council of Surat; dated 10th April 1697.

celebrity for enterprize and audacity, that the Lord Justices of England offered a reward of five hundred pounds for his apprehension, and the Company an additional four thousand rupees. Yet he seems to have escaped with impunity. After enriching himself and his crew in the Indian seas he sailed to the island of Providence in the Bahamas, where he sold his ship and dispersed the crew. Two of his followers being afterwards seized in Ireland, one at Rochester and others elsewhere, five of them were executed.

Little able as the natives were to defend themselves at sea, the risks of piracy were so trifling, and the prizes so rich, that it became more and more tempting. The Company's sailors soon began to discover that robbery was more lucrative than honest labour. Mutinous tendencies manifested themselves, and as the power of their officers to inflict punishment was but ill-defined, their disorders were not suppressed with sufficient promptitude. On the *Mocha* Frigate, the sailors openly made several complaints against Edgecomb, their Captain; but on this occasion Sir John Gayer acted with undue severity, and compelled them to sail for China before they had obtained redress. The consequence was, that they mutinied, shot their Captain in his cabin, turned pirates, induced the crew of the *Josiah* ketch to join them, and infested the straits of Malacca. They attacked the *Dorrel* as she was on her voyage to China, but Hide, her Commander, defended his ship so well, that although he lost sixteen men, he succeeded in beating them off. So disabled, however, were his ship and crew that he was obliged to end his voyage at Malacca. The President chose to attribute these mutinies to the intrigues of interlopers, but he was himself blamed for turning a deaf ear to the seamen's grievances. Whatever were the causes at work, a spirit of disaffection was so widely spread, that the Commanders of vessels feared even to send a boat's crew away, lest they should desert and take to buccaneering.*

The native rovers also were more numerous and bold than they had ever been before. So many of them were prowling about Swally, that the Captains of English vessels would not venture to land their cargoes, except under the protection of a guard. One of their small vessels, with eight guns, attacked the *Phœnix* Frigate, with forty-two guns, whilst she was on her voyage to Surat. The pirates supposed that she was a merchant ship, and did not discover their error until it was too late to sheer off. The Frigate's great guns soon sank their frail bark; but the desperate fellows refused quarter, and only about seventy were taken prisoners, whilst swimming for their lives. Sir George Byng, afterwards Viscount Torrington, who destroyed a Spanish fleet off Cape Passaro, was Lieutenant on board the *Phœnix*, and received a dangerous wound.†

We left the President and Factors under durance in consequence of the injuries which Avory had inflicted on the merchants of Surat. A native envoy, whom they despatched to the Mogul Court, with a message soliciting their release, found that Sir John Child's seizure of vessels was fresh in the remembrance of the Emperor's officers, and the late piracies had

* Bruce's Annals, 1696-97. Hamilton's "New Account," chap. xix.

† A relation of three years' sufferings of Robert Everard; Churchill's Voyages. Hamilton's "New Account," chap. xii.

revived their hatred of Englishmen. In spite of many protestations, an order was issued prohibiting Europeans from hoisting flags on their ships, wearing arms, or using palanquins. On the arrival of a report that another ship had been seized, all the Factors, except the President, two of the Council, and Captain Brown, were once more confined in irons. The order for their entire release and the restoration of the Company's property at Surat and its subordinate Factories did not arrive until the twenty-seventh of June 1696. Even then restrictions upon trade remained.*

In 1692 Captain, afterwards Sir John Goldesborough, was appointed Commissary General, and supervisor of all the Company's affairs in India, with power to dismiss all servants whom he should find after examination to be neglecting their masters' interests; and the next year he was made General. He died in January 1694, and having been in power so short a time he scarcely interfered at all with the affairs of Western India; we only find him calling President Annesley to account for not living within the walls of the Factory.†

On the dismissal of Vaux, Cook had been appointed by the Court Deputy Governor of Bombay, and as his death occurred the same season, Weldon succeeded him. Samuel Annesley was appointed President of Surat. One of his acts exhibited him as a man of singular meanness. It appears that the owners of native vessels being aware of Englishmen's courage and skill in the art of navigation, employed many of them as Commanders, and paid them salaries which in those days were considered handsome. Masters received from ten to fifteen, and mates from six to nine pounds *per mensem*, besides the privilege of carrying a certain quantity of merchandize without paying freight. Annesley insisted that a portion of such salaries should be considered his fee. Those who had no other resource complied with this unreasonable demand, and others who refused were ruined by his contrivance. Some of the latter joined the pirates, and all in revenge endeavoured to fill the minds of natives with contemptuous notions of the Company's servants. It may here be mentioned that in 1700 Annesley was dismissed the service by order of the Court, for breach of trust and fraudulent contracts made with native brokers. He was succeeded in the Presidentship by Stephen Colt.

In 1694 Sir John Gayer, Knight, arrived to be Governor of Bombay with the revived title of General. He was a man of good character and respectable abilities, but, as we shall see, his period of office was clouded with calamities and disgraceful rivalries. Some of his acts have been justly censured, and we shall find him shewing singular weakness in suffering himself and his wife to be made prisoner by the Governor of Surat. We must not anticipate events, but may simply remark that this negligence appeared at the time so impolitic and injurious to the Company's interests, that many attributed it, for those reasons alone, to some secret and mercenary motive.‡

* Bruce's Annals, 1695-97.

† Bruce, 1692-94. Letter from His Excellency Sir John Goldesborough to the President of Surat; dated 13th June 1693.

‡ Bruce, 1696-99. Hamilton's "New Account," chap. xix.

CHAPTER VIII.

1685—1697.

CONTENTS.—Ovington; his account of the Factory and Factors. The Company borrow of their servants. New regulations for Bombay. Low state of the revenues and garrison. Burdens on trade. Increasing ravages of disease. Everard; his visit to Bombay; adventures and sufferings. Manners of the English; their diet; dissolute morals; character given of the ladies. Sir John Gayer's ward; her first and second marriages; seduction. The Court attempts to check vice. Taverns, Poisoning, Consumption of spirits. The military; Captain Carr. Religion; special form of prayer; Divine Service. A Chaplain refuses to marry. Conversions to Romanism; Lieutenant Finch; persecution of a Priest. Reasons for this intolerance; treachery of the Jesuits. Punishment of the Portuguese. Newton's apostacy. Unsettled state of the country. Minor Factories; Amoy, Siam, Anjengo, Baroch. Sporting at Carwar. Young Goring and Lembourg. Dutch intrigues. Ships captured by the French. Spirited conduct of the Court. Armenians.

OVINGTON, a Chaplain in the Royal Navy who left England in 1689, and remained for several years on the coasts of India, has left us an account which shews that men and manners were changing, though not improving, with the times. He made particular inquiries into all matters connected with the Factory—or, as he calls it, the Lodge—at Surat, and we will give the result of them, as far as they can be interesting to the reader.

The building was held of the Emperor at a rent of sixty pounds a-year; but his Majesty was a liberal landlord, and expended nearly all this money in repairs. About forty Europeans resided within the walls.

The President was allowed three hundred pounds a-year, and as the prohibition against private trade had been cancelled, he and the other chief Factors could accumulate considerable wealth in a few years. Their profits were enormous, frequently amounting to fifty per cent; so that they could afford to commence business on a borrowed capital, for which they paid Banyás at the rate of twenty-five per cent. The council was composed of an Accountant, Storekeeper, and Purser Marine, in addition to the President, who had a double vote. After these ranked the Secretary, who usually succeeded to the first vacancy in Council; but it was tacitly regarded amongst the Factors as a rule of courtesy that the Chaplain should rank as third in the Factory.

All salaries were paid half yearly.* The second in Council received a hundred and twenty pounds a year; the Chaplain, as formerly, a hundred

* Ovington says annually; but the Accountant's charges in the Records shew that he was mistaken.

pounds, Senior Factors forty pounds, Junior Factors fifteen pounds, and Writers seven pounds. Forty or fifty peons were in attendance for general purposes, besides that several others were appointed specially to wait upon the President and each of the Factors. These men received monthly four rupees each, and their haváldár or serjeant six rupees. They were said to be remarkably honest; so much so, that not one had been accused of theft in the course of many years. At the gate of the Factory was a Porter, whose duty it was to see that no suspicious persons entered, and that the Writers and others were within walls at proper hours. Attached to the Factory were native brokers, who were allowed a commission of three per cent on all sales and purchases.

All Europeans dined at the public table, where they took their places according to seniority. The dinner service was sumptuous—all the dishes, plates, and drinking cups, being of massive and pure silver—and the provisions were of the best quality. Arak and wine from Shiraz were ordinarily drunk at table. There were an English, a Portuguese, and an Indian cook, so that every palate might be suited. Before and after meals a peon attended with a silver basin and ewer, which he offered to each person at table that he might pour water over his hands. On Sundays and a few other days high festival was kept. The choicest of European and Persian wines were then introduced.

On these festivals the Factors often accompanied the President, at his invitation, to a Garden which was kept for recreation and amusement. At such times they formed a procession. The President and his lady were borne in palanquins. Before him were carried two large banners, and gaily caparisoned horses of Arabian or Persian breed were led, their saddles being of richly embroidered velvet; their head-stalls, reins, and cruppers mounted with solid and wrought silver. The Council followed in coaches drawn by oxen, and the other Factors in country carts or on horses kept at the Company's expense.

There was a singular combination of pride and meanness displayed in the Factors' mode of life. None of them—not even the Chaplain—moved out of the walls of the city without being attended by four or five peons. At the Hindú feast of the Diválí, Banyás always offered presents to the President, Members of Council, Chaplain, Surgeon and others. To the young Factors these gifts were of great importance, as by selling them again, they were enabled to procure their annual supply of new clothes.

This was beggarly enough, but not so low as another practice which was in favour with these young gentlemen, as they were now styled in courtesy. They had a clever way of enjoying practical jokes, and at the same time indulging their mercenary propensities. One of them would enter the premises of a Banyá and pretend that he was shooting doves or sparrows. The horrified believer in metempsychosis would then come out, earnestly implore him to desist, and even offer him " ready money." He " drops in his hand a roupie or two to be gone," says the narrator. There, reader, is a picture of the representatives of a high-minded nation drawn by one of themselves. Poor Civilians! At least in your case necessity was the mother of invention.

In addition to their salaries, the Chaplain and Surgeon received fees for their services, and at Christmas both were accustomed to share "the President's bounty." The Chaplain was allowed his diet, lodgings, attendants, and he had at his disposal a coach or horse. With all these perquisites his income was raised to a considerable amount.* All were enjoined to treat him with great deference and respect. His duties on Sundays were to read prayers three times, and preach once; on other days to read prayers at six in the morning and eight in the evening in a room set apart for the purpose and "decently embellished." He was also required to catechize the lads of the Factory, to visit occasionally the subordinate Factories, and take care that Divine service was properly celebrated in his absence. As the Dutch were without a Chaplain, he was invited by them to baptize their children.†

Although the finances of the Factory were in an embarrassed state, the separate members seem to have been at no time more flourishing. The consequence was, that the Company were reduced to borrow money from their servants. The public debt amounted to twenty lakhs of rupees, and so much were the remittances from England below the sum required for investment, that it was necessary to raise a portion in India. The Company's credit was so low that they could not obtain a further loan of one lakh and eighty thousand rupees without drawing on the private funds of their Factors.‡

The Company, although thwarted for a time, yet steadily kept in view their object of raising an independent power in India, and on that account continued anxious to increase the commercial importance of Bombay. They ordered that regular markets for provisions should be established there, a dry dock built, and a duty of a dollar per ton levied on every ship which should be surveyed or repaired in it; that large quantities of iron should be sent out for building and repairing vessels; that a pier be constructed, and fixed rates charged for landing and shipping goods; that a progressive duty, varying from one shilling to two shillings and sixpence, be levied on every house; that all English inhabitants, not in the Company's service, be liable to pay duty for consulage; that a Post Office and an Insurance Office be established, and all the fortifications strengthened.

The uncultivated lands of the island had been divided amongst "a number of black soldiers" on condition that they should cultivate them and give half their produce to Government. These men had been engaged for military operations during the war, and it was thought that it would be imprudent to dismiss them. In order that the force of acclimatized Europeans might be strengthened, all such as were in the service of native powers were recalled to Bombay, "one seasoned man being worth two fresh ones."§

However, the Company's ability fell far short of their desire to repair the losses which they had suffered. When Sir John Gayer came to Bombay in 1694, he found the Government and trade in a most depressed

* On looking over copies of the remittance lists, I find that the Chaplains frequently remitted the whole of their salaries to England. How much more I cannot say.

† Ovington.

‡ Mill's History, Book i. chapter 5.

§ Bruce's Annals, 1688-91.

condition. The revenues had fallen from sixty-two thousand five hundred to seventeen thousand xeraphims, chiefly because the palm trees, from which a large portion was derived, had been neglected. The Garrison included sepoys, and only a hundred English, Dutch and French soldiers, who could scarcely overawe the inhabitants, exasperated as they were by the harsh treatment which some of their countrymen had received from English pirates. The Court supposed that they could fill up the ranks with Armenians, and "Madagascar blacks," but found that such were not to be had. All Gayer's efforts to keep the Garrison in an efficient state were futile. He increased it, but was soon compelled from lack of funds to disband three hundred and forty Gentoos, and sixty Christians, so that the native troops were reduced to seven Subedárs and four hundred rank and file. In 1697 they had no more than twenty-seven European soldiers.*

At the same time trade was oppressed with such heavy burdens that it could scarcely advance at all. For all goods exported from Bombay to the Mogul's dominions the Company themselves charged five per cent; a further duty of eight per cent was then demanded by the Portuguese at Thána, and arbitrary exactions were made by the Mogul Governor at Kalyán.†

The climate, instead of improving, grew more pestilential. Year by year the tragic story of disease and death is of heightening interest. The sword also had done its work, and so much were the constitutions of Europeans undermined by the deleterious air, that slight wounds were healed with difficulty, and severe wounds were usually mortal. The number diminished with a rapidity truly alarming. Of seven or eight hundred Europeans, who inhabited Bombay before the war, not more than sixty were left. There were but three civilians to carry on the Company's business, and it became necessary to close the Courts of Admiralty and Common Law. Children suffered equally with those who had reached maturity. Not one child in twenty survived the days of infancy. One of the pleasantest spots in India seemed no more than a garish graveyard. Such as remained in it murmured against their hard fate, and against the Company who would not listen to their request for permission to escape.‡

In addition to causes before stated the water of the island was now supposed to be unwholesome. Provisions too were scarce and bad. As the land produced little but cocoa-nuts and toddy, corn and cattle, usually of inferior quality, were imported. A sheep or two from Surat was the most acceptable present that could be offered to the Governor himself. Ovington tried to crack a melancholy joke on this pitiable state of things, and remarked that as some islands of the West were called Fortunate on account of their pure air and genial climate, "so the moderns may, in opposition to them, denominate this the unfortunate one in the East, because of the antipathy it bears to those two qualities." "It is certainly a mortal enemy to the lives of Europeans." Of twenty-four passengers who arrived with him in Bombay at the commencement of the rains, twenty, and fifteen of the ship's company, perished before the rains

* Bruce's Annals, 1694-97. † Bruce's Annals, 1697-98.

‡ Bruce's Annals, 1691-92. Ovington. Hamilton's "New Account," chap. xix. Hamilton's Hindostan, vol. ii.

had ceased. He declared that none would have escaped if they had remained till the end of October. The strictest temperance was of no avail. When they left the harbour neither the Commander nor himself had reason to hope that either would survive many days ; but contrary to all expectation, they were restored to health before they had sailed half way to Surat. Under such circumstances we are not surprised that when this reverend gentleman was invited by George Cook, the Deputy Governor, to become Chaplain of the place, he at once declined. He writes as if he would give the reader a nod and wink in approval of his own sagacity, adding, that one minister had been buried only a fortnight before, and three or four more in as many of the preceding years. It was a current proverb here, that "Two mussoons are the age of a man." Yet at Surat the health of Europeans suffered little. Not one Englishman was attacked by the plague in that place, at a time when three hundred natives were dying there each day. Such is Ovington's account.

Another writer who visited Bombay about the same time is not so well known, but his narrative deserves notice, not only from his allusions to Bombay, but as shewing the habits of English seamen and the dangers of a voyage to India. Robert Everard was merely an apprentice on board the ship *Bauden* which arrived in the Indian seas during the year 1686. The Captain was running into Versova supposing that it was the harbour of Bombay, and he only discovered his error when the Portuguese hoisted their national colours. As he was leaving Versova, the pilot ran his ship ashore, and again when entering the harbour of Bombay they struck upon the rocks. In both instances they escaped with difficulty. When in the harbour the mate and gunner having been tried and found guilty of disorderly conduct, were sentenced to a singular punishment. They were taken from ship to ship, and on each they received ten lashes. On their own ship they received twenty lashes. They were then taken ashore, and after the infliction of ten lashes under the wall of the fort, were discharged. When the *Bauden* had left India, she was treacherously attacked near the coast of Madagascar by the natives of Assada, who murdered the Captain, Mate, Purser, and many others of the crew. Everard himself was taken prisoner and kept in slavery for three years, during part of which time he endured great suffering. When he had regained his liberty, he visited Bombay a second time in another Indiaman. A widow lady came on board with a view of merely taking her passage to Surat, but during the short voyage the Captain made such good use of his time that he gained her heart, and when they arrived there, they were married amidst great rejoicing. Before they left Surat some Captains of other vessels and the gentlemen of the Factory came on board and held a carousal, firing guns and drinking healths. Being told of Everard's sufferings when in captivity, their hearts were moved to pity, and they made up for him a purse of fifteen rupees. On their return to Bombay the Captain engaged sailors at the rate of fifty shillings a head, and three pounds a month for wages. It is worthy of remark that the Lord's Day was scrupulously observed on board the ship in which Everard sailed, and the merchants refused on that day to employ themselves in traffic.*

* Everard's relation.

We may glean a little here and there regarding the manners of the English in this generation. Their diet appears at present in some respects singular even to their countrymen. Tea was drank in great quantities. Amongst the Dutch the tea pot, we are told, was seldom off the fire. The English do not seem to have usually taken it with sugar and milk, although sugar candy was occasionally dissolved in it. But it was more frequently drunk with hot spices, or "by the more curious with small conserved lemons." Khicharí, a mixture of rice and split pulse, was an ordinary article of food. In consequence of the scarcity of flesh meat, European sailors were required to fast one or two days in the week, just as good Churchmen were in England by the writers of the Homilies, in order that the Fisheries might not be ruined. On these days hungry tars were only permitted to eat khicharí; so, because they then conformed to the habits of Hindús, they called them "Banian days."

Immorality and dissoluteness were of the deepest dye, and added force to the assaults of the unhealthy climate. One who had been an eye-witness said after he had left Bombay, "I cannot without horror mention to what a pitch all vicious enormities were grown in this place. Their principles of action, and the consequent evil practices of the English, forwarded their miseries, and contributed to fill the air with those pestilential vapours that seized their vitals, and speeded their hasty passage to the other world. Luxury, immodesty, and a prostitute dissolution of manners, found still new matter to work upon." All kinds of vice were in the superlative degree, and the most detestable sins were indulged in to an almost unlimited extent.

Nor were individuals of the gentler sex such as could soften the hearts and elevate the minds of their husbands. "The Indian market" for ladies is now but an historical tradition; but at the close of the seventeenth century it was beginning to be a fact and reality. Women avowedly went there to gain husbands. The article when thus imported was finished in the most approved style; but as savages attach most value to beads and looking glasses, so the Factors did not look for solid acquirements or even accomplishments in their brides. "A modish garb and mien," we are assured, were all that was required, and if a lady could display these, she soon obtained the hand of some rich merchant.

One at least of these marriages *à la mode* turned out unhappily, and caused no little scandal to the virtuous part of the community. A young lady, daughter of Ward, the late Deputy Governor, and niece of Sir John Child, was residing on the island, and as she had no surviving relatives and a fortune of three thousand pounds, Sir John Gayer looked upon her as his peculiar charge. Not wishing that the family should lose such a prize, he intended that she should marry his son; but one day discovered to his great annoyance that she had been united clandestinely to Solomon Lloyd, a Factor. However, the will of a Governor had more of law in those days than at present, and no marriage was considered valid unless his consent had been previously obtained. In this case Sir John, without the least hesitation, transferred the dowried lady to his son. This was bad enough; but the worst part of the story remains to be told. On the principle of the French adage, that if a woman cannot get the man she loves, she must love the man she can get, the lady might have lived as a faithful and affectionate wife, if her husband had not been called away to China. But then she began to think of defects in her education, and proposed to employ her lonely hours in learning to write correctly. A schoolmaster, named Coleman, was engaged for the purpose, and taking advantage of his position, he communicated to her also lessons in unlawful love. A watchful mother-in-law discovered the intrigue; the wicked pedagogue was sent in chains to England, and all hopes of connubial bliss for Sir John Gayer's son and daughter-in-law were destroyed.*

It must be admitted that the Company did all in their power to arrest the progress of vice at Bombay, but as the English nation was in the midst of an iniquitous career, to which the first impulse had been given by that mean debauchee, miscalled "the merrie monarch," and his Court, it was not to be expected that a warning voice from London would gain respectful attention in India.† Yet the Directors did what they could and wrote thus:—"The Governor, Deputy Governor, and committees of the East India Company, having been informed of the disorderly and unchristian conversation of some of their Factors and servants in the parts of India, tending to the dishonour of God, the discredit of our Lord Jesus Christ, and the shame and scandal of the English nation," make certain regulations with a view to render "the religion we profess amiable in the sight of those heathens among whom they reside." Then follow directions for religious observances. The agents and chiefs of the several Factories were also strictly enjoined "to prevent all profane swearing, and taking the name of God in vain by cursed oaths; all drunkenness and intemperance, all fornication, and uncleanness." If any persisted in committing these sins, they were to be punished, and, if found incorrigible, sent to England.‡

Small as were the number of Europeans, taverns and grog shops were already established for them. We find from official papers that on the thirteenth of August 1694 John Wright applied for and gained permission to keep a tavern in Bombay. The prices of wines and spirituous liquors were then fixed by the Governor in Council. For a bottle of sherry two xeraphims were to be charged, and two lareens for a bottle of punch containing two quarts. An instance of the minutiæ to which legislation descended at that time is an order that, "if any man comes into a victualling house to drink punch, he may demand one quart of good Goa arak, half a pound of sugar, and half a pint of good lime water, and make his own punch. And if the bowle be not marked with the clerk of the market's seale, then the bowle may be freely broken without paying anything either for bowle or punch."§

Cases of poisoning were said to be frequent at these taverns. The rude

* Hamilton's "New Account."

† Burnet, who does not ordinarily make his statements in a few words, yet sums up his account of manners in England after the Revolution, concisely, thus:—"Upon the whole matter, the nation was falling under such a general corruption, both as to morals and principles, and that was so much spread among all sorts of people, that it gave us great apprehension of heavy judgments from Heaven." History of his Own Times, Book v.

‡ Ovington.

§ Order Book of the Bombay Government, 13th August 1694.

manners of British seamen led them to use a freedom with the dark ladies who frequented such places, for which they occasionally paid the penalty of their lives. A rough kiss given when a tar was under the excitement of liquor, or an offensive piece of raillery, would so disgust "the black wench" whose employment it was to make that "beloved mixture, punch of arak," that she would contrive with a subtle skilfulness to make the bowl fatal to the man who abused her, whilst his companions drank without the slightest injury to themselves.*

Liquor made in the country was drank by all classes of Englishmen. Sometimes they were contented with arak manufactured at Surat or Bombay; but the best was brought from Goa or Bengal. The strongest sort was called by Englishmen "Jagre" (jágrí), and was, I suppose, a liquor distilled like rum, from molasses. It was taken in drams and heated, or made lukewarm by a hot iron or wedge of gold dropped into it. A fondness for intoxicating spirits was carried even by superior minds to an astonishing degree of coarseness. Fryer, man of excellent education as he was, could not attend the banquet of a Mussulman officer, without having the bad taste to draw a flask out of his pocket, and qualify his sherbet with the more potent draught to which he was accustomed. This he tells us himself with an evident conviction that he had been knowing and clever †

As regards the military at this period, the Company had not been taught by bitter experience to treat them with liberality, and consequently they found that they themselves were treated by them with little respect. Their vexatious regulations infused a spirit of insubordination into the minds of all the troops, from the highest officer to the private soldier. Captain Carr, indeed, did not hesitate to insult the Deputy Governor in his Council Chamber. Unsummoned he appeared before his Honor to demand an inquiry into his conduct. He was told that he had not been sent for; but, as he had come of his own accord, he would perhaps be so good as to explain why he had not appeared on parade for two mornings. "I had business," was his laconic answer. The Deputy Governor mildly suggested that his business could not have been very urgent, and that it really appeared as if the Captain was not anxious to perform his duty. Upon that Carr began to swear "good mouth-filling oaths" at his Honor, and when threatened with punishment by him, shook his fist in the Deputy's face. The affair was terminated by the Captain being placed under arrest, and confined to his own quarters. Such an example thus set by an officer was, as might be expected, imitated by private soldiers, and at last all fell into such a disorganized state that the Governor could not find a man whom he would venture to make a Serjeant or Corporal.‡

The Company professed especial care for the religious instruction of their servants, and sent out strict orders that the Lord's Day should be observed, and prayers regularly offered. They also enclosed a form of special prayer, which taught their servants to implore in the first place the Divine favour for their honorable masters, and in the second place their

* Ovington's Voyage. An infusion of poppies called in Hindústání *post* is mentioned by Europeans of that time as a slow poison much used in India.

† Fryer, Letter iii. chap. v. Ovington.

‡ Letter from Bombay to Surat, dated 6th December, 1686. Bruce's Annals, 1696-97.

honorable masters' favour for themselves. The main objects of the prayer were such temporal blessings as are included in the promises made to the Patriarchs under the old dispensation. There was also a significant and suggestive allusion to the Factors' honesty, virtue, and general behaviour as Christians.* Divine Service was held twice every day at Bombay, and all the Factors were required to be present. A room was set apart for the purpose, but there was neither Church nor Chapel.

An affair in which Spencer, Chaplain of Bombay, was concerned, and which was made the subject of official inquiry, is a striking instance of the recklessness with which marriages were sometimes contracted. This gentleman was present one night at a convivial party, when he was suddenly asked by an amorous pair to make them man and wife. He regarded the application as a joke, and only supposed that they were enjoying themselves at his expense. However, he replied that he could not think of marrying them at that late hour; but if they continued in the same mind next morning, he would do as they required. What must have been his surprise to find that a charge against him for neglect of duty was grounded upon this refusal, and he was formally called upon by the President to state his reasons for not discharging the functions of his office.†

The reader will remember that at this time conversions to the Roman Catholic religion were fashionable in England, until checked by the arrival of William the Third, and the subsequent Revolution. The fashion had reached Bombay. Amongst the officers of the garrison was Lieut. Finch, who must have been no less a person than the son of Sir Heneage Finch, Attorney General and Lord Keeper in the reign of James the Second, created Lord Daventry in 1673, and Earl of Nottingham in 1681. Lieut. Finch's elder brother succeeded to his father's title, and was afterwards created Earl of Winchelsea. Although this young officer's relations were strict Protestants, he himself embraced the Roman Catholic faith soon after he reached Bombay. The circumstance was thought to call for the interference of government, and the Deputy Governor seized gladly the opportunity of shewing that he had once mixed in high society, by stating to his Council that having known Finch's Right Honorable father, and his no less Right Honorable brother, he could assure them that both

* The following is the prayer as printed in Ovington's work :—"O Almighty and most merciful God, Who art the Sovereign Protector of all that trust in Thee, and the Author of all spiritual and temporal blessings, we Thy unworthy creatures do most humbly implore Thy goodness for a plentiful effusion of Thy grace upon our employers, Thy servants, the Right Honorable East India Company of England. Prosper them in all their public undertakings, and make them famous and successful in all their governments, colonies, and commerce both by sea and land; so that they may prove a public blessing by the increase of honour, wealth, and power to our native country, as well as to themselves. Continue their favours towards us, and inspire their Generals, Presidents, Agents and Councils in these remote parts of the world, and all others that are intrusted with any authority under them, with piety towards Thee our God, and with wisdom, fidelity and circumspection in their several stations; that we may all discharge our respective duties faithfully, and live virtuously in due obedience to our superiors, and in love, peace, and charity one towards another, that these Indian nations among whom we dwell, seeing our sober and religious conversation, may be induced to have a just esteem for our most holy profession of the Gospel of our Lord Jesus Christ, to whom be honour, praise and glory, now and for ever. Amen."

† Letter from the Governor &c. of Bombay to Surat; dated 1st January 1686-7.

were steady members of the Church of England. The Council came to the resolution that they would not suffer Lieut. Finch to perform any military duty, for they would not "give the charge of the garrison into a man's hands of the Romish religion."*

So alarmed was the Government at the progress of Romanism, that they resolved to enforce against its professors the penal statute 23rd Elizabeth Chapter I, and having discovered that one John de Gloria, a Portuguese Priest, had baptized Matthew, son of Lieutenant Thorpe, deceased, they arrested him on a charge of high treason for persuading a person to be reconciled to the Pope. At first the over-zealous Priest was thrown into the common jail, but on the intercession of his clerical brethren, was kept a prisoner in his own Church.†

Some apology for this intolerance may be drawn from the relative position of the English and Portuguese. The latter hoped to regain their lost ascendancy in Bombay, and were known to hold a treasonable correspondence with the Jesuits of Bandora. During the war with the Dutch and Mogul they had refused to aid in defending the Island, claiming an exemption from military service, although it was shown that President Aungier had reserved to the Company a right to such service, and that the Company, as representatives of the English Crown, had become their lords paramount. It was even said that the Jesuits had first suggested to the Siddí the practicability of invading Bombay, and they certainly had supplied his army with provisions. It was not then altogether unnatural that the Government should regard with suspicion any Englishman who suddenly embraced the religion of their treacherous enemies, and that they should imagine him to be a fellow-conspirator with the Portuguese.

At this period all the property of the Jesuits on which the Government could lay their hands was confiscated. Their lands at Parell and Sion were never restored, because, when invited, they would make no promise to have the question of their guilt or innocence tried before a Court of Judicature. Other property belonging to Portuguese was given to its former owners, when, after inquiry, they were proved to have acted in good faith. It must be confessed that the English Government were hasty in their confiscations, and that the Court sanctioned their proceedings, because, as they candidly acknowledged, it had become necessary to improve, by every possible means, the revenues of the Island.‡

Annoyed as the English were at finding their countrymen embrace a faith which was in those days regarded as in itself treason to Church and State, they were shocked beyond measure when they heard that one had become an apostate to the religion of the false prophet. As has been stated, numerous Europeans deserted to the Siddí, and surely that shewed a degraded state of feeling. There were also instances of actual apostacy; but we have only one on record, and that may be told in the words of the

* Letter from the Deputy Governor &c. of Bombay to Surat; dated 21st February 1686-7. Burnet, in his "History of his Own Times," praises highly the integrity of these noblemen. Both were conscientious Protestants. The son wrote a "Defence of the Christian Faith" in reply to Whiston. He had thirty children, so could not be expected to do much for his brother, the Bombay officer.

† Letter as above, dated 13th April 1697.

‡ Bruce's Annals, 1690-93. Ovington.

Factors at Surat. "In addition of our troubles," they write, "there is one of our wicked Englishmen, by name John Newton, that came out in the *Royal James and Mary*, and came from Umbra yesterday, and went immediately to the Cossys, and declared his intention to turn Moor, and before we possibly could have an opportunity to send to the Governor, the business was done, and he circumcised, which was past our remedy of retrieving his wicked soul."*

The country about Surat was more unsettled than ever. There was a general expectation that civil wars were approaching, and that every one who had property must lose it, unless he could defend it, or side with the strongest. Aurangzíb was jealous of all his sons, each of whom was forming a cabal against his Government, or raising forces so as to assert his claims to the throne after his father's demise. So strongly did the Factors feel their insecurity, that they reduced their stock to the smallest possible amount. In February 1696, the city was thrown into the greatest consternation by a threatened assault of the Maráthás under Rájá Rám, who had approached as far as Nandarbár. The English, Dutch and French fortified their Factories, and Sir John Gayer sent twenty topasses with arms and ammunition from Bombay. The Native Governor also made great preparations, and seemed so determined to defend the place, that the marauders thought it advisable to retire.†

In 1685 Sir John Child had despatched a ship to establish a new Factory at Amoy, and another with Factors to re-settle trade at Siam. In 1695 Mr. Brabourne contracted with the Rání of Attinga for a regular settlement at Brinjan, and an attempt was made to open a trade with Sind and Moultan; but the Court disapproved of both these projects. They would not consent to the latter, because there was not sufficient depth of water in the Indus for ships to proceed higher than Tatta.‡

However, the same year were built the Factory and strong fortifications of Anjengo—about seventy-eight miles from Cape Comorin or Kúmárí—on a small strip of land which the English had obtained in 1684. Although protected by the sea on one side, and a small river on the other, the spot was injudiciously selected, for there was no good water within three miles; the anchorage was bad, and a continual surf rendered it inconvenient and even dangerous to land. But the country produced pepper in abundance, and the calicoes which the inhabitants manufactured were in those days considered of excellent quality.§ So the Factory flourished until 1813, when it was abolished. A few years after Anjengo had been selected for a settlement, the Factory at Baroch was closed for a time, and the Factors withdrawn.||

Carwar was celebrated amongst sportsmen for the game and wild animals with which its forests abounded. The Chief of the English Factory was held in great respect by the neighbouring Rájás, and when he issued on a hunting expedition they accompanied him with their followers. A

* Letter from the Factors of Surat; dated October 1691.
† Bruce's Annals, 1695-97.
‡ Bruce's Annals.
§ Hamilton's "New Account," chap. xxvi. Hamilton's East India Gazetteer.
|| "New Account," chap. xiii.

pack of twenty dogs was kept there in 1692, and each was allowed two pounds of rice *per diem* at the Company's expense. "But now," wrote a visitor not long afterwards, "they are better husbands of their money, and have discharged all their dogs, and other superfluities, except one good old custom of treating strangers that come there from Europe with pretty black female dancers, who are very active in their dancing, and free in their conversation, where shame is quite out of fashion."

This visitor, who had one eye for business, and another for pleasure, during one of these hunting expeditions saw killed within the space of twelve hours more than a dozen deer, two wild cows with their calves, and four or five hogs. At the close of day the Chief, like some Highland laird, was conducted home in state by his native attendants, who after delivering their compliments with strict formality parted from him at the Factory gate.

So great was the celebrity of this country for its game, that it attracted two young men to an enterprize, which must be considered more arduous than the excursions of modern sportsmen to the rocks and streams of Norway, or even the avalanches of the Himalayas and the plains of Southern Africa. A youth named Lembourg of the house of Lembourg in Germany, and a son of Lord Goring, without giving their friends notice of their intention, sailed from London to Carwar in one of the Company's vessels. As they had left letters behind them, bills of credit followed, and the Directors wrote to their Chiefs of Factories desiring that they would receive the young adventurers with hospitality and respect. They remained three years at Carwar, and then set off on their return home. Young Goring died four days after the ship sailed ; but Lembourg arrived safe in England.*

The memorable change which came over the English nation at this time placed the English and Dutch on a new footing. When the Factors first heard that the Prince of Orange had landed in England, they were evidently in doubt as to the issue, and with amusing caution only replied that "they trusted the true Protestant religion would be maintained and established." The Dutch hearing that the Revolution was complete, played the English a shabby trick in India, seizing the opportunity to represent Holland as a superior country to England. Mr. Baroon, having been sent by the Dutch Company as their Ambassador to the Emperor, and being honoured with an audience, maintained that the English were a contemptible people, and that a king had been sent from his country to rule over them. Aurangzíb, seeming to believe this plausible story, and encouraging the Dutchman in his boasting, gravely replied that as the Dutch were so superior, they had only to drive the English out of his dominions and appropriate the European trade to themselves. He strongly recommended them to take this step. But when Baroon excused himself on the plea that he could not act without instructions from home, the Emperor shewed that he was better acquainted with European affairs than the other had suspected. He plainly told him that Holland must be an insignificant country, for the King of France had conquered it in a few days, and would never have been expelled, if the English had not interfered ; that in reality England held the balance of power in Europe, and that if she did not,

* Hamilton's "New Account," chap. xxii.

the Emperor of Germany or King of France would conquer Holland in a single campaign.*

Again, when the English Factors were in confinement, the Dutch seized the opportunity to degrade them still lower in the opinion of the natives, and thus advance their own interests at the expense of their neighbours. One proposal of theirs' suggested an idea of which the English immediately availed themselves, and in course of time turned to their advantage. Having a powerful fleet in the Indian seas, the Dutch offered, if an exclusive trade were granted them, to convoy the pilgrim ships to Judda. This was probably the first hint which led the English Government eventually to demand and acquire the tanká or assignment on the revenues of Surat for protecting ships on their passage to the Red Sea. The Dutch had thirty-six ships of war, divided into six squadrons, cruizing in the Indian seas. One squadron remained between Surat and Bombay with a view of intercepting and attacking the ships of France.†

During the administration of President Harris, official information was received that England had declared war against France. On the eleventh of October 1692, the *Elizabeth*, East Indiaman, was captured within fifty leagues of Bombay by a French fleet of four ships mounting respectively sixty-six, sixty, forty, and twenty guns. To such a force the *Elizabeth* made a stout but of course fruitless resistance. In those days many an Englishman was tainted with the suspicion of treason, and Vaux was said to have held secret and traitorous communications with the enemy. Certain it is that he purchased from them the *Elizabeth*.‡

The French inflicted a more terrible blow on the Company in 1696. Four East Indiamen, the *Resolution*, *Defence*, *Princess Anne* and *Success*, with the *Seymour* an Interloper, to whom fear of the common foe had induced them to join themselves, were captured on their homeward voyage by a French fleet. We must all admire the spirit in which the Court announced this disaster to their President at Surat. Instead of desponding, they wrote with pardonable vanity, that they bore their loss " with a true Roman courage," and were resolved to increase their stock. One squadron of six French ships visited Surat and landed merchandize.

Now, for the first time, Armenians appear as mixed up with the Company's affairs at Surat. It was found that this industrious race could retail the woollens of England, or bring from the interior fine muslins and other articles at much less expense than English agents would have cost. Their services were therefore peculiarly valuable to the Company under their heavy embarrassments.§

* Bruce's Annals, 1688-89. Hamilton's " New Account," chap. xix.
† Bruce's Annals, 1695-96.
‡ Bruce's Annals, 1690-93.
§ Bruce's Annals, 1695-96.

CHAPTER IX.

1698—1701.

CONTENTS. — Necessity of referring to English politics—The House of Commons sanctions a new Company—Both parties bribe—The old Company exposed; ordered to be dissolved—A Bill passed in their favour—Consequent state of affairs in India—Additional rules of the New Company's Charter—Hope for the Old Company; their prospects and spirit—Fresh calamities of the Old Company—European piracy—Kidd sent to suppress it; turns pirate; his adventures; taken and executed—Sivers; his piracies; taken and brought to Bombay—Satisfaction demanded from the Factors—Low condition of the Factors — The two Companies prepare for a struggle—Lucas appears for the New Company; receives the Act of Authorization—Fresh arrivals of New Company's servants—Sir Nicholas Waite; his reception; contest for a flag—Waite's proceedings—The New Factory—Intrigues—Sir William Norris the ambassador; preparations for his reception; arrival at Surat; his public entry—Mutual injuries—Good times for the Mogul Officers—Sir John Gayer and others imprisoned—The ambassador proceeds to Court; offends the Minister; his grand procession and audience; result of his Embassy; he is insulted and injured; returns to Surat—Reflections on the ambassador's conduct—His departure, sickness, last words, and death.

THE state of affairs in India for the next few years was so extraordinary and confused,—conflicts being waged by subjects of the British Crown, each party claiming for itself the countenance of supreme authority, and each denying that the other party acted under the sanction of either King or Parliament—I say this state of affairs is such a labyrinth, that before we can find our way out of it, we must obtain for a clue not only information drawn from India, but also a little acquaintance with English politics.

Many merchants of London had for long been discontented with the monopoly granted to the East India Company, and their anxiety to have it abolished had sharpened their ingenuity in exposing its defects. The work of John De Witt, the celebrated Dutch statesman, had furnished their advocates with some of the soundest arguments, and the learned Pollexfen now brought his stores of knowledge and subtlety to their aid.* But their main hope had been placed in assailing the vulnerable points of their chartered adversaries and detecting their flagrant abuses. In the Parliament of 1691 numerous petitions were presented against the Company, whose replications were pronounced unsatisfactory, so that the House of Commons, in an address to the King, desired that it might be abolished, and a new Company established in its place. Early in 1693 the petitions

* John DeWitt wrote about the year 1662, and Pollexfen in 1697. Macpherson's History.

of malcontents were still more numerous, and a Committee of the whole House determined that a new Joint Stock Company should be formed. But then appears to have commenced that flagitious system of bribery which the world affected to regard with pious horror, but yet encouraged, and on which both parties relied more than on argument. Those who had avowed their conviction of the Company's abuses now opened their minds to reason and gold. They presented, indeed, another address to the King, praying him to dissolve the Company after three years ; but they were satisfied with the assurance, which in all ages has befriended dilatory statesmen, that the matter should *be considered.*

In the October Session of the same year, addresses were poured upon the House by clothiers, linen-drapers, and other tradesmen, as well as influential merchants, who undertook to prove that the transactions of the Company had tended to the scandal of religion, the dishonor of England, the reproach of its laws, the oppression of its people, and the ruin of its trade. The Directors were not contented with printing an answer to these charges; they also secretly purchased the favour of the Ministry. A new Charter was therefore granted by the King to the Company ; but an outcry was raised against the Government, the Commons resisting the Royal grant as an invasion of their rights, and passing a resolution that no persons could be prohibited from engaging in the East India trade, except by Act of Parliament.

In the Parliament of 1695, further measures were taken, and an inquiry was made into the means by which the Company had procured their new Charter. Their books were examined by a Committee, which fully revealed the system of corruption on which they had acted. The Company, chiefly through the agency of Sir Thomas Cooke, one of their Directors, had expended ninety thousand pounds in secret services. Cooke, having been committed to the Tower, promised to disclose all, on receiving an assurance of indemnity. The King endeavoured to stop inquiry by threatening to close the Session; yet it proceeded. The Duke of Leeds was strongly suspected of having received large bribes, and articles of impeachment were exhibited against him in the Upper House. At this stage the prosecution was stopped by a prorogation of Parliament.

However, these revelations so injured the Company, that when in 1698 a loan was required of them by the Ministry for the use of the State, and a rival association of merchants offered a larger sum than they could promise, it was decided that the old Company should be dissolved, and a new one established in its stead.

Still the old Company had influential supporters, and their case was defended by acute and powerful reasoning. Besides shewing the benefits which the country had derived from their trade, and the risk which would be incurred if it was intrusted to their inexperienced opponents, they argued that having become Lord Proprietors of St Helena and Bombay, they could not with justice be deprived of territory which had been conferred upon them by Royal grant ; that they had expended large sums on fortifications and Factories, and that justice and good policy would both be violated, if their chartered rights were infringed. Their remonstrances were thought by many to be highly reasonable, so that one and twenty members of the House of Peers formally protested against the hardship and injustice which they suffered. Moreover, it was quite clear that their opponents had succeeded by the corrupt means which had drawn so much obloquy on themselves, and the odium of corruption was pretty evenly shared by both Companies. Hence in 1700 the House willingly listened to the advocates of the original association, enlarging on the injuries which they had endured; and after hearing both sides of the case, once more passed a Bill in their favour.

A consideration of these transactions can alone explain the anomalous state of affairs in India. Two Companies appeared in the field. The old was now styled "The London Company," and had only obtained permission to trade for three years, when its accounts were to be wound up, and all its commerce was to cease. The new association, claiming to be more national in its spirit and undertakings, was styled "The English Company, trading to the East Indies." The servants of the two Courts of Directors made India the arena of a fierce struggle. One party claimed at one time the support of the King, the other the support of Parliament. One prevailed for a short period; the other seemed compelled to succumb. But the hopes of neither were crushed, nor was the cause of either proudly trimphant.*

In addition to the usual regulations, the Charter of the new Company, which became also the Charter of the old, when the two were amalgamated—contained special provisions for an educational and religious establishment. A Minister and Schoolmaster were to be maintained in every garrision and superior Factory, and a decent place appropriated exclusively to Divine Service. Moreover, it was ordered that every ship of five hundred tons burden and upwards, should carry a Chaplain. All clergymen, whether sent for duty on ships or in Factories, were to be approved either by the Archbishop of Canterbury or the Bishop of London, and care was to be taken that they were to be treated with respect. It was strictly enjoined also that all Chaplains who went to reside in India should learn the Portuguese language within one year after their arrival, and should also apply themselves to learn the language of the country "the better to enable them to instruct the Gentoos that should be the servants or slaves of the same Company, or of their agents, in the Protestant religion.†"

When their destruction was imminent, the old Company found one loophole through which they hoped to escape. Clauses in their rival's Charter had provided that all subscribers to the new stock might trade separately, and on their own account; also that other corporations might become holders of stock. Availing themselves of these privileges, the old resolved to subscribe largely to the funds of the new association, and thus to trade separately when the three years allowed them should have expired.

In the meanwhile they were reluctantly compelled to inform their Factors how altered was the state of their affairs. In 1695 their confident hopes of continued existence were for the first time undermined; and they

* Bruce's Annals. Smollett's History of England.

† Charter of King William the Third, A. D. 1698.

warned their servants at Surat, that as such violent prejudices were conceived against them, they did not know whether their Charter would be renewed or a new Company instituted. The words in which this information was conveyed are worthy of notice as proving that the feuds and mutual recriminations which will be recorded in this Chapter were not unforeseen. The Company rather looked forward with hope, that amidst the confusion something would turn up in their favour ; at all events, they had no intention of submitting quietly to defeat, and were resolved that they would either put down opposition with a strong hand or die fighting. In such a spirit they wrote :—" Two East Indian Companies could no more subsist without destroying one the other, than two Kings at the same time regnant in the same kingdom ; that now a civil battle was to be fought between the Old and New Company ; and that two or three years must end this war, as the Old or the New must give way ; that being veterans, if their servants abroad would do their duty, they did not doubt of the victory ; that if the world laughed at the pains the two Companies took to ruin each other, they could not help it, as they were on good ground, and had a Charter." And when their servants wrote from India in a timorous, desponding strain, the stout old Company told them that all this was only " as a blustering storm, which so far from tearing them up, only a little shook the roots, and made them thereby take the better hold, and grow the firmer and flourish the faster."* So as neither of the monopolist corporations would give way, they set to work, and a hard fight they had. Each got severe punishment and heavy falls. Then they ended by shaking hands, and dividing the stakes.

But what most distressed the old Company's Factors was, that their hands were tied, and instead of being left free to put forth all their strength against their adversaries, they were fettered by a calamity of another kind.

European piracy had been carried to such an extent, that the alternative now was—either honest trade or piracy must be suppressed. Anxiety, too, on the subject was heightened when it was found, that a remedy which had been prescribed was converted into a poison, and a man who professed to be a protector of Commerce had become its most dangerous enemy.

The Company having represented to the King of England that they were in constant fear lest the Mogul Emperor should make reprisals upon them for losses which pirates had inflicted on Natives of India, William the Third wished to send some men-of-war that they might attack and destroy the haunts of the buccaneers. As there would have been great difficulty in procuring a grant of public money for this purpose, it was proposed that the undertaking should be private. The Earls of Bellamont, Oxford, Romney, Lord Somers, Colonel Livingstone and others therefore agreed to form an association. Lord Bellamont had been just appointed Governor of New York and New England, and before he left for his seat of Government, Colonel Livingstone recommended to him Captain Kidd, a brave dashing fellow, who was said to have become remarkably well acquainted with the pirates' lairs—a circumstance which, strange to say, seems to have awakened no suspicions.

* Bruce's Annals, 1698-1700.

St. Augustine's Bay at Madagascar, and the neighbouring island of St. Mary, were chiefly looked to. Here the rovers had thrown up fortifications, and were supplied with stores from New York, and the West Indies. Six thousand pounds having been raised, a share of which Kidd himself contributed, he was placed in command of the *Adventure*, a galley with thirty guns and two hundred men, and in the year 1695 sailed to attack the robbers at Madagascar. He left that place, however, immediately after he had arrived at it, and went to cruize at the entrance of the Red Sea. There also he met with no success and again sailed for Cálicot.

These failures were mortifying. Kidd sought for remuneration ; but at this rate he and his association would never make their fortunes. So we may suppose that he reasoned like the shepherd's dog, which, according to an old proverb, considered that his watchfulness gave him a better claim than any one else to good mutton, and moreover that it was both easier and pleasanter to kill sheep than wolves. The policeman became thief; Captain Kidd appeared in the character of a most daring and successful pirate.

This change was suggested at Cálicot, where he was tempted by a small bark, the master and three or four sailors of which were Dutchmen, the rest Mussulmans. This sweet morsel he seized and took away to Madagascar, and four or five weeks after gorged his appetite with the *Quedah Merchant*, a ship of four hundred tons, having a cargo valued at four lakhs of rupees, and a crew of Mussulmans, commanded by an Englishman. His fame was soon spread far and wide, so that he was joined by other ships, including the *Mocha*, and *Josiah*, the crews of which had mutinied and renounced the Company's service. His whole force is said to have been composed of two frigates, each mounting thirty guns, which constantly cruized off Cape Comorin, and three of fifty, forty, and thirty guns respectively, which cruized off the Málabár Coast.* The *Mocha* frigate took or sank seven or eight ships belonging to Surat. A Portuguese ship engaged in the China trade was also taken. When the annual fleet of Mogul vessels arrived at Surat from the Red Sea, under convoy of a Dutch and English squadron, they learned that Kidd had been hovering near them, and had left them for Rájapúr, where he plundered a vessel belonging to Bombay. He then careened at the Laccadive islands, sailed to Cálicot, where he espied three armed vessels in the Company's service, escaped to Cochin, took three Dutch prizes of great value, and retired with his prey to his eyrie at St. Mary's.

The short, and brilliant career of this freebooter was now drawing to a close. He partitioned his gains amongst his crew, first appropriating forty shares to himself. Ninety of his men then took service in the *Mocha*, and he himself sailed with the rest to the West Indies. Going from thence to America he was seized by Lord Bellamont and sent to take his trial in England.

His reputation had arrived there long before him, and public indignation had been excited not only against him, but also against the noblemen and gentlemen who had sent him out, and who were charged with coun-

* Hamilton's Hindustan vol. ii. Letter from the President and Council ; dated 27th July 1700.

tenancing his piracies. However, his patrons seem to have been innocent, and to have acted only from good motives. Kidd was brought to the bar of the House of Commons, where he did not maintain his character; for Sir Edward Seymour remarked that " the fellow was not more a knave than a fool." Yet he at least observed a generous silence, and made no attempt to criminate others. The Court of Directors announced to the Governor of Surat that he was about to be tried at the Old Bailey, and the hope that he would be hung, drawn and quartered was a sustaining cordial to their harrassed minds. He and some of his companions in crime, having been convicted, were hung in chains at Tilbury. His property, to the value of six thousand four hundred and seventy-two pounds, was confiscated, and presented by Queen Anne to Greenwich Hospital.*

Another of these dreaded rovers was styled by the Deputy Governor of Bombay " that grand villain Sivers, commonly called Chivers." Having seized a vessel belonging to Hassan Amadan, he probably contributed more than any other individual to the troubles in which the Factors were involved. His luck, like Kidd's, failed him at the last moment. With fifteen others, who had followed the same courses, he had taken his passage on a small ship the *Margaret*, bound for New York. At the Cape of Good Hope they were so unfortunate as to meet with Captain Louth, who being in a large and well armed Indiaman, took their little vessel, with crew, passengers, negroes, goods and money to Bombay. The Mogul Governor of Surat demanded that all should be delivered to him ; but this was refused, and Louth made about six thousand pounds by his prize, his crew getting as much more. Of course the gallant Captain thought that he had performed a meritorious service ; but Bombay was full to repletion of European blackguards, and the Government was annoyed with him for bringing more. Sir John Gayer's grumbling letter lifts up the veil from a frightful state of Society. He plainly states, that he would have been better pleased if Louth had not been so officious, and had allowed the *Margaret* to proceed " rather than have filled our prison with twenty-one criminals in a place where we had before a sufficient number of such as would willingly side with such sparks."†

But now we approach the catastrophe. The owners of such vessels as had fallen into the hands of pirates, complained that they had been robbed by Englishmen, and insisted that the English ought to make them compensation. Without inquiring into the justice of these complaints, the Governor of Surat ordered the Factors to pay a million of rupees on account of one merchant's loss, and two hundred on account of another's. Annesley, the President, before replying to this unreasonable demand, consulted Sir John Gayer, who declared that not one rupee should be forthcoming. As the Governor had before succeeded by threatening that he would flog the Dutch and French brokers to death, if they did not grant the indemnity which he required, he now had the brokers of the English Factory seized, and when ropes had been fastened to their necks, they were led away, as though to be hung upon the green. At their earnest

* Bruce's Annals, 1697-98 and 1701-2. Burnet's History of his own Times. Naval History of Great Britain ; by Dr. John Campbell, vol. iii.

† Letter to the Court ; dated Bombay Castle, 20th September, 1700.

request, they were permitted to beg that the English would satisfy the Governor, and Annesley, being by this time intimidated, agreed to pay thirty thousand rupees. The General and his Council were so displeased with the President's pusillanimity and other offences, that they deprived him of his appointment, and made Stephen Colt President in his room. *

The Governor's partial success by no means abated his insolence. He demanded and obtained from the President a convoy for the Mocha fleet, and when it had returned in safety, dishonestly refused to pay the stipulated amount. The President had too hastily assured him that a force would be sent from England to clear the Indian seas of pirates, and when this was not done, the Governor affected to treat the English with profound contempt. As the mob followed his example, the Factors were spurned by all, and the poor President wrote that they were " as despicable as the Portuguese in India, and as odious as the Jews in Spain." †

At such a moment, when the affairs of the English in India were more depressed than they had ever been since prosperity first dawned upon them ; when they had lost credit with the Natives, and were victims of a local oppressor, they commenced an internecine strife amongst themselves, and two Companies engaged in a contest of commercial life and death. This war was waged with extraordinary animosity, each attributing blame entirely to the other. Fortunately the memoirs of both parties, written by themselves, are preserved in their diaries and official letters. The impression, which they leave on the reader's mind, is not favorable to the agents of either Company. It was of course to be expected that the old Factors, or the " veterans" as their master's style them, would look with envious eyes upon intruders, and would have rejoiced to see them discomfited. But they went much further than this. The old Company treated with utter contempt the privileges, which had been conferred upon their rivals by the English Government. They would not understand that they themselves were only continuing for three years on sufferance. And they carried faction to the highest point, when they prepared themselves not indeed openly to injure, but secretly to undermine the influence of an Ambassador, who came with Royal credentials, because he was in the pay and interest of others. On the other hand, the Ambassador, President, and Agents of the New Company were overbearing and insolent, ever active in endeavouring to exalt themselves, and little scrupulous about means, provided they could attain their end and degrade the servants of the old Company.

For some time a Mr. Lucas, who had come in an interloping ship called the *Mary*, resided at Surat as agent of the new Company, and in April 1699 the *Shrewsbury* galley, which was consigned to him, arrived with the intelligence that his Company was established by Act of Parliament. Interlopers were in extacies of delight. The days of monopoly, they trusted, were ended ; in the worst case, the new Company could not be more severe exclusionists than the old. Lucas communicated a copy of the Act to the President, and then with Bourchier and Dr. Leckie waited

* Letters from Sir John Gayer and Council to the President of Surat ; dated December 1698 and January 1699.

† Bruce's Annals, 1699-1700.

upon the Governor, who sent for the old Company's broker, to ascertain the truth of the matter. The President and Council informed the Governor that they had no information on the subject, but being obliged to appear before him, admitted the genuineness and authority of the Act of Parliament, only repeating that they had received no orders. The first idea which entered his mind was, that the Factors would disown their pecuniary engagements. He therefore desired their broker to find security that the President and Council would not leave the city, and ordered that they should be confined to their Factory until such security should be given. He also had their shroffs beaten to make them disclose the state of the Company's accounts. It should be observed, that the Governor's temper had been severely tried by the loss of two lakhs of rupees which he had on board the *Quedah Merchant*, when it was plundered by Kidd.

All this time Lucas was industriously spreading reports amongst the natives, that the King of England and his Parliament had deprived the old Company of their Charter, in consequence of their misdemeanours. By these means such a hostile spirit was aroused, that Sir John Gayer and his Council could scarcely write of him or his friends with decency, but in Scriptural language denounced them as their " Rabshaka adversaries."*

The disordered state of the old Company's affairs, the crimes and delinquencies of their Factors, and the intemperate use which their Presidents and Governors had made of their authority, these circumstances combined had led to the dismissal of so many of their servants, that the new Company found ready to their hands a body of men, whose integrity was in some instances certainly not unsullied, but whose experience and local knowledge were of the highest value, and whom revenge, as the Directors shrewdly but unamiably remarked, would stimulate to exertion. Such were Waite, Pitt, Master, Annesley, Bourchier, and others, all of whom had been originally servants of the old Company, and were now engaged with the utmost zeal in the cause of their opponents.†

On the 16th November 1699, fresh invaders of the Factory's peace arrived. Mewse and Brooke announced themselves as Factors of the new Company, and prepared Sir John Gayer for what was to follow. At last Sir Nicholas Waite made his appearance on the ship *Montague*, He had formerly been the London Company's Agent at Bantam, where he received the order for his dismissal. He was now President for the new Company, and in order that he might be superior to Sir John Gayer, the King had not only conferred upon him the honour of Knighthood, but had also declared him his Consul, thus placing him in a position which the President of the London Company could not occupy. He also styled himself his Majesty's minister, and by his subordinates was styled General.

We have letters from Sir Nicholas written after he had left the shores of England, one dated from Deal, and another from the Bay of Cadiz, in which he informs his masters, that he had devoutly asked God to vouchsafe His blessing to their undertaking, and for that purpose had, with the rest of the Company's servants, attended church on the day of sailing.‡

* Letter of Sir John Gayer &c. to Stephen Colt., &c., dated 23rd June 1699. Bruce's Annals, 1699-1700.

† Bruce's Annals, 1696-1700.

‡ Records of the English Company's Factory at Surat.

He reached Bombay on the eleventh of January 1700. Sir John Gayer refused to recognize him in any way, so he left immediately, and arrived at Surat on the nineteenth of the same month. Here his rights and pretensions were alike slighted by the old Factors, who in their addresses to him scarcely used ordinary courtesy, and in their correspondence with one another wrote of him in a style of the most vulgar insolence and contempt.

Sir Nicholas Waite commenced operations at Swally by insisting that his flag should be saluted as a Vice Admiral's, and that the old Company should strike theirs as a mark of respect for his Majesty's representative. Of course this modest demand met with a prompt refusal, on which the newly arrived dignitary sent two Commanders of ships and forty seamen to haul down the old Company's standard. This commission was speedily executed, and the captors were making off with their prize, when they were assailed by some of their rival's peons, supported by a party whom the Governor of the city, indignant at Waite's exercise of authority, had despatched to the scene of action. The flag was soon rescued and restored to its staff, where it waived, as in scorn of chartered interlopers, and thus led the Natives to infer, that the new Company were trading without the countenance of authority.

Waite being satisfied by this defeat that it was necessary to desist from open violence, hoisted the King's flag upon a house which he had hired, and endeavoured to injure his rivals by artifice and intrigue. Without waiting for the Ambassador, who was daily expected, he addressed a letter to the Emperor, accusing the old Company of being " thieves and confederates with the pirates." He took the opportunity also to intimate his own rank, and added, that he was expecting four men-of-war who would act under his authority and endeavour to destroy all pirates. His next step was to post notices about the city warning all persons against taking the London Company's passes for their ships ; but these were torn down by the Governor's orders. Afterwards he applied for and obtained permission to make a public entry. Accordingly he marched into Surat with an imposing procession, on which the servants of the old Company looked with silent sadness, feeling as they did that natives would augur from such a solemnity the approaching decline of the old Factory. These measures, and the disputes in which the members of the two establishments were incessantly engaged, had such a disheartening effect upon Sir John Gayer and Colt, that the former asked the Court's permission to resign their service, and the latter gave notice of his intention to resign in two years' time.*

The new Factory was established on the scale of the old one ; but Waite complained that his salary was inferior to that of the old Company's General, who now received five hundred pounds per annum, and had an allowance of five hundred more for the maintenance of his table. The second in Council received a hundred pounds per annum. The Chief Factors, including Benjamin Mewse " Chief for China," Jeremiah Bonnell, " Europe Warehousekeeper," John Lock, Secretary, and two merchants, received sixty pounds per annum ; the other five Factors forty

* Records of the London Company's Factory at Surat. Bruce's Annals, 1699-1700.

pounds each; fourteen Writers twenty pounds each; Lawrence Hackett, Chaplain, a hundred pounds; John Maxwell, Surgeon, thirty; and a Genoese cook twenty. These, and ten soldiers, who received four pounds each and a suit of clothes, and a trumpeter, were all the Europeans on the establishment.* All the servants of the Company were permitted to carry on private trade from port to port in India; but were prohibited renting farms or intermarrying with the natives. Diamonds only they might send to England for sale on paying a duty to the Company of five per cent, and five per cent to his Majesty.†

But now that the operators were on the spot, and all their apparatus prepared, they found a difficulty in beginning their experiment. Nothing could be done so long as the native Government supported their rivals, which they did—not from any regard for them, as they took every opportunity of oppressing them—but simply because they knew that they were not dangerous persons, whilst they were in the dark regarding the plans of the new comers. Waite, therefore, soon perceived that it was necessary to undermine the characters of the old Company's servants, and render them objects of suspicion.

In this design he succeeded, by turning the London Company's weapons against themselves, and also pointing a lance of his own. He contrived to represent them not only as interlopers; he also renewed the old insinuations of piracy, and, as it could be proved that there was some truth in his statement, no great address was required to make the Natives believe the whole. It was quite true as maintained by him, that the old Company's Charter was to terminate with the year 1702, and to this fact he cunningly pinned the suggestion that, unless they were sharply looked after, they would remove with all their goods and chattels, leaving no security for the payment of their debts. Thus were the native powers urged to seek reparation for the past, and to take precautions for the future. A false step taken by Sir John Gayer aided Waite's intrigues more than he could have anticipated. With a view of opposing his enemy on the spot and adjusting some affairs which Annesley had mismanaged, Sir John left the fortifications of Bombay and went to Swally—a measure as ill-timed as it was calamitous in its results.

Both parties now waited anxiously the arrival of Sir William Norris, a member of Parliament, who had been sent out with royal sanction at the English Company's expense, as Ambassador to the Great Mogul, in order that he might procure for them a firmán permitting them to trade in the Imperial dominions. The President of the new Factory of course felt that Norris would add great weight to his cause. On the other hand, the inmates of the old Factory were filled with apprehensions. They could scarcely make up their minds whether they should recognize the Ambassador as really accredited by their sovereign, or treat him as an enemy. On applying to Sir John Gayer to know how he was to be received, the answer was, that they and the commanders of European vessels were to shew him all marks of respect, so long as he conducted himself with impartiality, and did not exclusively favour the new Company. It is to be observed, that the President and his Council thus began by constituting

* Records of the English Company's Factory. † Bruce's Annals, 1698-99.

themselves judges of the Ambassador's behaviour, and determining beforehand to resist all his measures in favour of the new Company to which the Parliament of England had granted exclusive privileges. The resolution was unjustifiable, but it was more than acted upon at Masulipatam and Fort St. George, where the Ambassador first proceeded; there he was not recognized at all. At Masulipatam in particular the old Company's Factors treated him with mortifying indifference, and withheld from him all assistance, so that he was compelled to alter his intention of travelling from thence by Golconda to the camp of the Great Mogul.

Unable to reach the interior from the Eastern coast, and urgently invited by Waite to visit Surat, Sir William Norris arrived there on the tenth of December 1700. His presence was the signal for a commencement of squabbles, and a mutual infliction of injuries, the blame of which historians, who have only looked at one side of the facts, have thrown on the new Company. This, however, is not the true state of the case. If Sir William Norris, Sir Nicholas Waite, and all engaged in their cause, had been much better men than they were, and had shewn Christian forbearance, they could scarcely have helped resenting the insolent and factious behaviour of the old Company's servants.

Sir William Norris was convoyed by four ships of the Royal Navy, and his style was in every respect befitting his rank. His dignity as an Ambassador being superior to that of Sir John Gayer, he immediately ordered the Captain of the old Company's ship *Tavistock* to strike his Union Jack in token of respect. This was done; yet Sir John Gayer fearing that the old Factory would sink in the estimation of the Natives, ordered it to be re-hoisted. Norris then applied for permission to make a public entry into Surat; but the Governor had now learnt how to profit by the divisions of the English, and could not think of favouring either party gratuitously. For conceding this privilege he charged eighteen hundred gold mohars. One thousand he appropriated to himself, five hundred were given to his son, and three hundred to two principal officers. Then the embassy made its solemn entry.

Pleased with this little triumph, the Ambassador notified to Sir John Gayer that his diplomatic commission would be publicly read on the twenty-eighth of the month, and that it would be the duty of all the English to attend. Gayer in reply plainly disavowed his authority. Nor was he content with words; for he despatched an Armenian to Court as his Envoy, with orders to frustrate all the Ambassador's efforts. Enraged by this opposition, Sir Nicholas Waite brought a complaint before the Governor on the twenty-second of January 1701, and demanded that the Factors of the old Company should be placed in irons, as an atonement for the insults which they had offered to an Ambassador. Not feeling much interested in the matter, the Governor did not interfere, upon which Sir William Norris caused Wyche and Garnett, two members of Council in the old Factory, and Richardson their Secretary, to be seized. He then delivered them with their hands bound to the Governor, who detained them until they found security for their appearance when required.

This was a charming quarrel for the Mogul officers, and they saw that it was their interest to foment it in every way. Some notion of the golden harvest reaped by them may be formed by reading the following items, which I have collected. The entrance fee which Sir William Norris had paid, whetted the Governor's appetite for gold, and he took measures to sound the disposition of both parties. He first asked President Colt and then Sir Nicholas Waite whether each would give three lakhs of rupees to the Great Mogul. His son also intimated to Colt, that Waite had given him a written promise for four lakhs of rupees, but in consequence of his regard for the old Company's Factors he would be satisfied to receive three from them, in consideration of which he would write to Court on their behalf. The Armenian Envoy was allowed by Sir John Gayer and his party a credit of two lakhs to be spent in bribes at Court. Sir William Norris afterwards agreed to pay a lakh to the Mogul, and a lakh and a half to his ministers. To Gazedí Khán he gave two thousand three hundred gold mohars, and promised that he should have a lakh and a half of rupees on procuring the firmán. To the Khán's brother he also gave twenty thousand rupees. Lastly, he could only obtain permission to leave India by feeing the Governor with three thousand, and his officers with two thousand rupees.

As the new Company found the old Company burdened with debt, they gained a victory in this contest of bribes, and induced the Governor to strike a blow which it was hoped would be fatal to the old Factory. We have seen that Sir John Gayer had unwisely come to Swally, where he was unprotected. Taking advantage of this weakness the Governor's son marched in February 1701 from Surat with fifty horse and foot soldiers, seized him, his wife, and several Factors, conveyed them all to Surat and there closely confined them in the Governor's house. "This was done by an order from Court," wrote the servants of the old Company, "procured by SirNicholas Waite, the Hurcarra of Suratt, and others of that hellish crew." Sir William Norris had no concern in it, and demanded to know by what authority it was done. Indeed, Waite in the advices which he sent to England, admitted that the seizure was made at his solicitation, because the London Company's servants had spoken treasonably of the King, and had made use of their interest to oppose the privileges which Sir William Norris was endeavouring to obtain from the Emperor.*

After fourteen days Sir John Gayer and his friends were removed to their Factory, where in spite of their earnest remonstrances and moving appeals all remained confined for three years, and some much longer. We have a return of those who were in durance, made in January 1702. It includes the names of Sir John Gayer, General, Stephen Colt, President, six Senior Factors, six Junior Factors, seven Writers, six ladies, two children, two Surgeons, William Stephens, Captain Rayner and fifteen seamen, a Serjeant, thirty one soldiers, twenty four slaves, and three cooks—besides a Factor and Writer who were at Baroch, in all a hundred and nine persons.

The Ambassador had left Surat on the twenty-seventh of January

* The facts regarding these disputes are collected from diaries and a mass of official correspondence, copies of which are preserved in the books of the two Factories. Most of the facts are stated and repeated in different places, and I have not thought it necessary to give all the references.

1701, attended by a suite of sixty Europeans and three hundred Natives. His intention was to visit the Mogul's camp, and his easiest route would have been by Bombay; but he had already trusted too much to the hospitality of the old Company's servants, and prudently avoided their petty kingdom. If any had judged from the superior value of the presents which he took with him, they would have concluded that his prospects were fairer than Sir Thomas Roe's had been, but his personal qualifications were very inferior, and by no means fitted him for his delicate mission. After many alarms caused by the neighbourhood of Mogul and Maráthá armies,—which, we are told, the discipline of his followers kept in awe—and serious dissensions amongst his peons, he arrived at Birmapúri near Panderpúr on the Bíma, where Aurangzíb had established a permanent cantonment. The Emperor himself was encamped at Panála, but his minister Gazedí Khán was here, and Sir William requested permission to visit him in state with drums and trumpets. This was refused, on which the Ambassador being offended took his first false step, and proceeded without further ceremony, thus converting into an enemy one of the most influential men in the empire.

He reached Panála on the seventh of April, and demanded an audience of the Emperor, which was granted. There it became his study to make an imposing appearace, and to approach the Imperial presence in such a manner that an impression might be made both on the Court and people. A long procession was carefully arranged. First were drawn twelve brass guns, then came packages of glassware, and splendidly caparisoned steeds, all of which were designed as presents for the Emperor and his chief nobility. His Excellency next appeared in a palanquin, ornamented with embroidery, preceded and followed by heraldic insignia, flags, drums, trumpets, guards, servants in gorgeous liveries, all under the directions of a treasurer, secretary, master of the horse, and other officers of state. The whole was certainly calculated to strike with wonder a people like those of India, and it seems to have had for the time an effect upon the Imperial Court, as the firmáns, which the Ambassador demanded, were granted.* In gratitude he then paid his Majesty another visit, and presented him with two hundred gold mohars, which were graciouslyaccepted.

* The Ambassador's procession on the 28th April 1701:—
" Mr. Christor, Commander of His Excellency's Artillery, on horseback.
Twelve carts, wherein were carried the twelve brass guns for presents.
Five Hackerees, with the cloth &c. for presents.
One hundred cohors and messures, (coolies and gentlemen) carrying the glass ware, and looking glasses, for presents.
Two fine Arabian horses richly caparisoned, for presents.
Two ditto, without caparisons, for presents.
Four English soldiers, on horseback, guarding the presents.
The Union Flag.
The Red, White and Blue Flags.
Seven state horses, richly caparisoned, two with English furniture, and five with Indian.
The King's and His Excellency's crest
One state Palanquin, with English furniture of silver tissue brocaded.
Two other crests.
The Music, with rich liveries, on horseback.
Mr. Basset, Lieut. of His Excellency's foot guards, on horseback.
Ten servants in rich liveries, on horseback.

The event, however, proved that the Ambassador's success was unsubstantial. The Emperor required him to give security that his subjects should be protected from both European and Native pirates, to which Norris reasonably objected, saying that he could not undertake to keep in order the rovers of Málabár, and other inhabitants of the Mogul dominions ; but if the ever-ready resource of cash would be considered an equivalent, he would be glad to pay a lakh of rupees, and thus escape from the dilemma. In this instance money had no charm, and Sir William was curtly told that the "English best knew if it was their interest to trade, and if the Ambassador refused to give an obligation, he knew the same way back to England that he came." Norris made no further attempt at negotiation, but demanded his passports, and published a notice in the Persian, Hindústání, and English languages, requiring all persons to send in any claims which they might have upon the Embassy, as in five days he should commence his journey.

On the fifth of November, having received his passports, he set off on his return. After travelling three days he was overtaken by an Officer from Court, who declared that he must go back, as his papers were informal. This he refused, but agreed to halt for two days until the Emperor's pleasure should be known. Not hearing anything further he continued his march after the time specified had elapsed, and on the fourteenth reached Birmapúri, where his old enemy Gazedí Khán was on the look-out for him. With imprudent obstinacy he refused to pay the Khán a visit, although urgently pressed to do so, and on the twenty-second recommenced his journey. He had not advanced four miles before he and his suite were surrounded by a cloud of troops. His guard shewed courage and determination, so that he was not attacked ; but as his tents and baggage had been seized and resistance would have been hopeless, he was forced to comply with the demand that he should return to Birmapúri. When there, he protested against the outrage which had been offered to the representative of a great king, and was quietly told that he must wait till the Emperor's pleasure should be known. At last, on the fifth of February, the Khán informed him, that he had received from his Master a letter and sword for the King of England, and that the firmán would be forwarded in a short time. On the fifth the liberated Ambassador started again, and reached Surat on the twelfth of April, thus having occupied six months and

The King's and my Lord's Arms.
One Kettle Drum, in livery, on horseback.
Three Trumpetts, in liveries, on horseback.
Capt. Symons, Commander of H. E. guards.
Twelve troopers, every way armed and a·coutred after the English mode.
Mr. Beverley, Lieut. of H. E. horse guards.
The King's and my Lord's arms richly gilt, and very large, the first being borne by sixteen men.
Mr. John Mill, and Mr. Whitaker, on horseback, in rich laced coats.
Mr. Hale, Master of the Horse, richly drest, carrying the sword of state, pointed up.
His Excellency, in a rich Palanquin,—Indian embroidered furniture.
Four pages, two on each side of His Excellency's Palanquin, richly drest.
Edward Norris, Esq. Secretary to the Embassy, in a rich Palanquin, carrying His Majesty's letter to the Emperor, on each side Mr. Wingate, and Mr. Shettleworth, in rich laced coats on horseback.
Mr. Harlewyn, Treasurer, wearing a gold key, and Mr. Adiel Mill, Secretary to His Excellency, in a coach."— Bruce's Annals, 1701-2.

seven days in the journey from Panála. The distance is less than four hundred miles, and might have been easily accomplished by regular marches in a month. Vexatious indeed must have been the delays, painful the insults, to which he was subjected. Who, even after a century and a half have elapsed, does not feel some commiseration for the trials which the impatient and petulant, but yet highminded Norris had to brook? Who does not feel angry with the servants of the old Company, whose gold was the moving spring of all his troubles? Who is not disgusted with the sage Aurangzíb, the imperial persecutor of a stranger dependent on his generosity—Aurangzíb whose name stands high amongst the monarchs of India, but yet would not deserve the lowest place in a catalogue either of the heroes or the benefactors of the world?

When we consider the great expectations which were entertained of this embassy, the pomp for which it was distinguished, and the vast sums of money expended upon it, we are surprised to find that it has attracted so little the notice of historians. No account is given of it in the standard histories of India or England. Burnet, who tried to cull all the gossip of his day, has not alluded to it. There are certainly reasons why it deserved to sink into oblivion. It was really an abortive effort of one trading Company to ruin another. It was ill-conceived, worse planned, and still worse executed.

Although Sir William Norris was deficient in the coolness, astuteness, and decision which are necessary to render diplomacy successful, yet the failure of his embassy must not be altogether laid at his door. His position was one of extraordinary difficulty. The London Company left no stone unturned in their efforts to disgrace him. The advice which he received from the Presidents of the English Company in Bengal, Fort St. George, and Surat, could only confuse and perplex him. When he went to Masulipatam, Sir Nicholas Waite was jealous of Consul Pitt, who was there, and found that it was necessary for Norris to go to Surat, and Consul Pitt maintained, on the other hand, that he should not go to Surat as it would be derogatory for an Ambassador to be flitting from port to port instead of proceeding at once to Court. Then, when his expenses increased and he wanted money, Waite referred him to Consul Pitt, and Consul Pitt to Consul Sir Edward Littleton in Bengal. He consulted these troublesome Presidents as to the sort of firmán which he should procure, and each made a different proposition. When he had broken off negotiations with the Mogul, all complained of him, but each had a reason different from the others. Waite and his Council said he had no right to do so without their consent. From Masulipatam they plainly wrote and told him, that he had been rash, imprudent, and an absurd stickler for forms. At Húghli they charged him with being dilatory. In fact he had bitter enemies, false friends, and divided counsellors. It was no marvel that he fell a victim to a combination of adverse circumstances, to which many a wiser and more resolute man than he was would have succumbed.

He left Surat on the eighteenth of April 1702, after being on the worst terms with Waite, of whose violence he had always disapproved, and whose proposition that he should not negotiate the release of Sir John Gayer and his Factors he had repelled with indignation. Waite on the other hand accused him and his Secretary of being too favourably disposed towards the London Company. Having left his elephants, camels, horses, and oxen to be sold on the Company's account, and paid ten thousand rupees for his passage, he sailed on the *Scipio*, and reached the Mauritius on the eleventh of July, where the ship remained until the seventh of September. A few days after leaving that island he was seized with dysentery. Feeling that his end was approaching, he dictated to Harlwyn, the Treasurer of the Embassy, a vindication of his conduct, and pathetically expressed a hope, that notwithstanding his misfortunes his memory would be respected. With an unselfish and tender regard for a deceased friend, he called to mind the accusations which had been brought against Mill, his private Secretary, and declared that they were unfounded. He concluded by commending all persons who had been engaged in the Embassy to the Court's favour and protection. A few days later the poor sufferer expired.

CHAPTER X.

1698—1701.

CONTENTS.—Continued rivalry of the two Companies—The Emperor refers the question to a Múlá—Liberal conduct of the English Company—Terms of union arranged—Illustrative anecdotes—The new Company's Chaplain dies; interred in the Armenian cemetery; succeeded by Hackett; his martial commission—The Reverend Pratt Physon—Surgeon Maxwell—Disputes between the members of Council—Lock strikes the President—Mewse breaks Proby's head—The old Company's Surgeon—Statistics of crime for six months—Fight between Charles Peachey Esq. and the President; the President goes in and wins; Peachey severely punished—Offences of Walsh, Hartley, and Woodford—Captain Wyatt murders a sepoy—Provost Marshal Hall—Serjeant Bazett and other scabby sheep—Disease in Bombay—State of Bombay; frugality—The Moguls—Maráthás—Portuguese; dispute with them; their threats; ridiculous termination of the affair; they send an Envoy to Bombay; his proposals rejected—An Embassy from Abyssinia—The British Squadron—Queen Anne proclaimed.

THE departure of Sir William Norris did not in any way remove the bone of contention from the two Companies. Nor was either party so successful in petting and bribing the Great Mogul as to obtain any decided advantage over the other. So long as they continued to quarrel, they feed his Imperial Majesty and his officers so well, that it was impossible for him to say which ought to have the preference. If one party had paid for justice, and the other had not, the case would have been simple. But when both seemed to have inexhaustible treasures, and opened their coffers freely, the question of right became a knotty point.

Moreover, Aurangzíb was a religious Prince, and wanted to have the opinion of a Priest. So, after getting all he could for himself out of the English, and failing to discover the truth, he was willing to let a descendant of the prophet take his turn, and for that purpose commissioned a Múlá at Surat to find out which was "the real English Company." Saiyid Ṣedula, the Priest who was thus appealed to, began his inquiry in earnest, and was too shrewd a man to think that he could find his way through the maze without a golden clue. Sir Nicholas Waite calculated that a payment of ten thousand rupees would enable him to see quite clearly, and at this price he would draw up a report in the English Company's favour.

I may be thought presumptuous in going directly contrary to the opinion of all good writers on this subject, but yet I must say, that the new or English Company appeared throughout far more liberal and tolerant than the London Company. The Directors of the English Company were always inclined to peace, although their servants in India were far from carrying out their good intentions. No sooner did they hear of the disturbances and animosities at Surat, than they wrote out expressing their regret at such proceedings, which they feared might be destructive to both Companies. With prudent forbearance they desired that the system of competition should be changed, and that their servants should only endeavour "to out-trade" their rivals, at the same time treating all Englishmen with civility and respect. They were of opinion that Sir Nicholas Waite had no authority to remove the London Company's flag from their Factory at Swally, and that it was reasonable to expect the Mogul Governor would resent such an act. They condemned his malicious application to the Governor, leading, as it did, to the oppression under which Sir John Gayer and his friends suffered. They told Waite that his business was simply to procure for his Company the privileges which the others enjoyed, not to assail or injure them. In the same spirit they treated free traders. It really seemed their object to increase the commerce of England as well as their own, and with that view they permitted a certain De Paz to trade as a free merchant in India—an innovation of which the old Company had never dreamed.*

In 1700 the English Company made the first advances, and proposed that the two Companies should arrange terms of union; but to the factious Directors of the London Company this appeared only an evidence of weakness, and led them to suppose that by holding out a little longer they would bring their adversaries to unconditional surrender.† Losses and afflictions were still required to subdue their pride and rancour. Happily both parties were at last taught wisdom by their trials, and not driven to despair. Both took warning just in time, and made serious attempts to end their differences. If they had not, speedy ruin would have been the inevitable consequence. On the twenty-seventh of April 1702 the two Companies approved an instrument of union, and wrote to their servants desiring that their mutual disputes should be buried in oblivion. It was agreed that after the twenty-second of July all opposition should cease; that trade, with the exception of such as was afloat and contracted for, should be conducted on a general stock; that the servants of the two Companies should strive to forward each other's views, so as to assist each other in disposing of their European goods, and lowering the prices of Indian commodities. It was long before the Union was completed, but the work of reconciliation was now undertaken in earnest, and from this time we may date the commencement of a career which, after a necessary period of exhaustion, led the East India Company to wealth and power.

At the Union the affiliated Factories of Bombay were Surat, Baroch, Ahmedábád, Agra, and Lacknow; on the Coast of Málabár, the Forts and Factories of Carwar, Talichari, Anjengo and Cálicot; in Persia, the Factories of Gombroon, Shiraz and Ispahan.

We will now attempt to collect some facts which will give us a little further insight into the history of these three eventful years.

The new Company were very careful to provide their servants with

* Bruce's Annals, 1700-1702. † Ibid 1699-1700

ministers of religion, but did not always make a happy selection. Mr. Edwards, their first Chaplain, contracted a disease of the country, and died on the twenty-fifth of March 1700, after an illness of thirty days. Nothing can shew more painfully the bitterness—we may say the ferocity—of the spirit with which the two Companies were animated in their rivalry, than the fact that on this occasion Sir Nicholas Waite could not bury his dead in the ground where other bodies of his countrymen rested. There was the spacious cemetery of the old Company with the grand mausolea of its Chiefs, and a few generations of Factors sleeping around them ; but interlopers and competitors in trade might not rot there. Persons professing not only to hold the same religion but also observing the same forms, had been driven by commercial antagonism to set up altar against altar, and to hinder their clergy from associating even in death. They imitated the odious jealousy of the blindest superstition.

> " That mourn'd the dead ; and this denied a grave."

Probably Waite had as bitter feelings against the old Company's Factors as Young had, under similar circumstances, against Roman Catholics, and with a humanity denied to poor Edwards " *wished them all a grave.*"

It must be recorded to their credit that the Armenians came forward and offered the use of their burial ground. Their liberal proposal was gratefully accepted, and the Chaplain's body found a resting place with strangers.

Looking round to supply the place of the clergyman whom he had lost, Waite lighted upon Hackett, Chaplain of the ship *Norris*. The inducements which the President offered, and the consideration by which he was guided, shew us the value set at that time upon the services of sea-faring clergy. The owners of the *Norris* had arranged with Hackett that on his return to England he should receive a hundred pounds. When then he was invited to take duty at Surat,—it became necessary to engage that he should be indemnified for the loss which he would suffer on account of only fulfilling half his agreement. The President writes that he had stipulated for this, and adds, " I hope that he will by his piety and diligence in his station be such an example of virtue as may deserve this favour from your honours."*

Hackett was soon after employed on an errand for which his calling scarcely fitted him. He was sent to Birmapúri in charge of the brass guns which had arrived at Surat after the Ambassador had left, and this Priest of the Church militant marched at the head of ten soldiers, six writers, and two surgeons. However, he had episcopal authority for what he did, as eleven years previously Compton, Bishop of London, in buff-coat, jack-boots, with a sword at his side and pistols in his holsters—the dress of a Colonel of militia—had escorted the Princess Anne in her flight from the metropolis.†

On his return to Surat, Hackett, as we conclude from official letters, was engaged in instructing young persons ; but he soon left India. On this

* Letter from Sir N. Waite and Council to the English Company ; dated 9th April 1700.

† Macaulay's History of England.

occasion Sir Nicholas Waite, after making to the Court a modest application for one Bible and two Prayer Books, added in language which was fashionable even with disreputable men at that time :—"We shall be without a Chaplain for reading prayers and instruction of your youth, until your Honours please to send a pious and ingenious man, whose learning and behaviour may be exemplary to all your servants, and inform the world of the glorious mysteries as yet unknown amongst these people."

During Hackett's temporary absence, the Reverend Pratt Physon undertook the duties of the Chaplaincy for six months, but his example was by no means edifying to the gentlemen of the Factory. On the contrary, he did his utmost to bring them into disgrace by purchasing goods of considerable value, for which he had not the means of paying. And so passes off the scene this acting Chaplain, leaving a smell of brimstone behind him.

Nor was the Medical department of the new Factory better superintended than the Ecclesiastical. For some time Dr. John Maxwell, Surgeon, was in attendance on the Ambassador, but was dismissed for ill-behaviour. Returning thus disgraced to Surat, he there continued "his lewd debauched life," and was in consequence expelled the service. This reprobate then removed to Cochin, where he placed himself in communication with pirates, to whom, through means of correspondents, he gave information as to when and where vessels might be expected. He made no secret of these transactions, but with the utmost audacity boasted of the large sums which he had received in return for his treachery.*

But after all, the vices of subordinates were countenanced by the irregularity and indecency of their superiors. The Council Board was an arena of continual squabbles, which, in one instance at least, ended in blows. Jeremiah Bonnell was declared to be suspended from Council by his fellow members Benjamin Mewse and Callow Carey, and, as they were a majority, the President concurred. Soon afterwards John Lock, the fifth in Council, was suspended for the heinous offence of striking Sir Nicholas Waite, "her Majesty's publick minister and Consull," and he could not be brought to acknowledge his error, but steadily maintained that he had acted rightly. By this time Mewse had altered his opinion in Bonnell's case, and refused to attend Council till both he and Lock should be restored. He also complained that business was not transacted by a majority in Council, but merely according to the orders of Waite and Proby. He therefore absented himself from the Board.†

We shall meet with this Mewse again, when his turbulence brings him into notoriety, but we may now look at the sketch which Sir Nicholas Waite gave of his character, as we thus gain an idea of what the third member of Council *could* be. The President informs the Court that Mewse had the reputation amongst all the Company's servants, and indeed all Europeans at Surat, of being addicted to hard drinking, seldom sober, and above all reproof. The true reason of his absence from Council was not any well-grounded complaint ; but that his intellect was disordered by liquor, and he was "unfit for virtuous conversation." He compelled his

* Letter as above, and one dated 15th February 1703-4.

† Diary of the English Company's Factory at Surat ; 17th February and 14th May 1702.

subordinates to follow his example, and "would have nobody under him who would not drink." At last even in that society such dissipation became insufferable. One Sunday after dinner he invited Proby, the second in Council, to drink a glass of wine at his lodgings. He soon got very quarrelsome, began by flinging the glasses about, and concluded by breaking his senior's head with a bottle. Callow Carey, who was present at the time, deposed to this fact upon oath, and John Frost, and Thomas Moore, two writers, set their hands to a declaration that they had heard Mewse swear "he would pistole Mr. Proby." Such was a wine party of Councillors in the olden time. Number three gets drunk and breaks number two's head; at which number four looks on and takes notes. They only wanted number five, the pugnacious Lock, and number one, the intemperate Waite; they would then have formed a full Council. Truly "most potent, grave and reverend signors!"

Disgraceful as these intestine disorders were, they were not worse than those which preyed upon the inner life of the old Company. They, too, had a troublesome and unmanageable Doctor. Placing the same reliance as other Natives upon the medical skill of European practitioners, the Siddí had requested that the Government of Bombay would send a Surgeon to attend his wounded men. Dr. Thompson volunteered for the duty, and only desired—as the Deputy Governor wrote in the undignified style of the day—that he might take with him "that black fellow," who was an Assistant in the Hospital. As there were only three sick persons in all the Hospital, the Deputy Governor in Council concluded that Dr. Skinner, the Surgeon in charge, would not objeet to the temporary loss of the "black fellow's" services. The Secretary was therefore ordered to apply to Dr. Skinner, which he did in a polite note. The reply was simply a shower of abuse. This the Government bore with exemplary patience, merely stating in their official report that this "most scurrilous answer shews the pride and factiousness of that vain man."*

Possibly it will occur to the reader, as it has occurred to the writer—that the *dramatis personæ* in this Chapter are all men of bad character; that I only present offensive details which are relieved by no examples of goodness and honour. I can only say that I represent the matter faithfully as recorded by the best authorities of the age. Vices were then trifles; to be corrupt and to corrupt others was the fashion.† I do not find a word of any thing good in the local annals either written or printed. As soon as I do, it will be a pleasure to serve up what must be more agreeable to "the gentle reader" than depreciatory strictures. In the meanwhile it is not my fault, if nausea is created by a surfeit of disgraceful anecdotes.

Judge patiently, reader. Imagine yourself on the Bench for six months; see what culprits we shall bring before you, and then say whether you can-

* The Deputy Governor and Council to Sir John Gayer: March 1701.

† "Nemo illic vitia ridet; nec corrumpere ac corrumpi seculum vocatur." Thus Tacitus (De Mor. German.) writes of the ancient Germans, and of course hits Roman society. He is referring in the first place to adultery, but applies what he says generally. Might the special or general application be made to Anglo-Indian Society now? Persons in England who are interested in that society, would say that both might.

not form an opinion as to the statistics of folly and crime amongst Anglo-Indians in the Bombay Presidency at the opening of the eighteenth century. You will probably conclude that, sad as have been the delinquencies of which we have heard in late years, yet when we consider the vast number of persons employed now by the Indian Government, the cases are few indeed as compared with those which occurred in the year 1701-2, and between the months of October and March inclusive.

It will be remembered that President Annesley having been dismissed, was succeeded by Stephen Colt, who seems to have managed the Company's affairs at Surat with prudence. At least, I know of no charge brought against him, except the one I am now about to relate.

Mr. Charles Peachey was at this time lying in durance, to which he had been committed by the English authorities. He appears to have passed his many idle hours in giving vent to his indignation and writing letters, which are apparently the productions of a rational man, and, as such, were thought worthy of a place in the records of Government. Yet they expose a state of affairs which is calculated to awaken incredulity. The prisoner addresses, "The Right Honourable the President and Council for the affairs of the Right Honorable the East India Company," and then begins unceremoniously with telling them, that it is no use for them to think that by locking him up they can conceal their guilt. Complainant then proceeds to state that the Right Honorable President had broken his head, and lest that distinguished person should suppose the mischief had stopped there he further enters into details, pointing out that he had been in all respects punished very considerably,—in the language of the ring, "regularly doubled up." I am really afraid of being charged with exaggeration, and therefore quote the words of Peachey's extraordinary letter;—

"I have received from you two cuts on my head, the one very long and deep, the other a slight thing in comparison to that; then a great blow on my left arme which has enflamed the shoulder, and deprives me (at present) the use of that limb; on my right side a blow, on my ribs just beneath my pap, which is a stoppage to my breath, and makes me incapable of helping myself; on my left hipp another, nothing inferior to the first; but, above all, a cut on the brow of my left eye. The anguish thereof has caused a swelling, and that swelling destroyed my eyesight, which I should perfectly receive. There is a statute (which assuredly you shall take your triall upon); the sense thereof is, that whosoever shall mame another shall be thought culpable, and be punished with death."

It must be admitted that the Right Honorable pugilist had shewn considerable science, and planted his blows to some purpose. Imagine Charles Peachey Esquire in his prison house, with a deep gash on his head; his eye bunged up, his arm in a sling, stiff and wheezy from a blow beneath his fifth rib, and limping with a sprained hip joint. We must allow that although some Governors at the present time may have administrative abilities, none can have studied the noble art of self-defence with more success than had the gallant Stephen Colt.

Well, although Peachey cuts a sad figure and is certainly not fit to be seen, yet we must summon him to give evidence as to the cause of this singular outbreak. He admits that he had laughed at the President, but sets up as a plea of justification, that that high functionary had entirely forgotten his own dignity. For instance, the President had "cuffed" him, and when he took to his heels, flung his slipper after him. But the climax in this sanctimonious gentleman's estimation was, that the President had shewn no respect for the Sabbath, but ordered his victim's property to be removed from Mr. Wyche's lodgings on Sunday.

After receiving this severe punishment, and being expelled the Factory, Peachey was kept in prison "to plague" him, as the President expressed it. What follows shews that the President considered he had a good cause, and at least was not implacable. "I said," proceeds Peachey, "I would write to his Excellency. Your answer was, I might; but you would pass your word it should prove ineffectual, and thereupon offered me your hand."

After this, according to Peachey's account, the President saw him beaten by Mr. Robinson on the terrace, and when he was talking too loud in dispute with Mr. Deane, mocked and reviled him. From what follows it would appear that this unfortunate man was not without supporters :—

"When I returned with a sword, 'twas for no evil, but to rescue my companions, and had you assaulted me afresh, I should have killed you (as you pretend was my intent). I don't at all question but the law should have found it no otherwise than *se deffendendo*."

Four days later we have another letter from Mr. Peachey, who quotes the twenty-ninth article of Magna Charta, with observations by "Justice Cooke," to shew that no free man could be arrested or detained in prison without first resort being had to legal process.

On the whole, in the absence of evidence on the other side, we cannot find Stephen Colt guilty from this *ex-parte* statement. However, the existence of this paper on official records proves that there had been a disgraceful affray ; that Mr. Peachey had lost his temper, soundness of limbs, and liberty, and that the President had at least lost a portion of his dignity.*

The next month we have an account of a duel fought at Bombay by Mr. Enoch Walsh on the one side and Mr. Ralph Hartley on the other. The former gentleman had for long been a bad subject, notorious for idleness, deeply involved in debt, and generally of dissolute habits. The latter, as will be seen, was not much better. On this occasion he was the sufferer, being severely wounded. At first it was feared that his wound would prove mortal; but eventually he recovered.

The same month Mr. Thomas Woodford was guilty of embezzlement, having appropriated to himself the Right Honorable Company's cash to a considerable amount. He made his escape, but was taken and kept a prisoner. A few months later the Bombay Government report to the Directors that they should have sent this gentleman home in a ship, which was then sailing, "but that there were too many such order'd on her."

The above mentioned Hartley was concerned in fraud with Woodford.

* Diary of the London Company's Factory at Surat, containing copies of letters dated 4th and 8th October 1700.

Mr. William Howson, also, who had charge of the Custom House at Mahim, had appropriated to himself two thousand three hundred and two rupees from the public chest. When detected he made the usual excuse that he was driven by his exigencies to take the money, but that he had intended to return it in three or four days.* Such were the events of two months—October and November.

In December occurred a still more disgraceful and most tragical affair. On the twenty-third of that month Captain John Wyatt had command of the guards for the day, and about eleven o'clock at night left the apartments of Mr. Demetrius and Mr. Wright for his own quarters. At this time he was much intoxicated, although quite sober and rational when brought before the Council at five the next morning. After leaving his friends when he came near his own door, the sentry challenged him, upon which the Captain became extremely angry, drew his sword, and made a thrust at him. The sentry fled, and one who was stationed at Woodford's door followed his example. Both made for the main guard, pressed hard by their persecutor. Just at that moment the sand of the hour glass had run out, and the sepoy in whose charge it was, called to another to strike the gong. This seemed to add fuel to Wyatt's rage; he instantly ordered the Corporal of the guard to relieve and bring the sentry before him. He then commenced to beat the poor fellow, asking him how he dared to have the gong struck without waiting for his orders. The other meekly replied that he was merely acting according to established rule, but for the future he would only act as the Captain should think proper, and begged that he would cease beating him. Wyatt then took the man by the arm, deliberately turned him round, and run his sword through his side. The sepoy dropped down dead upon the spot. This savage madman added to the barbarity of his crime by kicking and otherwise abusing the corpse of his murdered victim. The Deputy Governor was immediately summoned from his bed, and had the murderer secured. The decision of the Governor in Council was, that Captain Wyatt should be deprived of his commission, confined in irons, and sent to England. The tragic issue of this affair made probably some impression even upon this turbulent community; for we do not find that any cases of a serious character were brought before Government during the following months of January and February.

In March 1701 we find John Hall, Provost Marshall, confined to the Fort of Dongarí.† There was once an intention of giving him an ensigncy; but he was then charged with being an infamous drunkard, and in other respects a bad character. When required to clear himself of these charges, he only cursed and swore at every one, from the highest to the lowest, expressing a hope that the time might come when he would have his revenge. The Government were obliged to put him in confinement at Dongarí, although, as they significantly remarked, "having too many such as he is in that or one fort or other, and with submission

* Letters to the Hon'ble Court from the Governor and Council of Bombay, dated 28th November 1700, and March 1701.

† Deputy Governor and Council of Bombay to Sir John Gayer and Council; dated 28th December 1700.

to your Excellency and Council, if they were all sent home, there would be a happy riddance of them." Hall was accordingly shipped off, but Sir John Gayer, the General, and his Council, thought that his masters had acted too precipitately. The reply to their advice was as follows :—

"As to Hall, had there been any hope of reclaiming him, by being reduced, as your Excellency and Council are pleased to direct, should have done it; but, as he is a restless, factious, and turbulent spirited man, ever promoting and carrying on his rascally designs, would be always reducing others to be confederates with him; therefore, as you were pleased to leave it to us, we thought it with submission much better to be rid of such a scabby sheep, that he might not infect the flock; so have sent him home."

However, by the shepherd's own admission, the flock were already infected. They seem to have been all "scabby." There was no soundness from head to foot. Amongst others, we find mentioned a Serjeant Bazett who had absconded. He must have been a stylish non-commissioned officer, for his wife disposed of her plate and jewels to satisfy his creditors. Besides these, a man named Scott, and several others who had formerly run away and become renegades, were sent back this month by the Siddí.*

It is some relief, after these numerous reports of crime and misdemeanours, to find it stated that Horbin, who had been one of the culprits, had been reclaimed, and was diligent in business, promising never again to be guilty of such errors. As Enoch Walsh and a number of other factious persons had been removed, the Government hoped to enjoy a season of quietness and moral decency.

When we would go on to inquire what punishment was inflicted on these grand offenders, and whether they met their deserts, we find ourselves in the dark. The Government would not venture to pass any more severe sentence than fine or dismissal, and so prisoners were shipped off in large numbers to England.

The thought occurs, what times those would have been for newspapers! They would indeed have had but a limited circulation; but their intelligence, how strongly spiced and exciting! Bombay is, it is true, still fertile in scandals and offences, and the fragrance from it, which steam and the public press carry with them, is not so sweet as that of "the perfumed isles;" but then consider how large our society is. Yet racy facts are comparatively rare. Governors conduct themselves with dignity; they won't fight, and are decorously dull. If a desire to *punch their heads* is sometimes expressed by disappointed candidates for their patronage, it is never put into execution. Heads of departments do not often take a felonious dip into their treasure chests, and we hope that there is but a solitary instance of a European murdering an unresisting native. But the first year of the eighteenth century was a stirring one. There are two Companies fighting with the Native Government, fighting with one another, and their servants fighting amongst themselves. The President of one is struck by a member of his Council, and the head of

* Letters as above.

the second member is broken in a drunken row by the third. As regards the other Company, lovers of gossip heard in six months how a Right Honorable President had been jeered at by one of his subordinates, to whom in return he gave a terrible drubbing; how a Collector of Customs had embezzled money, and other Factors had imitated him; how a Captain in the little army had stabbed to death a poor, defenceless, supplicating victim, and then spurned his lifeless corpse; how, after so many had committed crimes, it was *hoped* that *one* sinner had been reclaimed to honour. Those were stirring times in Bombay; and so are these. Then the sensation was often caused by the triumphs of vice, now, we trust, chiefly by its exposure and degradation.

As is usually the case, the weird sisters, crime and disease, appeared in company. A fearful mortality prevailed in Bombay. The Natives suffered much, and only seventy-six Europeans were left. Following this calamity was a violent storm, which destroyed the produce of the island, and wrecked the greater part of the shipping.*

Little was seen at this period of the pomp and grandeur for which the Factory had been distinguished in the days of Oxenden and Aungier. In Bombay people were compelled to be pedestrians, for Sir John Gayer wrote that there was only one horse on the island fit to be ridden, and but one pair of oxen to draw a coach. At Surat the public table was kept with the most wretched parsimony; so much so, that the Factors were almost driven to seek their meals at taverns and public houses. The members of Council sat down to an ordinary supper; but at the same time one joint of meat was all that was placed before the rest of the Company's servants. Here was another temptation to riotous living, for when so little comfort was to be found in their common home, the Factors and Writers naturally sallied out in search of good cheer. So little were they to be trusted, that it was feared they would fall into all kinds of mischief. Sir John Gayer attempted to remedy the evil, and remove all grounds of just complaint, by ordering that proper suppers should be provided for all at the public table; at the same time he was cautious in recommending frugality.†

These were "scambling and unquiet times" all over India; but so engrossed were the two Companies with their private feuds, and intrigues with the Mogul authorities, that they could turn little attention to other nations. Yet one or two transactions with foreign powers were not without interest. Great alarm was created in Bombay when the inhabitants heard that a Mussulman force was laying siege to Singhar, which was only five marches distant. The Mussulman powers of the whole peninsula were breaking up into parties, and anxiously expecting a dissolution of the Empire at Aurangzíb's death. The Maráthás were every year adding to their strength, and laying the country under contributions. Between Agra and Surat the districts had been kept in such alarm, that the Factors had not been able to procure from them a single bale of indigo.‡

* Bruce's Annals, 1702-3.

† Letters from Sir John Gayer and Council to Stephen Colt, Esq. and Council in 1699.

‡ Bruce's Annals, 1699-1700.

The fleet of the Maráthás, through the activity of Kanhojí Angria, its commander, had considerable success, and took many prizes from its native enemies. It was a troublesome and dangerous neighbour to Bombay, as the place now called Angria's Colaba was its rendezvous.*

The Portuguese, too, continued to cause much embarrassment, by intriguing with the Maráthás against the English, and also obstructing the transport of provisions. A serious dispute with them was opened, when the assault of a more cruel enemy than the English drove them to Bombay, not as invaders—which they had foolishly threatened that they would be—but as suppliants for protection. The story is as follows.

As a Portuguese manchua was firing guns off the harbour of Bombay, and the Commodore suspected her of being a pirate, he sent his boats to ascertain the real state of the case. The Portuguese, on their part, seeing the English giving them chase, as it were, may have supposed that they came with hostile intent. At all events, the English were fired upon, and in revenge they boarded the manchua, claimed her as their prize, and conveyed her to Bombay. Seeing that a mistake had been made, the English Commodore sent the captured vessel to the Portuguese Captain General of the North, who was furious at the insult offered to his nation, and threatened to attack the aggressors. The importation of provisions to Bombay from Salsette was prohibited, and a fleet of fifty manchuas was assembled off Mahim, as if with the view of invasion. The conclusion of this affair would have been simply ridiculous, if it had not brought suffering to others besides the boasters. Whilst the Portuguese were indulging their gasconade, an Arab fleet suddenly made its appearance, burned the shipping at Salsette, and landed an armed force, which took the Fort of Versova, putting all that they found of both sexes to the sword. A panic spread like wildfire. The Padre Superior and thousands of others came for refuge to Bombay. The Captain General's pride was brought down, and his tone softened. Instead of breathing out slaughter against the English, he humbly craved their assistance, remaining for some time in security at Bandora. The Arabs professed friendship for the English. However, they were not to be trusted. After a time they began to withdraw, and the re-embarkation of their whole force except three hundred men having been effected, they were about to set fire to the Church at Bandora when this residue was attacked by an overwhelming force of Portuguese. Three hundred more Arabs were speedily landed from the fleet, and a skirmish followed. Night only saved the Portuguese from an inglorious defeat, and the Arabs withdrew before morning, fearing lest they should be attacked by the English.

After this a Portuguese with the high sounding title of "Envoy for the Royal State of India" came to form a treaty with the Government of Bombay. His draft contained five articles, all of which were rejected. By the first it was to be engaged that such conditions should be observed as had been accepted by Captain Humphry Cook when he took possession of the island. This was refused because the conditions had been made by Cook under compulsion, and were subsequently disallowed by Charles

* Grant Duff's History, Chapter xi.

the Second. By the second article an offensive and defensive alliance was to be established between the English and Portuguese, such as had been arranged between the two Crowns in the original articles of capitulation; but it was declared that those articles were cancelled, when the King of Portugal had refused to assist the King of England in his war with the French and Dutch. The third declared that the lands of Portuguese residents in Bombay which had been confiscated should be restored: this was refused on the ground that the proprietors had run away and assisted the Siddí in making war against the English. The fourth proposed that the English should cease to demand customs from such subjects of the King of Portugal as imported goods from Bandora. This was refused, because the English claimed the customs as one of the royalties ceded to them by the Crown of Portugal. According to the fifth, all coolies and other natives who should run away from Salsette or Bombay were mutually to be given up by the contracting parties; but as the English did not see why they should send back to a state of slavery such as were discontented with the evils of Portuguese rule, this article was also rejected.*

Expectations were formed at this time of opening a lucrative trade with Abyssinia, an Ambassador from which country came to Bombay. In return for this visit, and the handsome presents which he had brought, the General provided him with the means of transport, and on sending him back to his country, delivered to him letters and presents for his master King Thoran. It is a matter of regret that we have only a gleam of light thrown upon these interesting communications, and have no means of obtaining further information about them.†

The British squadron which had accompanied the Ambassador effected little towards assisting the English in suppressing piracy. The Commodore, Littleton, was perplexed by the discordant claims of the rival Companies. Sir Nicholas Waite required his attendance when he made his public entry into Surat, but this was refused. Yet the Commodore recognized all the rights of the English Company, to the old Company's mortification. On the other hand, he disgusted Waite by holding communications with President Colt, and informing him that he would protect all vessels sailing under the old Company's license.‡

In Oct. 1702 Queen Anne was proclaimed in the room called the Chapel, at Surat, by the Secretary, after the minister had finished his sermon.§

* Letter from Sir John Gayer and Council to the Court; dated 1st February 1700.

† The following is a copy of the letter delivered to the Ambassador.

"John Gayer, General for affaires of the Right Honorable East India Company in India, residing at Bombay, sendeth greeting to his most excellent Majesty Thoran, King of Abissine, and Worshipper of Jesus, the Son of Mary, according to the laws of the Blessed Messias.

"Your Majesty's royal letters and present of seven horses, twenty slaves, and three horns of civit I was honored with in behalf of the Right Honorable East India Company, by your noble Embassador, Dumontre, whome received with all possible demonstration of honor, love, and affection, and have continued the same to him all the time of his abode in these parts, and now have taken care to transport him back to your territories with the President of the Right Honorable East India Company to your most sacred Majesty, an account of which comes with this. That your most Excellent Majesty will graciously be pleased to accept thereof, and to lay your royal commands on me for the future, as in your most serenely and princely wisdome shall seem meet, is most humbly desired" Diary of the London Company's Factory at Surat 1701-1704.

‡ Bruce's Annals, 1701-2.

§ Diary of the London Company's Factory at Surat.

CHAPTER XI.

1703—1708.

CONTENTS.—Continued disputes in India—Heavy liabilities of the London Company—Arrangements for the Government of Bombay—Factors still in confinement—Sir Nicholas Waite's malicious and selfish behaviour ; he offends all parties ; is dismissed ; impartial view of his character—Mewse causes disputes between the two Companies' servants—Eustace Needham—State of the two Factories—Fresh acts of piracy, and consequent injuries inflicted upon the old Factory—Wretched state of Bombay ; the revenues and garrison—Disease ; the European population dwindles away—Dr. Alexander Orme—Oppressions of the Mogul Officers ; Sir John Gayer's allegory—The Maráthás threaten fresh assaults—Contest at Sea—The Muscat Arabs—The Gennims—The Dutch successfully resist the oppression of the Moguls—Captain Green ; his piratical transactions—Suppression of European piracy—Union of the two Companies completed—New arrangements ; the Government—The state and system of trade : chartered ships ; import and export trade ; how conducted ; alarm at competition—Infringement of monopoly—Conclusion ; remarks on the East India Company ; on the Company's servants ; on their relations with the people of India.

ALTHOUGH the London and English Companies had arranged terms of union in England, and each had instructed its servants to treat the servants of the other with courtesy and respect, it was a long time before ainmosity was laid aside in India. A treaty of peace could not at once allay all hostile feelings, and during five years there were occasional skirmishes at the outposts, which sometimes grew so warm that there was danger lest the war should be renewed. As the instructions from home to live in peace and quietness were positive, neither party ventured at first to disobey them. Sir Nicholas Waite had pertinaciously endeavoured to prevent a union, and to persuade the Directors of his own Company that it would be to their detriment, but as soon as he heard that his remonstrances were unheeded and that a union would certainly take place, he wrote and assured the Directors of his resolution to "obliterate all past heats," and to hold friendly intercourse with Sir John Gayer and his Council.* The communication, however, between the two Chiefs and their Councils never went beyond formal civility. There was constraint on both sides ; nor did either place any reliance upon the good dispositions of the other.

Although the Directors of the English Company have been blamed for their conduct in these affairs, I think that they acted with prudent and

* Diary of the English Company's Factory at Surat, 7th February 1702-3.

consistent fairness. They found the London Company burdened with enormous debts—estimated at a hundred and forty lacks of rupees, chiefly incurred in Sir John Child's war, and other responsibilities which they took care should not fall upon their own shoulders. When both Companies appealed to Godolphin, Lord Treasurer of England, and he delivered an award which is admitted to have been as wise and solid a decision as is to be found in the political or commercial annals of England, he declared that the estate and effects of the London Company would not be sufficient to pay their debts, although when the stock of the English Company was joined to them, there would be a considerable balance in favour of the United Company, after paying all foreign demands. Moreover, the home debts of the London Company were very large, and altogether they were not, as their rivals were, in a solvent condition. The value of their stock had in consequence become so depreciated, that it had fallen from three hundred to thirty-seven per cent.

But there were also certain documents called Security Bonds, which were a heavy clog on the operations of the London Company at Surat, and for which the other Company prudently resolved not to be responsible. These had been extorted from the President and Council of the Factory by the Governor of Surat, in consequence of the piracies from which the native shipping had suffered so much, and they were intended as a guarantee to him that all future losses should be made good. It was not to be expected that the English Company would be ready to share with their new allies these serious responsibilities, and they of course cordially approved Sir Nicholas Waite's conduct, when he prevented their separate interests from being "embroiled in the Security Bonds, and in any demands which could be made on the London Company." They also urged him, but in consequence of superior management on the other side unsuccessfully, to see that in making the new appointments to official situations their own servants were taken as good care of as the other Company's. In these respects they looked vigilantly to the interests both of their constituents and dependents. But they also steadily required conciliatory behaviour on the part of their servants, regretted when old wounds were opened afresh, and, as we shall see, visited Sir Nicholas Waite with their severe displeasure, when he obstinately persisted in keeping alive the flame of discord.

In arranging the Government, it was settled that Sir John Gayer should be General and Governor of Bombay, Mr. Burniston Deputy Governor—both London Company's Servants—and Sir Nicholas Waite President at Surat. To all other appointments the servants of the two Companies were to be nominated according to their respective ranks. Such as were not so fortunate as to obtain any appointment had the option of returning to England or remaining as free merchants in India.. Burniston died in 1704, and Sir Nicholas Waite appointed Mr. Aislabie to succeed him, but the Court's orders were that Brabourne, Chief of Anjengo, should be Second in Council at Bombay, and Aislabie Third.

During all this time the General and Council of the old Factory were suffering a long and tedious confinement. They were not permitted to pass the gate of their own buildings, and could only receive a daily allowance of provisions. To Sir John Gayer this restraint must have been particularly irksome, as he was most anxious to visit his seat of Government, where he would be able to act independently. Moreover, an order had come from the Court, that unless he was liberated within three months after its arrival in India, Sir Nicholas Waite should act for him as General, and this order was highly objectionable to him, in consequence of the other's violent, restless, and saturnine disposition.

Although Sir Nicholas Waite had many provocations, yet his conduct was unjustifiable and injurious to all with whom he was concerned. He not only refused to be responsible for the Security Bonds of the London Company, but gave the Governor of Surat to understand that Sir John Gayer would be displaced, and he himself made General in his stead ; and that if the Governor wished to recover money for damages done by pirates, he had better place a strong guard over the Factory. Supporting these representations by a bribe of twenty-seven thousand rupees, he contrived that the three months specified in the Courts order should elapse, and he himself be installed as General. Burniston, and Harland, the new Commodore, in vain remonstrated with him for this ungenerous conduct, and declared to the Governor that he was acting in opposition to directions received from home. Harland, indeed, refused him a passage to Bombay ; so indignant was he at his selfishness.

Waite excused himself by declaring that Gayer owed his calamities to his own rashness, and that if instead of precipitately making known the union of the two Companies, he had concealed it for a time, their separate interests would have been adjusted, and he himself set at liberty. But certainly this spiteful Sir Nicholas gave no heed to his masters' positive orders that he should use every effort to procure Sir John Gayer's release. Indeed, when he had gone to Bombay, his broker assured Bonnell and Proby, the English Company's servants at Surat, that Waite had promised him fifty thousand rupees, if he would use his influence with the Governor to keep Sir John Gayer confined.

Waite was so unfortunate as to offend every person with whom he was in any way connected. He accused the two last named members of Council of embezzling eleven thousand rupees, and they in reply maintained that he had himself been guilty of fraud in overcharging thirty-five thousand rupees on the purchase of goods. Brabourne, who had gone to Fort St. George, when offered the Deputy Governorship of Bombay, refused it, because he would not serve under a man whose behaviour was so absurd that civilians on the other side of India said "they would rather be private centinels at Fort St. George than serve as Second in Council under Sir Nicholas Waite."

At last in 1708 this strange President was dismissed the service, or, as the Court mildly expressed it, "discontinued." They were fain to acknowledge that amidst all his follies and extravagancies he had shewn zeal for their interests, and therefore formally thanked him for his services. And in estimating his conduct, we must remember that although there is certainly much evidence against him which cannot be gainsayed, yet, to use his own strong language, the servants of the old Company took every opportunity of blackening his character with calumnious aspersions "as if

Hell were at liberty, and no God to be found."* Quaint as is the following defence of himself and his Council, showing too as it does, and all his writings do, that he was a man of imperfect education, it is not without truth :—

"We have hitherto governed all our actions in the whole managery of your affairs with soe much caution and a little expense, when your rivalls has been unlimited, and given away those emense and incredible summes for extinguishing your virtuous settlement, and vilely aspersing in your President and Councell that value ourselves upon our frugall and faithful services."†

Disputes between the servants of the two Companies were so warm, and at times carried to such a height on both sides, that it is difficult to say which were the most culpable. Sir John Gayer and his friends maintained that their opponents, instead of endeavouring to soften the rigours of their confinement, took advantage of it to embitter against them the native Governor, and on one occasion even went so far as to rob their messengers of the letters which they were conveying from Bombay.‡

An internal squabble amongst the servants of the English Company became in time a quarrel between the two Factories. We have seen that Benjamin Mewse, who was the Third in Council, complained that Waite and Proby managed affairs without caring for the majority, and from that date Mewse absented himself, refusing all invitations to attend the Council. At length he was ordered to be dismissed the English Company's service, and to give up his warehouse. This latter demand he met with a refusal. In consequence, the President and Council summoned him to appear before them and give an account of himself, but they "received no other reply than language unbecoming rationall creatures."§ A year afterwards Mewse meeting with no satisfaction in India proposed returning to England, and applied for a passage on board the old Company's ship *Regard.* Sir John Gayer and his Council therefore requested by messenger to know whether Sir Nicholas Waite and Council had any demands upon Mr. Mewse. Then followed a specimen of those singular communications which more than anything else mark the state of feeling prevailing between the two establishments.

To Mildmay, Gayer's messenger, Waite declared that his Company had been injured by Mewse to the extent of four thousand rupees, and, what appeared to him still worse, he had heard that Mewse had been frequently entertained in the old Company's Factory. Mildmay admitted the latter charge, but with regard to the former, inquired why Mewse's account had not been made up before, if he were really indebted so much to the new Company. Waite had other complaints to make against Gayer, but afterwards sent to him a Factor, named Crowe, with orders to say that Mewse would not be prevented from going home. By this time Sir John Gayer was waxing wroth, and told Crowe to inform Sir Nicholas that he need not make such ado about his power; he (Sir John Gayer) was intrusted

* Diary of the English Company's Factory at Surat, 5th October 1705.
† Id. 1st November 1705.
‡ Diary of the London Company's Factory at Surat, June 1704.
§ Id. 7th February 1702-3.

with greater powers, yet had "never used any of the Company's servants so barbarously as he had done Mr. Mewse, to turn him out of the Factory in a violent manner, and to send to all Europeans not to assist and help him, that he might hereby perish." Mr. Mewse, he added, had certainly been made welcome to the Company's table, and so at any time should any gentleman who belonged to the new Company. Then he concluded with recrimination, and opening an old sore asked, "if Sir Nicholas Waite thought so much of that, why did he entertain Bassett, a rascally fellow that ran away from his colours, when he was serjeant of his guard."*

Another troublesome subject in the new Factory was Eustace Needham, whom the Directors having taken into their service, had sent out as "a Factor experienced in business," and one who might be expected to prove useful in his vocation. No sooner, however, had he arrived than he was found to be a drunken sot, who could not safely be entrusted with any important business, and who, although there were so many to keep him in countenance, was yet declared to be a reproach to the Factory. Wholesome advice and instruction had been offered him in vain; he would have none of them. He had become so habituated, we are told, to his detestable vice, that he was irreclaimable, and therefore dismissed the Company's service.†

The immorality of the times seems not to have interfered with devotional forms. In fact, attendance at Divine Service was regarded by the Government as a public duty, although it was often reluctantly complied with. In the English Factory every member was required by a Minute in Council to attend at prayers eight times in the week, exclusive of Sundays. The eight times might be arranged as they pleased, and if the duty was thought a painful one, it might be discharged in four days, as there was service morning and evening. The clergyman was ordered to write down the names of such as did not attend, and a fine was inflicted upon them, which was deducted from their salaries.‡

The state of the two Factories at Surat was as follows. In the English Company's Factory were Sir Nicholas Waite the President, William Proby, and Jeremy Bonnell, Members of Council; one merchant, the minister, two Factors, nine writers, a Surgeon, and his mate, a trumpeter and an English cook. Between the thirtieth of November 1700 and the twenty-first of February 1704, no fewer than eight persons had died, and seven had been dismissed or suspended from the service.§ The monthly expenses of the Factory, including the Steward's disbursements, peons' wages, stationery, and other small charges, varied from fifteen hundred to two thousand rupees.‖

The servants of the old Company who were confined within the walls of their Factory were the Right Hon'ble Sir John Gayer, General, the Hon'ble Stephen Colt, President, the worshipful Ephraim Bendell, Ber-

* Diary of the London Company's Factory at Surat, 20th April 1704. See the account of the serjeant in the last chapter.

† Diary of the English Company's Factory at Surat, 7th February 1702-3.

‡ Diary of the English Company's Factory at Surat, 10th February 1703.

§ Diary of the English Company's Factory at Surat, 21st February 1703-4.

‖ Monthly statements in the Diary.

nard Wyche the accountant, and Purser Marine, the Chaplain, four senior and five junior Factors, six writers and one Surgeon.*

Instead of being encouraged to hope for a speedy release, these unfortunate persons were almost reduced to despair by hearing that some Europeans had committed fresh acts of piracy. Two piratical vessels had sighted five vessels belonging to Mussulmans, and immediately given them chase. Under cover of the night two of these merchant men proceeded on their voyage without molestation, a third had been compelled to alter her course, a fourth had been driven ashore at Swally, and the fifth captured. Great sensation was caused at Surat when these facts were known, and the Governor asserted that the pirates came from Bombay. Alarmed at his threats the Factors prepared to defend themselves within their walls. In anticipation that their usual supplies of provisions would be withheld, they had ordered a stock to be laid in, but sufficient time was not allowed them, and they were soon reduced to extremities. An ox, which they used for drawing water, was, with great difficulty kept alive by feeding it with the straw in which wine had been packed, and at last was killed for food. Meanwhile the infuriated Governor had seized the brokers of both the Dutch and London Companies, hung them up by their heels, and flogged them until he extorted from them a promise to indemnify the losses of the native merchants with a payment of seven lakhs of rupees. He then resolved to lay hold of the Factors, and that he might starve them out the sooner, drove into their Factory three English strangers whom he had apprehended, and who he trusted would help to consume their provisions. Nor did he spare threats, but vowed that he would have them alive or dead. They in reply declared they would never give themselves up, and would rather die than suffer again such misery as had been inflicted on them in their former confinement. At last after twelve days the Governor moderated his fury, and consented to allow them a small supply of provisions. As an aggravation of their sufferings they not only knew that their rivals, Waite and his friends, were at liberty, but could see that they had hoisted their Union Jack as if to flout at their misery. The perseverance which they manifested when their circumstances were almost desperate, was highly honorable to them, and their fortitude was a credit to the English name.†

The state of Bombay was described by Sir Nicholas Waite, when he had arrived there to assume the appointment of Governor, as wretched in the extreme, and he called it "this beggarly, ruined, but fertile island;" and this was in a measure true, although he clearly desired to enhance the value of his own reforms, by undervaluing the acts of his predecessors. In the year 1705 he let the tobacco farm for 26,500 xeraphims, which was more by two thousand xeraphims than it had yielded in the preceding year, six or seven thousand more than it had been twenty eight years, and seventeen thousand more than it had been thirty years before. The arak farm he let for five thousand xeraphims.

* Diary of the London Company's Factory at Surat, January 1703.

† Diary of the London Company's Factory at Surat from 30th August to 11th October.

But in 1707 both the tobacco and arak farms fell in value, and as no one would take them at a fair price, agents were employed instead of contractors. The garrison was very weak, and the three companies of Gentoos had been discharged for neglect of duty and disobedience of orders. Great alarm therefore was created, when in December 1705 the Mogul army came within three days march of the Coast, opposite Bombay; so that money and goods which had been brought in the *Josiah* from Persia were hastily landed and lodged in the Castle. As the Mogul had refused his consent to the establishment of a Mint, money was coined in the Castle, where only security was felt. The ill condition of the whole place may be concluded from the fact that the Deputy Governor was most anxious to prevent the visit of a merchant, who was expected on a mission from the King of Persia, because he feared to expose its weakness.*

Disease was, as usual, prevalent at Bombay, and when Commodore Harland, finding that he could not agree with Sir Nicholas Waite, was about to sail for England, he was obliged to impress sixty men, as his crew had suffered so much from sickness.† There were living but eight covenanted servants, including Members of Council, two persons more who could write, and two raw youths who had been taken out of English ships. Most of the survivors were in various stages of illness, so sad was the condition of what they called that year "the unhealthful, depopulated, and ruined island." In the following April the Civilians were reduced to seven, and some of those were invalids. There were but six commissioned officers, two of whom were frequently ill, and not quite forty English soldiers. In May the seven Civilians had dwindled to six, and these poor creatures deeply depressed by a sense of their desolation wrote: "It will be morally impossible to continue much longer from going under ground, if we have not a large assistance out before October." In the next January Henry Coster of the accountant's office was "wholly disabled by his unaccountable sottishness to hold a pen," and, although he could ill be spared, was dismissed. The Governor himself complains of his continued indisposition and want of assistance in that "very unhealthfull island;" yet he magnanimously assures the Directors that he feels bound in gratitude to exert himself, and inform them of all important matters, until he leaves the world or that place.‡

At such a time, the advent of Dr. Alexander Orme, the historian's father, must have been hailed with pleasure. He seems first to have come to India as an adventurer about the year 1706, and to have acted as Surgeon at Anjengo, where on his own application, backed by the Factors at Cálicot, he was received into the Company's service. The Factors when appealing in his favour say that he is "a very capable and ingenious person that would be extraordinarily serviceable to our masters and us in sickness." He was afterwards appointed Chief of Anjengo, where his second son the historian was born. §

* Bruce's Annals, 1704-8.

† Sir Nicholas Waite's letter to the Court, dated 3rd March 1706-7.

‡ Letters from Sir Nicholas Waite to the Court; dated Bombay Castle the 31st January 1705-6; 18th April 1706; 9th May 1706; and 23rd January 1706-7.

§ Memoir of Robert Orme, prefixed to his Historical Fragments.

In spite of the oppressions which the English suffered from the Mogul, and their own feebleness, the conviction that their only safety was in armed resistance acquired intensity. This, however, was impracticable so long as the Company's servants and their property remained within the reach and under the power of the Mogul Governor at Surat. They were compelled to endure the insolence or civility of natives in their various degrees, according as success made these tyrants overbearing or their fears brought them to be courteous and yielding. The Mohammedan force at Surat was quite insufficient for its protection, but strong enough to annoy the English. At one time an order came from Court to stop the trade of all topiwalas or hatmen ; at another the guards were removed from the London Company's Factory, although the Factors were not permitted to pass the gates. An idea of the continual fear under which they lived may be gathered from the fact, that when Aurangzíb died, and Sir John Gayer had heard the report of his demise, he felt that it would be dangerous to promulgate it, so communicated it to the Court of Directors in an allegory. He represented on the first of March 1707, "that the sun of this Hemisphere had set, and that the Star of the *second* magnitude, being under his meridian, had taken his place ; but that it was feared the star of the first magnitude, though under a remoter meridian, would struggle to exalt itself"—in other words, that the Emperor had died, that Prince Azim, his second son, had assumed the Imperial title, and marched towards Delhi, and that Prince Alam or Moazim, the eldest son, was marching to dispute the throne with him. This actually occurred, and a great battle was fought near Agra in June, in which Prince Azim was killed. Moazim then became Emperor, with the title of Bahádur Shah.*

The Maráthás were almost as much to be feared as the Moguls. Although Sivají was dead, yet the terror of his name survived.† When Kanhojí Angria was harassing the English with his ships, he was described as "a Sevagee or Maratha pirate." In 1703 the Factors of the English Company wrote that Sivají was expected at Surat, and that his army had actually fired the suburbs. The Factory was consequently placed in a state of defence. William Proby, Second in Council, was appointed first Captain, William Beawes, a seafaring man, second Captain, Jeremy Bonnell, Captain Lieutenant, John Lock, Lieutenant, Callow Carey and William Martin, Ensigns. The Writers were ordered to stand as sentinels, but they were so unpatriotic as to refuse, and leave the whole of this duty to sixteen sailors. They were all put under

* Bruce's Annals, 1703-8. Elphinstone's History, Book xii. chap. i.

† Indeed the Factors at Bengal seemed to doubt whether he *could* die. On the thirteenth of December 1680, having heard of his death from the Governor and Council of Bombay, they wrote thus :—"Sevagee has died so often, that some begin to think him immortal. 'Tis certain little belief can be given to any report of his death, until experience tell the waining of his hitherto prosperous affairs, since when he dies indeed, it is thought he has none to leave behind him that is capacitated to carry on things at the rate and fortune he has all along done." Orme's Fragments. By the by, it is rather surprising that this hero has not yet had his apotheosis. His success was greater than Ráma's, and his conquests more permanent. The ancestor of the Satára Rájás would make quite as respectable a god as the founder of the *Saturnia regna*.

arrest. Two, who continued refractory, were dismissed the service, and the rest then returned to their duty. Happily the Maráthás retired.*

Three years afterwards, on the third of May 1706, having defeated the Mogul army near Ahmedábád, they invested Surat for nine days, but as they had no cannon, and only a small proportion of fire arms, were unable to carry the entrenchments, which the Governor had thrown up. In their retreat they plundered the villages, and destroyed all kinds of provision, so that the prices of the necessaries of life were raised "from two to three hundred per cent." A year after Sáhují,† or as he is called in the English records, "the Sow Rajah," made a formal application to the General at Bombay for a supply of arms, ammunition, European troops and money.

The Maráthás were becoming more formidable at sea, and Kanhojí Angria's force increased. Having equipped sixty vessels, they pretended to no nice discernment of friend or foe, but attacked all who could not make a fair show of resistance. They also sometimes took roving Arabs into their pay. Captain Hide, commanding the ship *President*, was attacked on his passage to Bombay off the Málabár coast by two ships and four grabs from Muscat. Three of the grabs grappled with the *President*, and the crew of one boarded her; but they were beaten off, and their vessel sank. One of the others was blown up, so that several of the English crew were scorched, and their ship set on fire in sixteen places. The third grab was sunk. The rest of the enemy's fleet then made off, leaving eleven of the *President's* men killed and thirty-five wounded. It was afterwards discovered that the Arab fleet had been hired by the Maráthás.‡

These pirates from Muscat were added to the long established enemies of trade, and, cruizing as they did constantly on the Indian coasts, caused great annoyance to the English. The Court therefore declared that armed ships must be equipped "to root out that nest of pirates, the Muscat Arabs." Instead of contenting themselves with arming only one or two vessels at a time, and cruizing off the coast of Málabár, these people were now forming a regular system of aggression, having obtained permission from the King of Pegu to build ships in his ports, and spreading their fleets over the Indian Seas. Some of their ships carried from thirty to fifty guns, and with these they had made several descents on towns and villages.§

Various tribes of plunderers also now found their opportunity in the weakness of the Mogul Empire, and became more formidable on account of their numbers. From this time we find the *Gennims* frequently mentioned in the Records, as a continual source of uneasiness

* Diary of the English Company's Factory at Surat, 10th February 1702-3.

† Grant Duff calls this Prince *Shao*. The word is the Hindústání *sáh*, which is from the Sanskrit *sádhu*, and becomes the Maráthí *sáv*. It means the opposite of thief, and was originally given by Aurangzíb, who designed to signify by it in a coarse joke his opinion of Sáhují's father and grandfather. So English officials improved upon the joke and called him the "Sow."

‡ Orme's Fragments.

§ Bruce's Annals, 1704-8.

to the Factory at Surat. Under this name were included numerous tribes of freebooters, such as Vádavals, Kolís, Rájpúts, and Patháns.*

The Dutch Factors had, like the English, been required by the Governor of Surat to deposit security against piracy, and their brokers had been seized. But as they themselves contrived to escape his clutches, they acted a bolder part, and sought redress by more decided measures. Retiring to Swally, they blockaded the river with six large vessels, and demanded two millions of rupees as a compensation for the sums which had been extorted from their agents, or eight lakhs, and permission to form a settlement at "Roan" near Surat. They also insisted that they should be liable in future to pay only two and a half per cent. for customs, and should have a firmán granting them free trade. As they could not obtain what they demanded, they continued the blockade, and in March 1705 made prizes of Mogul Ships to the value of two millions of rupees. Things were in this state when a new Director of their trade and a new Council having arrived off Surat, opened on the sixth of January 1707 a negotiation with the Governor for the adjustment of disputes. In this they met with considerable success, for the Governor agreed to pay them eight hundred and eleven thousand rupees, on condition that they should deliver up the ships and other property which they had seized. He engaged also that one per cent on the customs should be abated, and that they should be free from payment of customs at Baroch. If the Emperor refused to ratify this agreement, the Dutch had the option of leaving the port, and taking such measures as they thought proper to obtain redress.†

Great as were the efforts made to suppress piracy, it was still committed, and even by persons who professed to be lawful traders. When Captain Alexander Hamilton was at Cálicot in February 1703, he found there the ship of a Captain Green, who was afterwards hanged in Scotland. This worthy having a fellow feeling for the interloping Hamilton, came on board his ship with several others—all in a state of intoxication. In the course of conversation he said that he had disposed of a large quantity of arms and ammunition to the pirates at Madagascar, and when warned that his candour might bring him into trouble, showed that he despised all such advice. At night his chief mate Mather came to Hamilton in a melancholy mood, and wished to exchange situations with one of the mates on board his ship. On meeting with an indirect refusal, he burst into tears, saying that he was undone, for Green and his crew had perpetrated acts which if brought to light would end in their shame and punishment, and, what was worse, the crew were such a drunken set that they could keep no secret, but would divulge every thing although their ruin would be the consequence. Hamilton sympathized with him, and drew from him an admission that they had plundered some Moor's ships, and sunk a sloop with ten or twelve Europeans on board. Next day Hamilton met Green and his supercargo. It was before dinner time, but both

* The word is from the Arabic *ghanîm* a plunderer. Hamilton refers to them ; "New Account," chap xiii.

† Bruce's Annals, 1704-1707.

were drunk, and the supercargo boasted that he would make the best voyage ever made from England on a small stock. Hamilton wished him joy, and quietly remarks, "We Indians understood none of those profitable voyages, but were well content with thirty or forty per cent." After this he prudently resolved to shun their society, and his account of them concludes thus :—"Whether Captain Green and Mr. Mather had justice impartially allowed them in their process and sentence I know not. I have heard of as great innocents condemned to death as they were.*"

A proclamation sent from England and published as far and wide as possible by Commodore Littleton had more effect in suppressing piracy than any other measure. By this a pardon was offered to all pirates who surrendered themselves, and a reward to all such as would secure and deliver up their commanders. Suspicions and divisions were by these means sown amongst the buccaneers. Some were bought off; others were destroyed, and at last security was given to navigation.†

All this time the union between the English and London Companies had been only partial. Probably, each did not understand its own circumstances, and certainly not the circumstances of the other ; so that it was impossible to arrive at a complete agreement as to terms, and in India their servants had rival interests, which gave rise to incessant bickerings. At last they consented to appeal to the Earl of Godolphin, Lord High Treasurer of England, who, after a most patient investigation of the questions in dispute, published on the twenty-ninth of September 1708 his famous award. From that date the two Companies were made one, which assumed the title of THE UNITED COMPANY OF MERCHANTS OF ENGLAND TRADING TO THE EAST INDIES.

It was arranged that there were to be three Presidencies in India—at Calcutta, Madras, and Bombay. A new Governor, with the title of General, and a Council, were appointed for Bombay. The Members of Council were all selected from the class of Civilians, who continued to discharge other duties, and of course took care that they held the most lucrative offices. The number was not fixed by law, and varied at different times, the Members being appointed to the government of subordinate Factories, and yet nominally holding their seats in Council. All important business was transacted by the Governor and Council. Where a difference of opinion arose, the question was decided by a majority of votes. Aislabie was the new General, Proby second in Council, Rendall third, Goodshaw fourth, Wyche fifth, Mildmay sixth, Boone seventh, and Oakley eighth. These were to select four of their number to be a President and Council at Surat, and to nominate such Factors and Writers as they might think the service required. Poor Sir John Gayer still languished in confinement. The only comfort he received was, to be assured by the Court that the General, by whom he had been superseded, had been instructed by them to use every effort for his liberation.‡

* Hamilton's "New Account," chap. xxv.
† Campbell's Lives of the Admirals, vol. ii.
‡ Bruce's Annals, 1707-8.

As the trade was now very different from what it had been when the English first came to India, we may endeavour to explain the system on which it was conducted. An important change was made at this time in the shipping. The Company's goods were chiefly conveyed in hired or chartered vessels, and not, as formerly, in vessels which they built and owned. A ship-owner's was gradually becoming a separate branch of business. The Company possessed only some swift sailing packets, and a very few trading vessels.

The Import Trade chiefly consisted of Bullion, Lead, Quicksilver, Woollen Cloths, and Hardware. It had long been the custom for European adventurers to carry their goods up the country for sale, but soon after the union, travelling had become more insecure than ever, and no European was permitted to go into the interior without special leave obtained from the Governor and Council. The disposal of goods, therefore, was for the most part left to native dealers.

The Export Trade consisted chiefly of Calicoes and other woven manufactures of India, Diamonds, Pepper, Drugs and Saltpetre. As there were no manufacturers in the country to whom the English could give large orders for goods, and who would deliver them, when required, at the ships, agents were employed, who collected the different articles and brought them to the warehouses, called Factories, which in time became Forts mounting heavy guns and defended by garrisons. For the purchase of Cloths a complicated system had been devised. As the weavers lived for the most part in poverty, before they could be set to work at their looms, it was necessary to advance them money for the raw material and their own subsistence. For this purpose the Company's brokers were sent into the districts, where they employed a second class of agents called gumáshtas, on a monthly salary. These men established a kachari, or house of business, in the various towns, where they were attended by peons and other servants, who summoned to their presence dalâls or small brokers. These again employed inferior agents to transact business with the weavers. Thus, it would appear, that four agents stood according to a regular system of gradation between the English Factor and the native operative. Each of these deducted, as a matter of course, a certain percentage for commission from the money advanced by the Company, and consequently whilst the weaver was ill remunerated for his labour, the price of his fabric was considerably raised even before it left the shores of India.*

It is curious to observe the different effects which have been produced by an increase of trade in the nineteenth century, and at the beginning of the seventeenth century. No one can now read the encouraging returns of imports and exports between India and England without being satisfied that they shew the flourishing condition of both countries. The conclusion drawn from similar returns a hundred and fifty years ago was diametrically opposite. Through the competition of the two Companies, and the efforts of private traders, sixty ships were employed in the Indian trade. This was a large number as compared with former years ; but

* Mill's History, vol. iii chap. i.

was the advance hailed as a national benefit? Far from it. Complaints were made that the exportation both of bullion and merchandise was excessive. European goods were transported to India in such large quantities, that they sold much too cheaply. Then by a singular inconsistency, it was urged on one side that the merchants had been led by their rivalries to pay too highly for goods in India, and yet on the other side it was declared that they had glutted the English market with them, and sold them at rates which were unreasonably cheap. There was perplexity on all sides. The manufacturers of London, Norwich, and Coventry were being ruined by the introduction of Silks and Calicoes. The industrious Huguenots, who having been expelled from France by the bigotry of Louis the Fourteenth, had effected vast improvements in the Silk and Linen Manufactures of England, found now that their trade was falling into neglect. The retail dealer went to market and was delighted to lay in a stock of Indian goods at a low price, but no sooner had he returned home than he found that a neighbour had been yet more fortunate, and in the rival shop Oriental manufactures were still cheaper. What could he do? He must sell at par with his neighbours, and either sacrifice part of his capital, or be altogether ruined. Interested parties were thrown into the greatest alarm. Competition, which is often a public benefit, was looked upon as a national calamity. Government was appealed to, and Parliament supposed that it was alleviating the general distress by enforcing sumptuary laws, and prohibiting the subject from wearing the silks and calicoes of India.*

However, there is no doubt that on the whole improved liberality in trade resulted from the disputes of the two Companies, and monopoly was never again shut up so closely as it had been in preceding years. The United Company made a remarkable concession in permitting supernumeraries to remain in India as free merchants. Whilst the animosities of the two Companies had been raging, there had been organized a separate stock—apparently unobserved by them—with which independent adventurers engaged in trade. Sometimes it suited the Company's servants to connive at this innovation, and such as were discontented with their masters embarked their persons and effects in vessels belonging to the separate stock. It is worthy of notice, that Sir William Norris, when leaving India, took his passage in such a vessel, the *Scipio*, preferring it to the English Company's. Three of these ships, the *Great London*, *Little London* and *Windsor* were at the close of this period trading on the Western side of India.†

The Union of the two Companies is an epoch which properly closes the Early History of the English in India. From this time the United

* By the Act 11, 12 Gul. III. chap. 10, which states in the premises that "It is most evident that the continuance of the trade to the East Indies, in the same manner and proportions as it hath been for two years last past, must inevitably be to the great detriment of this kingdom, by exhausting the treasure thereof, and melting down the coin, and taking away the labour of the people, whereby very many of the manufacturers of this nation are become excessively burdensom and chargeable to their respective parishes, and others are thereby compelled to seek for employment in foreign parts." Macpherson's History of Commerce, p 160. This writer does not doubt the validity of all the arguments then urged against competition.

† Bruce's Annals, 1702-1708.

Company commenced a new and more wonderful career. Past struggles had left it in a state of exhaustion; so its advance was at first feeble and tardy. But it never receded a step; never even halted. Movement imparted fresh health, and it acquired strength by progress. Whilst yet an infant of days it walked timidly; but with increasing size assumed a bolder front, and at last in a gigantic form strode fearlessly across the whole continent of India.*

And now I crave the reader's favour whilst I draw his attention to three matters in conclusion.

First, with regard to the East India Company. It is a singular fact that as yet no writer who has analyzed their records, and drawn from them the materials of his history, has ventured to express an impartial opinion respecting their affairs. Bruce is the only author who has composed a connected narrative derived solely from these sources. His diligence has been great, and his accuracy, as to the facts which he records, unquestioned. But he wrote for the Company, and as their humble servant, at a time when they would have considered it perilous to admit the whole truth regarding themselves. Hence, throughout his three quarto volumes, but one or at most two adverse criticisms on their conduct of affairs are to be met with; and many circumstances which reflect discredit upon them are omitted. The result has been the opposite of what was anticipated. People would not believe in the spotless virtues of a dynastic oligarchy, and they felt sure that the Directorial succession could not have preserved themselves quite free from vice for a whole century. Facts oozed out. The prejudiced narratives of foreigners and interlopers were seized greedily and swallowed entire. The enemies of the Company then attacked them violently, misrepresented them unscrupulously, and suffered imagination to supply the place of truths which the Company had themselves unwisely concealed.

The Court of Directors were neither much better nor much worse than the age in which they lived. Be it remembered that the Company began to trade in a reign during which the Lord Chancellor of England was accessible to bribes, and a false judgment could be purchased from "the most exquisitely constructed intellect that has ever been bestowed on any of the children of men."† They struggled for existence at a time when Charles the Second supported himself in extravagance and debauchery by receiving secret service money from France. And a little before the crisis of their affairs which we have just related, they had purchased the good will of William the Third with ten thousand pounds, and of the Duke of Leeds with five thousand guineas.‡ So that the immorality of the age may be urged as an excuse for many charges of corruption brought against them; but, on the other hand, to represent their career as altogether honorable and highly creditable, is to palm upon the public a prodigious imposture.

* "Mobilitate viget, viresque acquirit eundo;
Parva metu primo; mox sese attollit in auras." Æn. iv. 175.

† Macaulay's Essay on Lord Bacon.

‡ Burnet's History of His Own Times, Book vi.

In their corporate capacity the Company never laid any claim to the higher order of virtues. They professed to be honest and enterprising; but their aims were limited by their own interests. Sometimes, indeed, they made use, but very awkwardly, of ethical phrases. When they had reduced the size of a bale of cotton, and saved themselves a charge for freight, they called it patriotism;* and before each renewal of their Charter they magnified the advantages which the country derived from their commerce. But gain was their one object. To advance a people's happiness, to encourage the growth of their knowledge and intelligence, to sow the seeds of moral greatness, to provide for the security of future generations—all these objects of good government came not within the scope of the Company's efforts, and evoked no disinterested and sublime virtues. Yet in the hands of Providence their mercenary project has been made an instrument for the civilization, and we trust for the moral elevation of two hundred millions of people. God has sent the Company to import the energies and virtues of the North to the enervated and barbaric East. Let them be satisfied with this. Let their advocates boast of His goodness, which has selected them to be His servants in such a cause, and not falsely ascribe to them transcendental purity. There are, it is true, periods of their early history when their conduct was almost magnanimous. The Court of Directors lived and laboured for themselves; but when they resisted so stoutly the open assaults of doughty adversaries, countermined the concealed approaches of secret foes, rallied their fainting troops, and from their own unfailing fires rekindled the extinguished energies of their servants—such an indomitable spirit claims our admiration, for the vulgar instinct of self-preservation appears then in an imposing dress as heroic glory.

With regard to the Company's servants in India, during this first century, is it not singular that so little has been known of them? When I attempted to form an idea of the first Englishmen who lived in India, it seemed to me impracticable. The learning of Europe had blown away much of the mist which obscured Hindú and Mussulman annals. We have caught glimpses of As'oka, Sandracottus or Chandragupta, and the Græco-Bactrian Kings. Our authors have given laborious and faithful narratives of Mogul and Maráthá dynasties. But what sort of people were they who first quarried out and prepared for others to chisel into shape an Anglo-Indian Government? I could not answer this question. Our standard histories say little, in many cases literally nothing about them. They in no way enable us to comprehend their characters or appreciate their efforts. They only condescend to enter into details of times when heroes and Governor Generals flourished, when Clive conquered or Warren Hastings ruled.

But what sort of persons were Clive's and Hastings' forerunners? "All, all honourable men," says printed history. There was a Captain named Best, who fought like a bull-dog; an Ambassador, Sir Thomas Roe, "a man of discernment and temper," Boughton, a generous Doctor; Oxenden, Child, and a few others—of whom particulars not known. But

* See page 71 of this book.

what of the rest? What of their employments, manners, and characters? There was no regular account of them. The ordinary reader had no means of making their acquaintance.

We have tried to lift the veil, to see them in their hours of business and recreation, and have been sorry to find that they were not all honourable. We gladly indeed seized and brought to light the virtues of a few, but generally found it our duty to deprive vice of an immunity which truth should not permit it to enjoy, and remove from it the covering under which it had lain concealed. Here again, writers who enjoyed the Honorable Company's patronage, had collected from their records certain wise and chivalrous deeds of Oxenden, exaggerated the abilities of Child, disparaged Norris and Waite, because they were zealous rivals; but they never hinted at the piracies which their Captains were proved to have committed, the follies of some, and the enormous vices of others.

In particular, the preceding work will probably remove one mistake into which many writers have fallen. It will show that the English did not leave their forms of Religion behind them. Like the ancient colonists of Greece, who carried with them the unquenchable fire of their Prytaneum, and the Priests who ministered to their Gods; so the English imported their Bibles and Liturgies, their Gospellers and Chaplains. Twice each day did they meet at the throne of grace, and on Sundays the President and Senior Factors repaired thrice to their pews, where they and their dames sat in burgher dignity whilst writers and apprentices listened, prayed, or dozed at a respectful distance.*

But, then, candour requires the painful admission that religion was without a soul. The larger portion of these Chapel-goers were dissolute or dishonest. Anglo-Indian Society was, as it has ever been, one degree worse than English. Now that the world bears itself more morally, there is still rather a lower standard of principle, together with more shamelessness and disregard of propriety in Bombay than in England. There seems to have been a similar ratio of morality, when after the restraint which the Puritans had placed upon them, the evil passions of Englishmen broke forth with ungovernable fury; when public opinion was no longer a check, for there could not be wit and fashion without a violation of decorum, when ridicule did not raise a blush on the forehead of guilt, but only aimed its shafts at innocence. When such was the state of things in England, *a fortiori* was it so in Bombay.†

With regard to the people of India, it must be confessed that Europeans had up to the period which this narrative has reached, only exercised an evil influence upon them. A man who was highly esteemed in his generation and had much experience of Indian life—President Pitt of Madras—declared this, tracing the cunning, suspicion, and disobliging behaviour for which the natives whom he had observed were distin-

* Sir John Gayer in a letter to President Annesley, dated 16th September 1698, settles a question of precedence which had been referred to him, and which had evidently given rise to heart-burnings. Mrs. Colt had been excluded from her seat in Chapel by Mrs. Vaux, on the ground that the rank of the latter's husband was inferior to the former's. Gayer, without fearing the consequences of Mrs. Vaux's displeasure, decided that she must give way.

† See Macaulay's History of England, Chapter ii.

guished, to the example of Europeans.* But in other respects the people of the country gained much by European connexion. Encouragement was given to the labour and skill of their operatives. The Manufactures of England could not compete with those of India. Woollens from the former country were not in sufficient demand to pay for the calicoes of the latter, and consequently so much bullion was exported, that Pollexfen on that ground alone built his arguments against the East India Company, and attempted to prove that they were inflicting an injury on the British nation.

It would be well if discontented Natives could be brought to compare their position under British rule with that of the English under Native rule. There is now at least security for life and property. The tax which the subject pays for the support of Government is small—when we consider that really it is the rent of his land—and its rate is being fixed. He has the most absolute control over his own movements. He may travel North, South, East, or West, and be safe from injury and insult. If his journey be on land, the tribes, such as Bhils and Kúlis, which formerly would have plundered him, are now the Police which protect him; if his course be over the sea, he no longer fears lest behind each headland there should lurk some ferocious rover, and that to double it will be his death or ruin. His religion is tolerated, and his person respected. The oppressions of petty tyrants are restrained by equitable laws, and he meets with consideration and politeness from that dominant people, whom he still regards as outcastes and unfit to share his social enjoyments.

How widely different was the life of an Englishman under a Native Government! There was no power sufficient to protect the merchant either by land or sea. If he wished to convey his goods from Surat to Agra, he could only hope to defend them against plunderers by mustering a strong party, and setting regular guards at each camping place, as though he were in an enemy's country. Even then he might be overpowered by the free lances of Hindustan. Still more dangerous were the paths of the ocean. There he must entirely depend upon his own resources, for it would be vain to seek protection from the law. Nay, the proud Emperor appealed to the despised strangers that his shipping might be protected, and they were expected not only to defend themselves, but also the mariners and traders of a vast Empire. Yet he and his subjects, helpless haughty barbarians, affected to despise the English, wronged them incessantly, imprisoned their Chiefs, insulted their envoys, fleeced their merchants, and drove them to turn upon their oppressors in despair. Thus the evils of native rule compelled English merchants to protect their warehouses with battlements, and all the muniments of war. Then, as they still suffered injuries, the facility with which they managed to defend themselves suggested offensive operations, and these led to territorial aggran-

* This President Pitt was grandfather of the great Earl of Chatham, and owner of the celebrated Pitt diamond. He wrote thus :—"When the Europeans first settled in India, they were mightily admired by the natives, believing they were as innocent as themselves; but since by their example they are grown very crafty and cautious, and no people better understand their own interest, so that it was easier to effect that in one year which you shant do now in a century, and the more obliging your management, the more jealous they are of you." Bruce's Annals, 1707-8.

dizement. Some politicians now think, or rather say, that because it is an age of commerce it cannot be an age of conquest. But the fact is, the necessities of commerce throw open the door to conquest, and the defence of their trade first suggested to the English a policy which ended in the subjugation of India.

Short as this history is, it yet seems a labyrinth of human follies and errors. Religion, however, which is the only solid basis of all knowledge, enables us to trace through it all a mysterious clue of Divine Providence and Divine direction. European vices and native vices bear an overwhelming proportion on the record, and the catalogue is relieved by few items of virtue. But as two negations make an affirmative, so the vices of Europeans and Natives have produced a positive good. The thirst for riches, the unscrupulous efforts of ambition, the reckless violence which often struck Hindús with terror—all these were the disgrace of the English, but yet they hurried them on to Empire. The perfidy, the cunning which overreached itself, the cowardice, the exclusive bigotry, which disgraced the natives, smöothed the way to their subjection; and surely these two results are being directed by the Universal Benefactor to good. We know of no other way in which India could have been regenerated. Had the English in India been a set of peaceful saintly emigrants, what impression would they have made upon the country? Had the natives placed confidence in each other, and been united under a common faith, how could they have given way to the encroachments of a few foreigners?

But, although Providence has thus brought good out of evil, we have certain indications that for the future they who sow vices will not reap a harvest of blessings. Moreover, all history teaches one certain truth, which is this, that between conquering and conquered peoples there must be mutual forbearance, frankness, and liberality, or there is no hope of permanence, much less of progress and improvement. Where these are wanting, good policy, energy, and courage cannot long be of any avail. We may take a lesson from Sparta in ancient, and Spain in modern times. The Spartans would admit no conquered people to the rights of naturalization, and the consequence was, that as their power spread, the boughs soon became too heavy for the trunk, and it was uprooted by a tempest. The Spaniards treated most illiberally the natives of South America, and consequently their conquered territories were wrested from them. Widely different was the manner in which the Romans discharged their duties towards the people which they subdued. Whole families, cities, even nations, were admitted to all the rights of Roman citizenship;* so that, as has been said, "it was not the Romans that spread upon the world, but it was the world that spread upon the Romans." Hence conquerors and conquered rose in company to greatness. Amalgamation like theirs cannot indeed take place between Európean and Oriental races. The example of the Portuguese has satisfied us that it is not desirable. But there can be no reason why there should not be mutual esteem and regard. These, however, can never be built up securely unless they have for a

* *i. e.* Not only to the jus commercii, jus connubii and jus hereditatis, but also to the jus suffragii, and jus honorum.

foundation growing intelligence, a more fervent and disinterested love of truth, a nobler morality, a juster appreciation of immutable principles than formerly distinguished Natives or Europeans. When truth is represented on both sides with intellectual vigour as a living principle, Natives will have a claim to receive, and Europeans will have a disposition to give, both political and social privileges. Then indeed, we shall plant, and posterity shall gather greatness and happiness for both the English and the Native multitudes of Hindustan.

THE END.

INDEX.